PRESIDENTIAL APPROVAL

Presidential Approval

A SOURCEBOOK

GEORGE C. EDWARDS III

with Alec M. Gallup

The Johns Hopkins University Press
Baltimore and London

To Larry Edwards, Mary Beth Moody, Susan Darling, and
   Barry Edwards
   and
   George H. Gallup and Paul K. Perry

The Johns Hopkins University Press, 701 West 40th Street, Baltimore, Maryland 21211
The Johns Hopkins Press Ltd., London

The paper used in this book meets the minimum requirements of American National Standard
for Information Sciences—Permanence of Paper for Printed Library Materials,
ANSI Z39.48-1984.

LIBRARY OF CONGRESS CATALOGING-IN-PUBLICATION DATA

Edwards, George C.
    Presidential approval: a sourcebook / George C. Edwards III with
  Alec M. Gallup.
        p.   cm.
    Includes bibliographical references (p.   ).
    ISBN 0-8018-4085-6
    1. Presidents—United States—Public opinion. 2. Public opinion—
  United States. I. Gallup, Alec. II. Title.
  JK518.E27   1990
  353.03'13—dc20   90-4160 CIP

CONTENTS

TABLES

ACKNOWLEDGMENTS

This is an unusual book. It provides a large data set on the principal figure in American politics, along with a discussion of the data. It is our hope that scholars, journalists, and others interested in American politics will find the data useful for a wide variety of projects.

Preparing and checking the results of six hundred Gallup Polls taken over a period of thirty-six years (1953–88) requires a substantial effort. Several people have been essential to the completion of the volume and deserve special recognition. Sarah Van Allen of the Gallup Organization provided invaluable aid in searching for and checking poll results and always maintained a delightful sense of humor. Everett Ladd and Marilyn Potter of the Roper Center not only gave their moral support to the project but also provided much of the data from Roper's archives. This book would not exist without their cooperation, and we are very grateful.

Richard Burkholder, Diane Colasanto, Harry Cotugno, Don DeLuca, George Gallup, Jr., Fred Greenstein, Graham Hueber, Larry Hugick, Andrew Kohut, James Shriver, and Martin Wattenberg read the entire manuscript and made useful suggestions, for which we are appreciative. Carl Richard provided skilled computer support. Finally, Carmella Edwards spent weeks in the painstaking task of coding the data for use on the computer, and we are indebted to her.

INTRODUCTION

This volume has two goals. The first is to make available to scholars the results of six hundred Gallup Polls on presidential approval from the presidencies of Dwight Eisenhower through Ronald Reagan (1953–88). The results of a few polls have been lost, and occasionally only the figures for the entire nation have been retained. Usually, however, the poll results include the presidential approval ratings of a number of important demographic groups. The number of polls for each administration is shown in table I.1, and the number for each president in each year of his tenure in office is shown in table I.2.

The data in this volume probably represent the largest set of public responses to a single question asked over an extended period of time. Scholars can use the data to investigate many fundamental questions regarding presidential approval, including which segments of the public approved of the president (or disapproved or had no opinion), the levels and timing of their approval, and the conditions under which their opinions were expressed—for example, conditions of media coverage, White House efforts to lead the public, the economy, war or peace, international tension,

TABLE I.1   Presidential Approval Polls for Each President

President	Polls
Eisenhower	119
Kennedy	40
Johnson	83
Nixon	96
Ford	36
Carter	91
Reagan	135
TOTAL	600

TABLE I.2 Presidential Approval Polls for Each Year and President

Year	Polls	President
1953	13	Eisenhower
1954	16	Eisenhower
1955	15	Eisenhower
1956	13	Eisenhower
1957	15	Eisenhower
1958	16	Eisenhower
1959	14	Eisenhower
1960	17	Eisenhower
1961	14	Kennedy
1962	13	Kennedy
1963	13	Kennedy
1963	2	Johnson
1964	14	Johnson
1965	18	Johnson
1966	17	Johnson
1967	17	Johnson
1968	14	Johnson
1969	1	Johnson
1969	18	Nixon
1970	18	Nixon
1971	13	Nixon
1972	10	Nixon
1973	20	Nixon
1974	17	Nixon
1974	8	Ford
1975	19	Ford
1976	9	Ford
1977	24	Carter
1978	25	Carter
1979	25	Carter
1980	17	Carter
1981	19	Reagan
1982	19	Reagan
1983	22	Reagan
1984	21	Reagan
1985	15	Reagan
1986	13	Reagan
1987	11	Reagan
1988	15	Reagan

domestic turmoil, or scandal. Researchers can compare presidents or examine individual presidential terms. They can also employ the data as independent variables in order to examine whether approval provides the president with leverage with members of Congress or other political actors.[1]

The second goal of this book is to provide a brief analysis of the data that will be useful for a broad range of students and scholars. The substantive chapters describe the data in summary form and examine explanations of presidential approval.

The Question

The Gallup Poll began asking about presidential approval in 1935 (we hope to make the results for the Roosevelt and Truman presidencies available in the future). For the first three years the poll experimented with different wording of the question, seeking to avoid responses that represented "liking" the president. Since 1945 the approval question has read as follows: "Do you approve or disapprove of the way [president's name] is handling his job as president"? Most other polling organizations have adopted this wording as well. A discussion of the evolution of the approval question can be found in Appendix A.

To prevent responses to the presidential approval question from being contaminated by responses to subsequent questions, the Gallup Poll has almost always asked the approval question first.

Occasional polls did not ask the approval question. It was especially likely to be omitted during presidential election campaigns, when Gallup concluded it could not be asked along with trial-heat questions on presidential candidates because the responses to the trial-heat questions contaminated responses to the approval question and vice versa. In addition, sometimes Gallup did not ask for certain demographic characteristics, such as union membership. In such cases the relevant spaces in the tables are blank.

Gallup has also asked questions designed to elicit responses regarding the strength of presidential approval and opinions about the president's handling of specific aspects of his job, such as the economy and foreign policy. At a later date, we intend to make this data available as well.

The Demographic Groups

Measurement of most of the demographic variables, including race, sex, and age, is straightforward. Others require some explanation. Party identification and religious affiliation are determined by the self-identification of the respondent. Union membership is recorded according to household. Even if the respondent is not a union member, if his or her spouse is, the respondent is placed in the union household category.

Educational groups are defined by the broad level of schooling attained. A respondent who attended but did not complete high school is placed in the high school category. Although the grade school category once included large numbers, few people fall in it in the 1980s. On the other hand, the college-educated category was small in 1953 but has grown substantially as educational attainment has increased in the United States. Care should be taken in interpreting these figures when the sample sizes are small.

The states included in each region are as follows:

East

Maine, New Hampshire, Vermont, Massachusetts, Rhode Island, Connecticut, New York, New Jersey, Pennsylvania, Maryland, Delaware, West Virginia, District of Columbia

Midwest

Ohio, Michigan, Indiana, Illinois, Wisconsin, Minnesota, Iowa, Missouri, North Dakota, South Dakota, Nebraska, Kansas

South

Virginia, North Carolina, South Carolina, Georgia, Florida, Kentucky, Tennessee, Alabama, Mississippi, Arkansas, Louisiana, Oklahoma, Texas

West

Montana, Wyoming, Colorado, New Mexico, Idaho, Utah, Nevada, Arizona, Washington, Oregon, California, Alaska, Hawaii

The Gallup Poll also coded data on the occupation of respondents (an open-ended question), their income, and the size of the community in which they lived. Because of a lack of comparable data across presidents, the results of these questions are not included in this study. The wording of each question on demographics is found in Appendix B.

The Sample

During the period covered by this study, the Gallup Poll sample has been designed to represent the adult civilian population of the United States living in private households or, in the case of telephone surveys, households with a telephone.

The sample consisted of fifteen hundred or more personal interviews until 1984. The margin of error for most findings in a sample of this size is plus or minus three percentage points for results based on the entire sample. In 1984 Gallup began conducting a few polls by telephone based on samples of about one thousand persons. Following a few trial runs during 1986 and 1987, the Poll in 1988 reduced the sample size for all its personal interview surveys from 1,500 to approximately 1,000 cases. The dates of the surveys with samples of this size are listed in table I.3. The margin of error for most findings in a sample of one thousand is plus or minus 4 percentage points for results based on the entire sample.

After the survey data have been collected and processed, the results are weighted so that the demographic characteristics of the total weighted sample of respondents matches the latest estimates of the demographic characteristics of the adult population according to the U.S. Census Bureau. Telephone surveys are weighted to match the characteristics of the adult population living in households with a telephone.

Researchers should not make too much of differences in approval levels that may represent no real change at all. Small fluctuations in presidential approval between two points in time may be due to sampling error or other polling limitations. Moreover, often the range of opinion fluctuation during a year is rather small. Some perspective is useful in claims of "explaining" opinion change. Explaining a large portion of a small change in approval is not necessarily very meaningful. It is also

TABLE I.3   Surveys with Samples of About One Thousand

Date of Poll	Date of Poll
1984	1987
May 3–5	March 6–9[a]
June 6–8	March 14–18
	June 8–14
1985	August 24–September 2
August 13–15	
August 16–19[a]	1988
September 13–16[a]	March 4–7[a]
November 1–4[a]	March 8–12
November 11–18	May 2–8
	June 24–27[a]
1986	July 1–7
March 4–10	July 15–18[a]
May 16–19[a]	August 19–22[a]
June 9–16	September 25–October 1
August 8–11[a]	October 21–24[a]
September 12–15[a]	November 11–14[a]
September 13–17	December 27–29
December 4–5	

[a] Personal interviews; all other surveys were made by phone.

probably less important to explain variation in opinion in such circumstances than to explain the basic, relatively stable level of approval. A
more detailed discussion of sampling, weighting, and sampling tolerances
can be found in Appendixes C and D.

Holding Opinions

Given the prominence of the presidency, it may seem surprising that
millions of Americans do not have an opinion of the incumbent's performance. Yet on the average about one of every eight citizens falls into
this category. The percentage is generally highest early in a president's
term.

Over the period 1953–88 those expressing no opinion about the president have averaged 13 percent, with little variation across administrations
(table I.4). There are two exceptions, however. The first is the tenure of

TABLE I.4 No Opinion on Presidential Approval (%)

Group	Eisenhower	Kennedy	Johnson	Nixon	Ford	Carter	Reagan
All	14	13	14	14	17	15	10
Male	11	10	11	11	13	13	9
Female	16	15	16	17	19	17	12
White	13	13	14	14	16	14	10
Nonwhite	22	11	13	19	23	19	13
East	13	12	13	14	17	15	11
Midwest	13	12	13	13	15	16	10
South	17	16	15	14	18	15	11
West	12	11	13	15	18	15	9
Republican	7	17	13	10	13	13	6
Democrat	17	9	12	15	17	14	11
Independent	15	16	16	14	17	16	13
Protestant	13	14	14	14	16	15	10
Catholic	14	8	12	14	16	14	11
Union	14	10	13	14	16	14	10
Nonunion	14	15	14	14	17	15	11
Grade school	18	16	17	20	22	20	17
High school	13	11	13	14	17	16	12
College	8	9	10	8	11	11	7
Under 30	14	10	11	11	15	14	11
30–49	14	11	13	14	17	14	9
Over 50	13	15	15	16	18	16	12

Gerald Ford, when the number of those expressing no opinion was high. Ford was not well known to the American people when he became president, and the figure for his short term disproportionately reflects the early period of a presidency. In his last year he averaged a 13 percent no-opinion rate. At the opposite extreme was Ronald Reagan. As a polarizing force in American politics (discussed below), Reagan evoked evaluations from a larger percentage of the public than any of his six immediate predecessors.

Traditionally, women have been more reluctant than men to express an opinion of the president, but the early gap between the sexes of 5 or 6 percentage points narrowed to only 3 under Reagan. Nonwhites have been less likely than whites to express opinions during Republican presidencies, but this difference disappeared with Democrats in the White House. Again, the gap narrowed to 3 percentage points under Reagan.

Two factors related to whether people express opinions about presidential performance are education and political party identification. The more education a group has, and presumably the better informed it is about public affairs, the more likely it will be to express an evaluation of the president. The differences between the least and best educated groups in expressing opinions averaged 10 percentage points over the span of this study. Nearly one of every five people in the lowest education group for each poll typically did not express an opinion of the president's job performance.

The relationship with party identification is more complicated. Independents do not vary much over time in stating opinions, except that they are more likely to express opinions about Reagan than about other presidents. Those who identify with either major party, however, vary considerably across administrations in holding opinions. In general, adherents of the party occupying the White House are most likely to evaluate the president. The differences are often sizable. The exception is Jimmy Carter's tenure, in which a larger percentage of Democrats than Republicans expressed no opinion about the president.

Holding opinions about the president has not varied notably among regions since the mid-1960s, and religion has only been important under Kennedy, when few Catholics failed to articulate opinions about the first president who shared their faith. A union member in the household has also made a difference only during the Kennedy administration, when nonunion households were more likely to withhold judgment. Age has not been an important factor in determining whether an opinion is expressed, although the oldest cohort is always the least likely to express an evaluation. The lower level of opinion expression for the oldest cohort is the result of its also being the age cohort with the lowest level of education.

PART ONE

Presidential Approval Polls, 1953–1988

PRESIDENTIAL APPROVAL POLLS, 1953–1988

In the tables that follow, the following abbreviations appear:

A% = Percent approving the president's handling of his job
D% = Percent disapproving the president's handling of his job
N% = Percent expressing no opinion of the president's handling of
   his job

EISENHOWER: 1953

	February 1-5			February 22-27			March 28-April 2			April 19-24			May 9-14			July 4-9		
	A%	D%	N%	A%	D%	N%	A%	D%	N%	A%	D%	N%	A%	D%	N%	A%	D%	N%
National	68	07	25	67	08	25	74	08	18	73	10	17	74	10	16	69	15	16
Male	71	07	22	68	08	24	74	09	17	73	11	16	74	11	15	66	19	15
Female	66	07	27	67	07	26	73	07	20	72	09	19	74	10	16	71	12	17
White	69	07	24	68	08	24	75	08	17	75	09	16	75	11	14	71	15	14
Nonwhite	55	08	37	61	10	29	53	09	38	55	15	30	58	11	31	48	20	32
East	72	04	24	67	07	26	74	10	16	71	12	17	74	10	16	71	14	15
Midwest	65	09	26	70	07	23	75	06	19	73	09	18	74	12	14	70	17	13
South	70	09	21	69	06	25	70	08	22	73	06	21	74	07	19	62	15	23
West	67	05	28	62	13	25	77	07	16	77	10	13	71	15	14	75	14	11
Republican	84	02	14	85	02	13	87	03	10	87	03	10	89	03	08	87	04	09
Democrat	60	12	28	57	12	31	64	12	24	64	15	21	64	17	19	56	25	19
Independent	65	04	31	68	08	24	74	08	18	72	09	19	76	09	15	68	14	18
Protestant				71	06	23	74	07	19	75	08	17				65	18	17
Catholic				65	09	26	74	09	17	71	11	18				70	14	16
Union										67	12	21	70	13	17	65	18	17
Nonunion										74	09	17	75	09	16	70	14	16
Grade School	65	09	26	62	08	30	66	09	25	63	11	26	68	12	20	61	16	23
High School	70	05	25	69	07	24	76	08	16	76	10	14	75	11	14	72	15	13
College	74	07	19	77	10	13	84	06	10	84	08	08	85	07	08	76	15	09
Under 30	71	05	24	67	09	24	75	08	17	73	08	19	72	12	16	69	17	14
30-49	66	07	27	66	08	26	73	09	18	73	11	16	72	11	17	69	15	16
Over 50	71	08	21	69	07	24	74	06	20	72	09	19	76	09	15	68	16	16

EISENHOWER: 1953

	July 25-30			August 15-20			September 12-17			October 9-14			November 1-5			November 19-24		
	A%	D%	N%	A%	D%	N%	A%	D%	N%	A%	D%	N%	A%	D%	N%	A%	D%	N%
National	73	13	14	74	14	12	61	20	19	65	19	16	61	26	13	59	25	16
Male	73	15	12	73	17	10	59	25	16	63	23	14	61	28	11	58	30	12
Female	72	11	17	75	12	13	63	17	20	66	16	18	62	23	15	60	20	20
White	74	12	14	75	14	11	61	21	18	66	19	15	62	26	12	60	24	16
Nonwhite	59	16	25	63	18	19	53	19	28	47	25	28	54	23	23	42	38	20
East	71	14	15	76	14	10	63	20	17	68	17	15	66	22	12	57	26	17
Midwest	74	11	15	76	13	11	58	23	19	67	20	13	56	27	17	63	23	14
South	71	13	16	68	17	15	62	18	20	57	22	21	67	22	11	53	27	20
West	79	11	10	77	12	11	62	19	19	65	19	16	55	34	11	67	21	12
Republican	91	03	06	90	04	06	84	07	09	89	03	08	84	07	09	84	05	11
Democrat	63	19	18	60	25	15	48	30	22	49	32	19	44	43	13	42	40	18
Independent	70	11	19	75	13	12	60	21	19	64	18	18	65	19	16	62	20	18
Protestant										66	18	16	63	24	13	62	23	15
Catholic										66	17	17	62	26	12	55	25	20
Union										58	24	18	53	30	17	54	28	18
Nonunion										68	17	15	64	24	12	61	23	16
Grade School	71	12	17	66	17	17	51	27	22	58	21	21	54	27	19	52	27	21
High School	74	12	14	77	13	10	65	17	18	66	20	14	64	25	11	60	23	17
College	73	16	11	76	16	08	68	18	14	73	15	12	69	22	09	68	26	06
Under 30	75	11	14	76	13	11	62	17	21	65	16	19	67	22	11	58	23	19
30-49	73	12	15	72	15	13	61	21	18	64	21	15	61	25	14	61	25	14
Over 50	71	14	15	74	15	11	61	21	18	64	20	16	59	28	13	57	26	17

EISENHOWER: 1953-1954

	December 11-16			January 9-14			January 28-February 2			February 25-March 2			March 19-24			April 8-13		
	A%	D%	N%	A%	D%	N%	A%	D%	N%	A%	D%	N%	A%	D%	N%	A%	D%	N%
National	69	22	09	71	19	10	70	17	13	67	21	12	66	22	12	68	21	11
Male	67	25	08	72	21	07	69	21	10	67	22	11	66	22	12	68	22	10
Female	71	18	11	71	16	13	71	14	15	66	21	13	66	21	13	69	20	11
White	70	21	09	72	18	10	71	17	12	68	21	11	68	21	11	69	21	10
Nonwhite	53	32	15	60	26	14	55	28	17	51	25	24	51	25	24	60	25	15
East	72	20	08	69	21	10	69	18	13	64	25	11	64	25	11	71	19	10
Midwest	69	18	13	73	16	11	69	18	13	68	22	10	68	22	10	66	25	09
South	65	26	09	71	17	12	73	15	12	68	19	13	68	19	13	66	20	14
West	70	21	09	69	21	10	70	19	11	68	15	17	68	14	18	71	20	09
Republican	91	06	03	92	03	05	90	04	06	88	06	06	88	06	06	91	05	04
Democrat	54	34	12	55	32	13	54	29	17	52	35	13	52	35	13	50	37	13
Independent	66	22	12	74	14	12	75	14	11	69	14	17	69	14	17	73	15	12
Protestant	71	20	09	73	16	11	72	17	11	69	19	12	69	19	12	73	17	10
Catholic	70	20	10	69	22	09	71	14	15	65	24	11	65	24	11	57	30	13
Union	64	27	09	69	21	10	62	23	15	57	29	14	57	29	14			
Nonunion	70	20	10	72	18	10	73	16	11	70	19	11	70	19	11			
Grade School	63	23	14	69	18	13	62	22	16	61	22	17	61	22	17	65	22	13
High School	71	21	08	71	19	10	72	16	12	67	23	10	67	23	10	67	22	11
College	71	22	07	75	17	08	80	14	06	73	17	10	74	17	09	76	17	07
Under 30	68	22	10	75	15	10	69	20	11	67	21	12	67	21	12	65	22	13
30-49	65	25	10	65	22	13	69	18	13	65	23	12	65	22	13	67	24	09
Over 50	74	18	08	76	15	09	71	16	13	69	19	12	69	19	12	73	16	11

EISENHOWER: 1954

	May 2-7 A%	D%	N%	May 21-26 A%	D%	N%	June 12-17 A%	D%	N%	July 2-7 A%	D%	N%	July 16-21 A%	D%	N%	August 5-10 A%	D%	N%
National	60	22	18	61	24	15	62	24	14	65	21	14	75	20	05	67	19	14
Male	58	27	15	62	25	13	61	30	09	66	22	12	71	23	06	69	20	11
Female	63	17	20	61	22	17	64	18	18	64	20	16	78	17	05	65	17	18
White	62	22	16	63	23	14	64	23	13	65	22	13	75	20	05	68	19	13
Nonwhite	55	20	25	38	35	27	39	38	23	55	15	30	67	23	10	55	21	24
East	58	27	15	61	26	13	61	28	11	65	26	09	73	22	05	64	23	13
Midwest	64	18	18	61	24	15	62	24	14	67	18	15	76	18	06	70	16	14
South	57	20	23	59	22	19	60	22	18	60	20	20	73	20	07	65	18	17
West	65	21	14	69	19	12	69	22	09	69	20	11	73	21	06	72	16	12
Republican	86	06	08	83	09	08	82	08	10	84	09	07	92	05	03	91	03	06
Democrat	42	36	22	45	38	17	46	39	15	51	31	18	61	32	07	51	32	17
Independent	62	19	19	61	21	18	67	18	15	66	19	15	79	15	06	69	13	18
Protestant				63	22	15										69	17	14
Catholic				57	28	15										65	21	14
Union													71	24	05	61	23	16
Nonunion													75	19	06	70	17	13
Grade School	54	22	24	52	28	20	56	26	18	58	23	19	73	23	04	60	18	22
High School	63	22	15	65	21	14	63	25	12	66	21	13	74	19	07	69	19	12
College	66	24	10	71	23	06	74	18	08	73	18	09	77	18	05	77	19	04
Under 30	60	24	16	63	21	16	60	28	12	63	21	16	72	21	07	66	21	13
30-49	57	24	19	60	25	15	61	24	15	64	22	14	74	21	05	67	19	14
Over 50	67	17	16	63	22	15	66	22	12	67	19	14	76	18	06	69	17	14

EISENHOWER: 1954-1955

	August 26-31			September 16-21			October 15-20			November 11-16			December 2-7			December 31-January 5		
	A%	D%	N%	A%	D%	N%	A%	D%	N%	A%	D%	N%	A%	D%	N%	A%	D%	N%
National	63	24	13	66	21	13	61	26	13	57	23	20	69	23	08	70	18	12
Male	62	27	11	65	23	12	62	30	08	59	26	15	70	24	06	70	21	09
Female	65	20	15	67	20	13	61	21	18	55	21	24	68	22	10	70	15	15
White	65	23	12	67	21	12	62	25	13	58	23	19	70	22	08	71	18	11
Nonwhite	49	30	21	56	22	22	53	30	17	51	28	21	57	30	13	62	13	25
East	63	22	15	68	22	10	59	28	13	58	23	19	69	24	07	71	16	13
Midwest	65	24	11	68	19	13	58	27	15	57	24	19	69	22	09	72	18	10
South	60	25	15	62	23	15	68	20	12	59	23	18	65	28	07	66	21	13
West	67	22	11	67	22	11	60	29	11	52	24	24	78	14	08	72	15	13
Republican	87	06	07	89	05	06	88	06	06	85	04	11	89	06	05	86	07	07
Democrat	46	38	16	48	35	17	45	40	15	41	37	22	54	37	09	58	28	14
Independent	67	17	16	71	15	14	71	15	14	58	20	22	68	23	09	74	14	12
Protestant	66	22	12	67	20	13	66	23	11	59	23	18	73	19	08			
Catholic	63	23	14	65	22	13	53	28	19	57	21	22	63	29	08			
Union	52	32	16	61	24	15	50	36	14	52	27	21	61	30	09	69	18	13
Nonunion	68	20	12	68	20	12	66	22	12	59	22	19	72	21	07	71	18	11
Grade School	59	24	17	62	23	15	57	27	16	48	24	28	63	26	11	65	16	19
High School	64	24	12	66	21	13	63	24	13	59	23	18	71	22	07	71	19	10
College	69	21	10	73	20	07	68	26	06	70	23	07	71	24	05	78	17	05
Under 30	66	22	12	69	20	11	60	27	13	59	19	22	65	26	09	71	14	15
30-49	60	26	14	63	23	14	59	27	14	54	25	21	70	24	06	67	21	12
Over 50	68	20	12	68	20	12	65	23	12	58	24	18	71	20	09	74	16	10

EISENHOWER: 1955

	January 20-25			February 10-15			March 3-8			March 24-29			April 14-19			May 12-17		
	A%	D%	N%	A%	D%	N%	A%	D%	N%	A%	D%	N%	A%	D%	N%	A%	D%	N%
National	70	17	13	73	15	12	71	17	12	66	21	13	70	14	16	68	16	16
Male	67	20	13	73	17	10	73	17	10	66	23	11	69	17	14	68	20	12
Female	72	14	14	73	13	14	69	17	14	65	20	15	70	12	18	68	13	19
White	70	17	13	74	15	11	72	17	11	67	20	13	70	14	16	68	16	16
Nonwhite	58	17	25	63	20	17	54	19	27	55	30	15	63	11	26	75	08	17
East	66	18	16	72	17	11	72	16	12	62	25	13	66	17	17	66	16	18
Midwest	71	17	12	73	14	13	69	19	12	67	21	12	71	14	15	72	15	13
South	67	20	13	72	17	11	65	18	17	66	19	15	67	11	22	63	17	20
West	75	14	11	75	12	13	84	10	06	67	23	10	80	13	07	74	17	09
Republican	92	03	05	90	04	06	89	06	05	87	07	06	89	04	07	90	03	07
Democrat	53	30	17	61	24	15	54	30	16	50	33	17	58	22	20	52	27	21
Independent	71	11	18	79	11	10	74	12	14	69	17	14	68	14	18	69	13	18
Protestant	72	16	12	75	15	10	73	15	12	67	21	12	73	12	15	70	15	15
Catholic	61	20	19	70	15	15	66	20	14	64	20	16	65	17	18	66	16	18
Union							67	21	12									
Nonunion							73	15	12									
Grade School	62	19	19	66	17	17	66	17	17	58	26	16	67	14	19	62	18	20
High School	72	16	12	73	16	11	72	17	11	65	22	13	70	14	16	69	17	14
College	72	19	09	84	11	05	77	15	08	81	14	05	74	15	11	77	10	13
Under 30	66	20	14	75	15	10	73	17	10	60	23	17	67	14	19	70	15	15
30-49	70	17	13	70	17	13	69	18	13	66	21	13	69	14	17	68	15	17
Over 50	70	17	13	76	13	11	73	15	12	65	23	12	72	15	13	68	17	15

EISENHOWER: 1955

	June 3-8 A%	D%	N%	June 24-29 A%	D%	N%	July 14-19 A%	D%	N%	August 4-9 A%	D%	N%	August 25-30 A%	D%	N%	September 15-20 A%	D%	N%
National	70	16	14	67	15	18	72	18	10	76	11	13	71	16	13	71	16	13
Male	71	18	11	71	16	13	71	20	09	77	13	10	71	19	10	71	20	09
Female	69	14	17	64	14	22	74	15	11	74	10	16	70	13	17	71	13	16
White	71	15	14	68	15	17	74	17	09	76	11	13	71	16	13	72	16	12
Nonwhite	60	19	21	53	22	25	66	18	16	66	07	27	64	13	23	60	19	21
East	68	19	13	68	13	19	71	19	10	78	10	12	73	14	13	73	15	12
Midwest	71	18	11	67	17	16	73	18	09	77	11	12	70	17	13	73	17	10
South	69	14	17	66	14	20	70	18	12	70	14	16	64	19	17	65	17	18
West	75	09	16	66	18	16	81	12	07	75	10	15	80	10	10	72	17	11
Republican	92	03	05	87	04	09	93	04	03	93	02	05	92	03	05	92	05	03
Democrat	54	27	19	52	25	23	57	29	14	64	18	18	54	28	18	52	31	17
Independent	76	11	13	68	13	19	76	14	10	75	10	15	75	09	16	77	06	17
Protestant	73	13	14	69	14	17							71	15	14	71	16	13
Catholic	65	19	16	66	16	18							70	17	13	73	15	12
Union	65	20	15															
Nonunion	73	14	13															
Grade School	69	15	16	63	15	22	67	21	12	70	13	17	63	18	19	62	19	19
High School	67	17	16	68	15	17	74	16	10	76	10	14	71	16	13	73	15	12
College	81	14	05	75	14	11	81	15	04	82	11	07	84	11	05	78	16	06
Under 30	63	19	18	66	15	19	72	17	11	78	10	12	72	14	14	69	15	16
30-49	73	14	13	63	18	19	72	19	09	75	11	14	70	18	12	70	17	13
Over 50	70	17	13	72	12	16	73	17	10	74	12	14	71	14	15	72	16	12

EISENHOWER: 1955-1956

	November 17-22			December 8-13			January 6-11			January 26-31			February 16-21			March 8-13		
	A%	D%	N%	A%	D%	N%	A%	D%	N%	A%	D%	N%	A%	D%	N%	A%	D%	N%
National	78	13	09	75	13	12	76	12	12	77	14	09	75	15	10	72	18	10
Male	76	16	08	73	15	12	76	14	10	75	18	07	74	17	09	72	20	08
Female	80	11	09	76	11	13	77	10	13	78	11	11	76	14	10	72	15	13
White	78	13	09	75	13	12	78	12	10	77	14	09	75	15	10	74	16	10
Nonwhite	74	16	10	67	16	17	67	08	25	71	11	18	70	18	12	58	28	14
East	81	11	08	80	10	10	79	11	10	81	13	06	77	14	09	77	14	09
Midwest	77	14	09	73	13	14	73	12	15	77	15	08	76	13	11	71	18	11
South	78	14	08	71	16	13	75	12	13	70	15	15	69	21	10	69	18	13
West	78	14	08	77	12	11	80	12	08	78	11	11	77	13	10	70	22	08
Republican	93	03	04	91	04	05	92	03	05	93	03	04	93	02	05	95	01	04
Democrat	67	21	12	61	23	16	63	21	16	61	25	14	58	29	13	52	32	16
Independent	81	11	08	78	09	13	81	09	10	80	11	09	80	09	11	77	13	10
Protestant				75	14	11							76	15	09	73	17	10
Catholic				75	11	14							76	15	09	74	14	12
Union	76	14	10	71	15	14	74	13	14	73	18	09	73	16	11	66	22	12
Nonunion	79	13	08	77	12	11	78	11	11	77	13	10	76	15	09	75	15	10
Grade School	75	14	11	70	18	12	70	12	18	72	15	13	69	17	14	69	19	12
High School	79	13	08	76	12	12	79	10	11	77	14	09	75	16	09	73	16	11
College	81	11	08	79	08	13	81	14	05	82	12	06	83	10	07	77	17	06
Under 30	80	10	10	75	10	15	81	08	11	77	12	11	76	16	08	74	16	10
30-49	76	14	10	75	12	13	74	14	12	76	13	11	72	15	13	70	18	12
Over 50	80	14	06	75	16	09	77	11	12	77	16	07	78	15	07	73	17	10

EISENHOWER: 1956

	March 29-April 3			April 19-24			May 10-15			May 31-June 5			June 15-20			July 12-17		
	A%	D%	N%	A%	D%	N%	A%	D%	N%	A%	D%	N%	A%	D%	N%	A%	D%	N%
National	73	17	10	69	19	12	69	17	14	71	19	10	73	18	09	70	20	10
Male	72	20	08	68	22	10	68	20	12	71	22	07	72	21	07	68	23	09
Female	73	15	12	71	16	13	71	13	16	72	16	12	73	16	11	72	17	11
White	74	17	09	68	22	10	71	17	12	73	18	09	75	17	08	70	20	10
Nonwhite	59	17	24	71	16	13	59	16	25	58	25	17	51	28	21	63	23	14
East	78	13	09	75	16	09	77	11	12	75	16	09	78	13	09	74	16	10
Midwest	73	17	10	72	17	11	69	18	13	72	20	08	71	20	09	66	23	11
South	64	21	15	62	22	16	60	22	18	67	20	13	69	21	10	66	24	10
West	75	19	06	66	24	10	68	17	15	70	20	10	71	21	08	73	18	09
Republican	95	02	03	90	04	06	92	03	05	92	04	04	95	02	03	92	04	04
Democrat	56	30	14	51	34	15	52	30	18	55	32	13	55	33	12	49	36	15
Independent	74	13	13	76	12	12	68	13	19	73	14	13	76	13	11	75	16	09
Protestant										72	18	10	74	17	09	71	21	08
Catholic										72	17	11	74	17	09	68	18	14
Union	66	21	13	65	22	13	66	18	16	72	19	09	67	22	11	69	21	10
Nonunion	75	16	09	71	18	11	71	16	13	71	18	11	75	16	09	70	20	10
Grade School	66	19	15	63	21	16	65	17	18	67	20	13	69	19	12	63	22	15
High School	75	17	08	70	19	11	70	17	13	73	17	10	73	18	09	71	19	10
College	80	14	06	83	15	02	75	15	10	75	21	04	79	17	04	75	20	05
Under 30	72	17	11	70	17	13	70	14	16	75	15	10	75	14	11	77	16	07
30-49	75	16	09	70	19	11	67	19	14	70	19	11	72	20	08	68	21	11
Over 50	71	19	10	69	20	11	72	16	12	72	19	09	73	18	09	69	21	10

EISENHOWER: 1956-1957

	August 3-8			November 22-27			December 14-19			January 17-22			February 7-12			February 28-March 5		
	A%	D%	N%	A%	D%	N%	A%	D%	N%	A%	D%	N%	A%	D%	N%	A%	D%	N%
National	68	19	13	75	15	10	79	11	10	73	14	13	72	16	12	72	17	11
Male	68	22	10	77	16	07	79	14	07	71	17	12	72	18	10	69	21	10
Female	67	17	16	73	14	13	78	10	12	76	11	13	73	14	13	74	14	12
White	69	19	12	75	15	10	79	12	09	75	13	12	73	16	11	72	17	11
Nonwhite	57	19	24	76	10	14	69	08	23	65	19	16	68	16	16	67	18	15
East	71	17	12	78	14	08	81	10	09	78	12	10	72	16	12	78	15	07
Midwest	68	19	13	77	14	09	80	11	09	73	14	13	78	13	09	68	17	15
South	64	20	16	66	17	17	72	14	14	70	15	15	69	18	13	67	18	15
West	66	23	11	79	13	08	78	14	08	74	14	12	71	18	11	71	21	08
Republican	91	04	05	94	03	03	95	02	03	91	05	04	92	03	05	90	05	05
Democrat	49	34	17	57	27	16	67	20	13	57	25	18	57	28	15	56	30	14
Independent	70	13	17	81	09	10	78	11	11	82	08	10	77	11	12	73	13	14
Protestant	70	18	12	75	14	11	79	12	09	75	13	12	72	16	12			
Catholic	66	19	15	79	13	08	79	10	11	74	13	13	75	13	12			
Union	61	24	15	72	16	12	79	10	11	72	15	13	71	17	12			
Nonunion	70	18	12	76	14	10	79	12	09	75	13	12	73	16	11			
Grade School	65	18	17	71	14	15	75	13	12	70	12	18	68	17	15	64	21	15
High School	67	20	13	77	13	10	80	10	10	75	14	11	74	14	12	75	15	10
College	75	18	07	76	20	04	82	13	05	77	18	05	78	18	04	75	16	09
Under 30	67	18	15	79	13	08	78	11	11	76	13	11	74	14	12	75	14	11
30-49	67	20	13	74	15	11	78	12	10	74	14	12	74	15	11	72	16	12
Over 50	69	19	12	75	15	10	80	11	09	71	15	14	70	18	12	68	21	11

EISENHOWER: 1957

	March 15-20			April 6-11			April 25-30			May 17-22			June 6-11			June 27-July 2		
	A%	D%	N%	A%	D%	N%	A%	D%	N%	A%	D%	N%	A%	D%	N%	A%	D%	N%
National	65	20	15	67	21	12	64	23	13	62	23	15	64	22	14	63	23	14
Male	66	23	11	65	25	10	66	25	09	62	25	13	61	28	11	63	27	10
Female	65	17	18	68	18	14	62	21	17	62	21	17	66	18	16	64	19	17
White	68	18	14	68	20	12	66	22	12	63	23	14	64	23	13	63	23	14
Nonwhite	41	33	26	55	28	17	45	33	22	52	21	27	60	20	20	61	23	16
East	68	18	14	72	18	10	64	22	14	64	22	14	71	19	10	67	21	12
Midwest	65	21	14	65	23	12	65	23	12	63	23	14	61	23	16	67	22	11
South	61	22	17	62	21	17	62	23	15	55	24	21	61	23	16	52	25	23
West	69	17	14	67	23	10	65	25	10	65	23	12	60	27	13	67	24	09
Republican	87	06	07	85	07	08	86	07	07	86	06	08	85	08	07	85	07	08
Democrat	48	33	19	51	35	14	49	35	16	43	38	19	48	36	16	45	37	18
Independent	69	14	17	68	17	15	62	21	17	66	19	15	65	18	17	64	22	14
Protestant	66	20	14							63	21	16						
Catholic	69	15	16							63	24	13						
Union				64	24	12												
Nonunion				68	20	12												
Grade School	63	19	18	62	23	15	60	23	17	58	25	17	62	21	17	60	21	19
High School	66	20	14	68	20	12	64	24	12	64	20	16	64	23	13	63	24	13
College	68	20	12	71	22	07	69	21	10	65	26	09	67	23	10	69	23	08
Under 30	68	17	15	78	11	11	70	16	14	66	17	17	64	21	15	69	19	12
30-49	63	22	15	64	23	13	64	23	13	61	23	16	66	22	12	63	23	14
Over 50	67	19	14	64	23	13	61	26	13	61	25	14	60	25	15	61	24	15

EISENHOWER: 1957

	July 18-23			August 8-13			August 29-September 4			September 19-24			October 10-15			November 7-12		
	A%	D%	N%	A%	D%	N%	A%	D%	N%	A%	D%	N%	A%	D%	N%	A%	D%	N%
National	65	22	13	63	20	17	59	23	18	59	26	15	57	27	16	58	27	15
Male	62	28	10	60	24	16	59	26	15	58	30	12	58	28	14	60	29	11
Female	67	17	16	65	16	19	60	20	20	60	23	17	56	26	18	56	26	18
White	66	22	12	64	20	16	60	23	17	59	27	14	56	28	16	56	30	14
Nonwhite	53	25	22	56	17	27	51	26	23	58	25	17	64	14	22	71	09	20
East	72	19	09	68	15	17	62	22	16	67	22	11	66	21	13	63	24	13
Midwest	65	24	11	61	19	20	62	23	15	58	29	13	63	20	17	61	26	13
South	58	20	22	56	26	18	51	23	26	49	31	20	36	43	21	48	33	19
West	59	30	11	64	22	14	62	24	14	63	23	14	62	26	12	59	28	13
Republican	86	07	07	85	05	10	84	06	10	81	10	09	82	08	10	85	09	06
Democrat	45	37	18	46	33	21	44	37	19	42	40	18	38	44	18	41	42	17
Independent	70	19	11	65	16	19	54	22	24	63	23	14	56	23	21	61	22	17
Protestant	65	21	14															
Catholic	66	24	10															
Union	57	29	14	61	19	20	54	28	18	58	27	15						
Nonunion	67	20	13	63	21	16	62	20	18	59	26	15						
Grade School	65	20	15	59	19	22	52	23	25	53	27	20	49	29	22	57	23	20
High School	63	24	13	62	20	18	62	22	16	61	26	13	58	25	17	58	29	13
College	69	22	09	71	22	07	69	23	08	64	27	09	68	27	05	59	33	08
Under 30	71	16	13	60	17	23	66	18	16	63	24	13	63	22	15	58	27	15
30-49	61	24	15	63	20	17	60	22	18	59	25	16	58	27	15	56	29	15
Over 50	65	24	11	62	22	16	57	25	18	57	29	14	54	29	17	61	26	13

EISENHOWER: 1958

	January 2-7			January 24-29			February 14-19			March 6-11			March 27-April 1			April 16-21		
	A%	D%	N%	A%	D%	N%	A%	D%	N%	A%	D%	N%	A%	D%	N%	A%	D%	N%
National	60	30	10	58	27	15	54	33	13	51	33	16	48	36	16	54	31	15
Male	57	34	09	55	33	12	53	39	08	50	38	12	47	40	13	51	36	13
Female	64	26	10	59	23	18	56	26	18	52	28	20	50	32	18	58	26	16
White	60	31	09	58	28	14	55	33	12	50	34	16	49	37	14	55	31	14
Nonwhite	64	19	17	53	27	20	52	29	19	59	25	16	41	30	29	50	25	25
East	65	27	08	65	20	15	57	29	14	57	28	15	50	32	18	60	25	15
Midwest	65	25	10	62	24	14	55	34	11	51	33	16	53	33	14	60	28	12
South	53	36	11	46	36	18	53	34	13	43	36	21	38	46	16	43	37	20
West	57	35	08	56	33	11	52	32	16	54	38	08	52	32	16	56	35	09
Republican	85	12	03	84	09	07	84	09	07	79	09	12	81	09	10	83	07	10
Democrat	45	43	12	39	43	18	39	46	15	31	52	17	28	54	18	36	47	17
Independent	60	29	11	55	26	19	55	30	15	58	23	19	51	30	19	57	28	15
Protestant							55	32	13	52	32	16	50	35	15			
Catholic							56	31	13	52	34	14	49	36	15			
Union	54	35	11															
Nonunion	64	28	08															
Grade School	58	30	12	51	28	21	52	32	16	46	34	20	43	38	19	47	32	21
High School	62	28	10	59	27	14	55	32	13	52	32	16	49	36	15	54	32	14
College	60	36	04	64	28	08	59	34	07	59	33	08	55	33	12	69	26	05
Under 30	61	30	09	59	25	16	59	29	12	55	29	16	54	28	18	59	25	16
30-49	59	30	11	56	30	14	53	32	15	51	33	16	47	37	16	54	31	15
Over 50	62	30	08	59	26	15	55	34	11	50	35	15	47	38	15	53	33	14

EISENHOWER: 1958

	May 7-12			May 28-June 2			July 10-15			July 30-August 4			August 20-25			September 10-15		
	A%	D%	N%	A%	D%	N%	A%	D%	N%	A%	D%	N%	A%	D%	N%	A%	D%	N%
National	53	32	15	54	31	15	52	32	16	58	27	15	56	27	17	57	29	14
Male	51	37	12	50	37	13	50	36	14	61	28	11	55	31	14	54	36	10
Female	54	28	18	57	26	17	54	28	18	55	26	19	58	24	18	59	23	18
White	52	33	15	54	32	14	53	31	16	59	27	14	56	28	16	56	30	14
Nonwhite	52	27	21	47	24	29	46	39	15	45	26	29	60	21	19	55	22	23
East	59	25	16	57	29	14	56	27	17	63	24	13	60	24	16	58	29	13
Midwest	52	35	13	57	30	13	51	35	14	56	28	16	57	26	17	63	24	13
South	47	37	16	42	37	21	48	34	18	50	30	20	50	32	18	46	34	20
West	49	35	16	62	27	11	53	34	13	65	27	08	59	26	15	58	33	09
Republican	80	09	11	79	13	08	81	12	07	83	08	09	82	08	10	81	08	11
Democrat	32	52	16	35	49	16	35	47	18	41	40	19	39	42	19	40	44	16
Independent	55	27	18	53	26	21	55	26	19	58	27	15	59	23	18	60	25	15
Protestant	54	32	14	55	29	16	52	33	15	59	26	15	56	28	16	58	28	14
Catholic	51	33	16	54	31	15	56	27	17	62	24	14	60	23	17	59	28	13
Union																51	34	15
Nonunion																59	27	14
Grade School	49	32	19	45	33	22	46	32	22	52	27	21	55	25	20	55	26	19
High School	52	33	15	55	31	14	53	32	15	59	27	14	56	26	18	55	31	14
College	63	32	05	67	27	06	61	32	07	64	28	08	59	34	07	64	31	05
Under 30	50	35	15	60	27	13	55	27	18	56	26	18	63	21	16	54	30	16
30-49	50	33	17	51	33	16	51	34	15	57	29	14	52	29	19	57	29	14
Over 50	55	32	13	53	32	15	53	31	16	60	25	15	57	28	15	56	30	14

EISENHOWER: 1958-1959

	September 24-29			October 15-20			November 7-12			December 3-8			January 7-12			February 4-9		
	A%	D%	N%	A%	D%	N%	A%	D%	N%	A%	D%	N%	A%	D%	N%	A%	D%	N%
National	54	28	18	57	27	16	52	30	18	57	32	11	57	27	16	59	26	15
Male	51	33	16	55	30	15	52	33	15	56	36	08	55	33	12	58	30	12
Female	58	23	19	59	24	17	52	27	21	58	29	13	60	21	19	60	22	18
White	56	28	16	58	27	15	53	29	18	58	32	10	59	26	15	59	27	14
Nonwhite	44	25	31	46	27	27	46	35	19	46	40	14	45	35	20	56	17	27
East	58	26	16	67	18	15	58	25	17	58	31	11	62	23	15	61	25	14
Midwest	54	26	20	62	25	13	51	30	19	64	28	08	58	27	15	62	26	12
South	50	32	18	39	38	23	43	34	23	45	42	13	52	30	18	51	26	23
West	56	28	16	54	31	15	56	32	12	62	26	12	55	31	14	63	26	11
Republican	81	10	09	86	07	07	80	10	10	85	10	05	85	08	07	86	07	07
Democrat	38	41	21	37	42	21	35	44	21	37	50	13	42	39	19	39	43	18
Independent	54	26	20	54	27	19	52	26	22	61	28	11	57	27	16	61	20	19
Protestant	55	28	17	55	28	17	53	29	18	59	31	10	58	27	15	61	23	16
Catholic	58	25	17	64	21	15	51	31	18	57	32	11	56	27	17	57	30	13
Union	51	29	20	51	32	17	48	34	18				49	34	17			
Nonunion	56	27	17	59	25	16	54	28	18				60	25	15			
Grade School	50	29	21	53	27	20	48	29	23	54	34	12	53	27	20	52	25	23
High School	57	26	17	58	27	15	53	30	17	57	32	11	57	27	16	59	27	14
College	57	32	11	62	27	11	56	32	12	63	30	07	65	31	04	70	25	05
Under 30	56	23	21	62	24	14	49	29	22	67	23	10	60	24	16	60	21	19
30-49	54	29	17	58	25	17	54	30	16	55	34	11	54	29	17	58	28	14
Over 50	55	29	16	54	29	17	50	31	19	57	33	10	60	27	13	62	24	14

EISENHOWER: 1959

	March 4-9			April 2-7			April 29-May 4			May 29-June 3			June 25-30			July 23-28		
	A%	D%	N%	A%	D%	N%	A%	D%	N%	A%	D%	N%	A%	D%	N%	A%	D%	N%
National	58	26	16	62	23	15	60	24	16	64	21	15	62	23	15	61	26	13
Male	60	27	13	63	25	12	61	27	12	63	24	13	60	27	13	60	30	10
Female	57	24	19	61	21	18	59	22	19	66	18	16	65	19	16	62	23	15
White	60	24	16	63	23	14	62	24	14	66	20	14	64	22	14	61	27	12
Nonwhite	43	35	22	56	19	25	45	26	29	48	30	22	51	29	20	63	23	14
East	66	23	11	68	17	15	60	25	15	66	20	14	65	20	15	61	25	14
Midwest	59	25	16	66	20	14	62	23	15	65	22	13	59	26	15	67	23	10
South	46	28	26	51	29	20	56	25	19	57	23	20	58	25	17	54	31	15
West	62	25	13	61	27	12	64	25	11	70	19	11	67	21	12	62	26	12
Republican	85	07	08	87	06	07	87	05	08	87	07	06	90	04	06	88	06	06
Democrat	44	38	18	46	36	18	45	38	17	51	33	16	44	37	19	44	42	14
Independent	62	19	19	66	15	19	61	19	20	63	18	19	64	20	16	67	19	14
Protestant	58	25	17	62	22	16	61	24	15	67	19	14	62	24	14	64	24	12
Catholic	64	24	12	65	22	13	62	22	16	63	22	15	66	19	15	62	26	12
Union										57	26	17	55	28	17	59	28	13
Nonunion										66	20	14	65	21	14	62	26	12
Grade School	53	24	23	53	25	22	55	26	19	56	24	20	61	22	17	55	27	18
High school	60	25	15	64	21	15	61	24	15	67	19	14	62	23	15	62	27	11
College	63	29	08	71	23	06	67	25	08	70	21	09	66	25	09	70	23	07
Under 30	64	23	13	64	19	17	61	23	16	63	22	15	68	17	15	65	23	12
30-49	56	27	17	62	24	14	58	25	17	65	20	15	60	24	16	62	25	13
Over 50	60	24	16	63	22	15	62	25	13	64	22	14	64	24	12	59	29	12

EISENHOWER: 1959

	August 20-25			September 18-23			October 16-21			November 12-17			December 3-8			December 10-15		
	A%	D%	N%	A%	D%	N%	A%	D%	N%	A%	D%	N%	A%	D%	N%	A%	D%	N%
National	67	20	13	66	20	14	67	19	14	65	21	14	67	18	15	77	15	08
Male	67	23	10	65	23	12	66	22	12	65	25	10	66	21	13	75	17	08
Female	67	17	16	68	16	16	68	17	15	66	17	17	67	16	17	78	13	09
White	68	20	12	67	19	14	68	19	13	65	22	13	69	17	14	77	15	08
Nonwhite	55	23	22	63	25	12	55	20	25	67	16	17	45	28	27	78	14	08
East	72	16	12	70	16	14	69	20	11	65	23	12	69	17	14	76	16	08
Midwest	65	20	15	70	18	12	63	21	16	64	21	15	66	19	15	79	13	08
South	64	22	14	55	27	18	63	21	16	65	20	15	60	23	17	75	18	07
West	64	23	13	71	17	12	76	13	11	69	20	11	73	13	14	77	13	10
Republican	87	07	06	88	04	08	88	05	07	89	06	05	89	05	06	94	03	03
Democrat	51	33	16	51	33	16	52	31	17	49	34	17	53	28	19	66	24	10
Independent	71	15	14	67	16	17	74	13	13	66	17	17	67	17	16	78	12	10
Protestant	67	20	13	68	19	13	65	20	15	66	20	14	67	19	14	78	15	07
Catholic	70	18	12	68	18	14	72	17	11	68	21	11	71	12	17	77	13	10
Union	61	24	15				62	23	15	57	28	15	58	23	19	73	20	07
Nonunion	69	19	12				69	18	13	68	19	13	71	16	13	78	14	08
Grade School	59	23	18	56	22	22	58	24	18	57	24	19	57	23	20	74	16	10
High School	70	19	11	70	18	12	67	19	14	69	20	11	70	16	14	78	15	07
College	76	17	07	73	20	07	81	13	06	72	16	12	77	17	06	78	15	07
Under 30	68	19	13	72	17	11	68	19	13	70	18	12	68	14	18	77	17	06
30-49	65	21	14	66	20	14	68	17	15	63	21	16	66	19	15	76	15	09
Over 50	67	20	13	65	20	15	65	22	13	67	22	11	67	19	14	78	15	07

EISENHOWER: 1960

	May 26-31			April 28-May 3			March 30-April 4			March 2-7			February 4-9			January 6-11		
	A%	D%	N%	A%	D%	N%	A%	D%	N%	A%	D%	N%	A%	D%	N%	A%	D%	N%
National	65	22	13	62	22	16	65	22	13	64	22	14	64	22	14	66	19	15
Male	64	26	10	62	24	14	63	26	11	62	29	09	61	26	13	66	23	11
Female	66	19	15	62	20	18	68	18	14	65	17	18	67	18	15	67	14	19
White	67	21	12	63	22	15	66	22	12	65	22	13	64	22	14	68	18	14
Nonwhite	49	26	25	54	21	25	60	22	18	51	24	25	62	15	23	50	21	29
East	67	19	14	67	21	12	69	22	09	66	21	13	66	23	11	70	18	12
Midwest	70	20	10	64	21	15	67	22	11	63	24	13	69	18	13	65	20	15
South	58	28	14	57	23	20	63	22	15	56	23	21	56	23	21	62	18	20
West	65	21	14	59	25	16	60	23	17	70	20	10	66	24	10	70	16	14
Republican	91	05	04	87	07	06	89	05	06	88	07	05	91	06	03	91	02	07
Democrat	48	36	16	44	36	20	50	36	14	47	34	19	42	37	21	54	29	17
Independent	71	14	15	69	14	17	66	15	19	68	20	12	71	15	14	67	15	18
Protestant	66	21	13	63	22	15	68	21	11	66	20	14	65	21	14	67	17	16
Catholic	69	20	11	63	22	15	63	23	14	63	22	15	66	22	12	68	19	13
Union	63	24	13	56	27	17	55	31	14	59	28	13	56	30	14			
Nonunion	66	21	13	64	20	16	69	19	12	65	20	15	67	18	15			
Grade School	60	23	17	62	20	18	61	22	17	55	26	19	56	22	22	55	22	23
High School	68	21	11	61	23	16	66	22	12	68	20	12	68	20	12	71	16	13
College	70	22	08	67	24	09	74	22	04	71	22	07	71	24	05	73	17	10
Under 30	67	18	15	61	24	15	70	21	09	68	20	12	68	17	15	69	14	17
30-49	66	24	10	60	23	17	64	24	12	61	24	15	63	25	12	66	20	14
Over 50	64	21	15	65	21	14	66	21	13	64	22	14	64	20	16	66	18	16

EISENHOWER: 1960

	June 16-21			June 30-July 5			July 16-21			July 30-August 4			August 11-16			August 25-30		
	A%	D%	N%	A%	D%	N%	A%	D%	N%	A%	D%	N%	A%	D%	N%	A%	D%	N%
National	61	24	15	57	27	16	49	33	18	63	26	11	63	24	13	61	28	11
Male	61	27	12	55	31	14	46	38	16	61	30	09	65	26	09	59	33	08
Female	61	22	17	60	22	18	52	29	19	64	23	13	62	23	15	64	24	12
White	65	23	12	59	26	15	52	32	16	64	26	10	65	23	12	62	28	10
Nonwhite	39	29	32	45	26	29	34	39	27	55	30	15	54	32	14	55	33	12
East	65	21	14	67	21	12	54	32	14	62	27	11	67	22	11	65	24	11
Midwest	67	23	10	59	25	16	52	33	15	69	21	10	64	26	10	62	28	10
South	51	24	25	45	33	22	41	33	26	55	31	14	58	26	16	58	28	14
West	61	30	09	57	28	15	49	36	15	63	29	08	64	20	16	56	39	05
Republican	86	07	07	82	09	09	79	10	11	88	06	06	87	07	06	87	09	04
Democrat	46	37	17	43	39	18	34	47	19	40	46	14	45	39	16	43	44	13
Independent	67	19	14	61	21	18	51	29	20	68	21	11	64	22	14	64	25	11
Protestant	60	24	16	54	28	18	50	32	18	67	23	10	66	22	12	65	25	10
Catholic	70	16	14	69	20	11	53	32	15	58	30	12	56	29	15	58	31	11
Union	57	31	12	55	28	17	45	38	17	55	31	14	62	27	11	55	34	11
Nonunion	63	22	15	58	26	16	51	31	18	66	25	09	63	24	13	64	26	10
Grade School	56	22	22	52	27	21	48	29	23	63	24	13	58	26	16	60	27	13
High School	64	24	12	60	25	15	50	33	17	61	28	11	65	24	11	60	29	11
College	65	25	10	64	28	08	50	43	07	69	26	05	70	23	07	65	29	06
Under 30	60	27	13	62	20	18	49	34	17	59	30	11	65	23	12	60	28	12
30-49	62	25	13	59	27	14	50	32	18	63	26	11	64	25	11	61	29	10
Over 50	62	21	17	54	28	18	50	33	17	65	24	11	62	24	14	61	28	11

EISENHOWER: 1960

	September 9-14			September 28-October 2			October 18-23			November 17-22			December 8-13		
	A%	D%	N%	A%	D%	N%	A%	D%	N%	A%	D%	N%	A%	D%	N%
National	58	28	14	65	26	09	58	31	11	59	26	15	59	28	13
Male	57	32	11	61	32	07	58	34	08	57	30	13	58	33	09
Female	60	25	15	69	21	10	58	29	13	61	22	17	61	22	17
White	60	27	13	66	26	08	61	30	09	61	25	14	62	26	12
Nonwhite	48	34	18	55	28	17	38	43	19	47	33	20	48	33	19
East	57	30	13	66	26	08	64	25	11	59	26	15	60	28	12
Midwest	63	29	08	71	21	08	57	33	10	60	26	14	63	28	09
South	53	30	17	59	30	11	54	33	13	55	27	18	58	22	20
West	59	23	18	62	31	07	57	36	07	67	24	09	55	33	12
Republican	85	08	07	88	09	03	90	07	03	90	04	06	88	06	06
Democrat	40	42	18	46	41	13	36	50	14	40	40	20	43	41	16
Independent	61	29	10	74	19	07	62	27	11	55	27	18	56	29	15
Protestant	60	26	14	69	24	07	61	30	09	63	23	14	64	23	13
Catholic	59	29	12	62	26	12	57	30	13	52	31	17	52	34	14
Union	52	35	13	62	30	08	53	37	10				54	37	09
Nonunion	60	26	14	67	25	08	59	30	11				62	24	14
Grade School	53	28	19	63	26	11	51	35	14	53	27	20	57	25	18
High School	61	27	12	66	27	07	61	30	09	62	24	14	61	26	13
College	60	33	07	69	25	06	64	28	08	64	29	07	61	34	05
Under 30	64	21	15	73	21	06	60	26	14	64	22	14	62	24	14
30-49	54	33	13	59	30	11	54	35	11	59	25	16	59	30	11
Over 50	62	26	12	70	23	07	62	30	08	58	28	14	59	26	15

KENNEDY: 1961

	February 10-15			March 10-15			April 6-11			April 28-May 3			May 4-9			May 17-22		
	A%	D%	N%	A%	D%	N%	A%	D%	N%	A%	D%	N%	A%	D%	N%	A%	D%	N%
National	72	06	22	73	07	20	78	06	16	83	05	12	77	09	14	75	10	15
Male	71	07	22	75	07	18	80	06	14				77	11	12	77	12	11
Female	72	06	22	71	08	21	76	06	18				78	06	16	72	09	19
White	71	06	23	73	07	20	76	07	17				77	09	14	74	11	15
Nonwhite	80	05	15	73	08	19	86	01	13				84	03	13	79	03	18
East	74	04	22	74	05	21	80	07	13				79	07	14	79	08	13
Midwest	72	07	21	72	07	21	80	05	15				78	10	12	77	11	12
South	68	07	25	71	11	18	74	05	21				72	10	18	70	10	20
West	73	07	20	77	06	17	76	10	14				81	07	12	70	13	17
Republican	52	14	34	60	13	27	63	15	22				60	18	22	57	21	22
Democrat	85	02	13	85	04	11	89	02	09				89	03	08	86	04	10
Independent	67	06	27	69	07	24	75	03	22				75	09	16	68	12	20
Protestant				69	08	23	74	07	19				74	10	16	70	12	18
Catholic				84	05	11	86	04	10				86	05	09	89	04	07
Union							85	03	12				84	06	10	79	06	15
Nonunion							76	07	17				75	09	16	73	12	15
Grade School	70	05	25	71	07	22	73	06	21				75	07	18	75	09	16
High School	72	07	21	72	08	20	82	06	12				79	08	13	75	09	16
College	72	06	22	80	06	14	78	08	14				79	13	08	71	18	11
Under 30	74	05	21	79	03	18	86	05	09				80	07	13	77	07	16
30-49	73	05	22	77	06	17	78	07	15				82	07	11	76	10	14
Over 50	68	08	24	67	10	23	74	06	20				71	11	18	72	12	16

KENNEDY: 1961

	May 28-June 2 A%	D%	N%	June 23-28 A%	D%	N%	July 27-August 1 A%	D%	N%	August 24-29 A%	D%	N%	September 21-26 A%	D%	N%	October 19-24 A%	D%	N%
National	74	11	15	72	14	14	75	12	13	76	12	12	79	10	11	77	12	11
Male	72	14	14	73	15	12	77	14	09	79	13	08	80	13	07	80	12	08
Female	76	08	16	71	13	16	73	10	17	73	12	15	78	08	14	75	12	13
White	74	12	14	70	16	14	75	12	13	77	12	11	76	12	12	76	13	11
Nonwhite	68	04	28	84	01	15	75	10	15	72	12	16	94	03	03	93	04	03
East	76	07	17	74	14	12	80	09	11	77	12	11	81	09	10	79	11	10
Midwest	76	11	13	68	16	16	75	14	11	79	11	10	81	10	09	78	13	09
South	63	16	21	80	10	10	67	11	22	67	16	17	76	12	12	79	09	12
West	82	10	08	66	13	21	77	15	08	84	09	07	75	11	14	71	19	10
Republican	55	23	22	56	29	15	60	23	17	59	25	16	61	24	15	57	30	13
Democrat	87	04	09	84	06	10	86	04	10	88	05	07	87	06	07	90	03	07
Independent	68	12	20	64	15	21	70	14	16	70	11	19	78	08	14	75	12	13
Protestant	70	13	17	68	17	15	69	15	16	73	13	14	76	12	12	73	15	12
Catholic	85	06	09	81	06	13	90	04	06	87	06	07	86	06	08	91	04	05
Union																		
Nonunion																		
Grade School	70	11	19	73	11	16	71	10	19	75	10	15	80	06	14	76	10	14
High School	77	09	14	74	12	14	78	10	12	78	12	10	79	11	10	81	10	09
College	71	19	10	62	25	13	71	23	06	73	18	09	75	17	08	69	25	06
Under 30	74	09	17	80	10	10	75	11	14	85	09	06	81	09	10	82	08	10
30-49	79	09	12	74	12	14	78	11	11	77	12	11	83	08	09	79	12	09
Over 50	68	14	18	66	18	16	72	13	15	72	14	14	72	14	14	74	14	12

KENNEDY: 1961-1962

	November 17-22			December 7-12			January 11-16			February 8-13			March 8-13			April 6-11		
	A%	D%	N%	A%	D%	N%	A%	D%	N%	A%	D%	N%	A%	D%	N%	A%	D%	N%
National	79	09	12	77	11	12	79	10	11	78	11	11	79	12	09	77	13	10
Male	81	09	10	79	11	10	78	13	09	78	12	10	78	17	05	76	16	08
Female	77	08	15	76	10	14	80	07	13	79	10	11	81	07	12	78	10	12
White	79	10	11	77	12	11	78	10	12	78	12	10	80	12	08	76	14	10
Nonwhite	82	00	18	76	05	19	85	04	11	83	03	14	78	08	14	86	03	11
East	82	09	09	80	09	11	76	10	14	79	12	09	83	09	08	78	14	08
Midwest	82	08	10	80	09	11	81	08	11	80	08	12	81	12	07	80	12	08
South	73	10	17	70	14	16	81	11	08	76	14	10	75	14	11	73	11	16
West	78	08	14	80	12	08	76	11	13	78	12	10	79	12	09	80	14	06
Republican	64	20	16	55	27	18	59	24	17	62	25	13	67	25	08	57	30	13
Democrat	89	03	08	84	04	12	91	02	07	89	04	07	89	04	07	90	04	06
Independent	73	10	17	80	10	10	74	11	15	72	14	14	78	11	11	73	13	14
Protestant	76	10	14	73	13	14	75	12	13	75	13	12	76	14	10	73	15	12
Catholic	89	04	07	89	05	06	89	04	07	87	06	07	91	06	03	88	07	05
Union																		
Nonunion																		
Grade School	78	06	16	75	08	17	78	08	14	77	09	14	76	12	12	74	12	14
High School	81	09	10	80	11	09	80	08	12	81	10	09	83	10	07	80	12	08
College	77	13	10	75	17	08	76	18	06	75	21	04	78	17	05	76	18	06
Under 30	79	08	13	84	09	07	88	05	07	86	06	08	88	09	03	87	07	06
30-49	82	07	11	79	10	11	79	10	11	80	11	09	82	10	08	81	10	09
Over 50	76	11	13	72	13	15	76	11	13	74	14	12	73	15	12	70	18	12

KENNEDY: 1962

	May 3-8			May 31-June 5			June 28-July 3			July 26-31			August 23-28			September 20-25		
	A%	D%	N%	A%	D%	N%	A%	D%	N%	A%	D%	N%	A%	D%	N%	A%	D%	N%
National	74	16	10	71	19	10	69	19	12	66	23	11	67	20	13	63	22	15
Male	74	18	08	73	18	09	67	24	09	67	25	08	68	23	09	64	24	12
Female	74	14	12	69	19	12	70	15	15	66	20	14	67	17	16	62	21	17
White	72	18	10	68	21	11	68	20	12	64	25	11	66	21	13	61	24	15
Nonwhite	90	03	07	90	04	06	79	07	14	84	05	11	95	00	05	79	08	13
East	76	15	09	74	18	08	76	14	10	77	16	07	66	21	13	72	18	10
Midwest	76	14	10	71	19	10	68	22	10	65	25	10	71	18	11	60	26	14
South	68	20	12	69	16	15	60	23	17	58	24	18	65	20	15	53	24	23
West	75	18	07	69	23	08	74	16	10	62	28	10	69	21	10	69	20	11
Republican	53	31	16	44	42	14	44	41	15	39	47	14	42	40	18	37	46	17
Democrat	86	08	06	85	07	08	84	05	11	82	10	08	84	08	08	79	10	11
Independent	73	17	10	73	16	11	64	26	10	66	22	12	60	24	16	62	21	17
Protestant	70	18	12	67	20	13	63	23	14	59	28	13	63	23	14	57	26	17
Catholic	91	05	04	82	13	05	85	09	06	83	11	06	84	08	08	82	10	08
Union	81	13	06				69	21	10									
Nonunion	71	18	11				69	15	16									
Grade School	78	11	11	72	13	15	70	13	17	66	18	16	67	16	17	63	18	19
High School	74	16	10	73	18	09	71	19	10	68	22	10	70	20	10	63	23	14
College	66	28	06	62	32	06	60	34	06	60	36	04	64	29	07	62	31	07
Under 30	81	13	06	77	12	11	77	16	07	77	15	08	80	12	08	75	13	12
30-49	79	12	09	74	18	08	70	18	12	69	21	10	71	18	11	67	20	13
Over 50	66	22	12	66	22	12	64	22	14	59	28	13	62	23	15	54	29	17

KENNEDY: 1962-1963

	October 19-24 A%	D%	N%	November 16-21 A%	D%	N%	December 13-18 A%	D%	N%	January 11-16 A%	D%	N%	February 7-12 A%	D%	N%	March 8-13 A%	D%	N%
National	61	25	14	74	14	12	76	13	11	74	14	12	70	18	12	67	20	13
Male	62	29	09	76	15	09	74	15	11	73	18	09	69	22	09	69	22	09
Female	61	21	18	72	13	15	77	12	11	74	11	15	71	14	15	64	18	18
White	60	26	14	73	15	12	74	14	12	73	15	12	68	20	12	64	22	14
Nonwhite	80	09	11	81	05	14	93	05	02	80	08	12	92	02	06	84	06	10
East	68	21	11	78	10	12	80	06	14	79	12	09	78	13	09	71	19	10
Midwest	61	21	18	77	12	11	80	11	09	77	13	10	70	17	13	69	19	12
South	52	33	15	65	20	15	69	22	09	66	15	19	63	21	16	60	22	18
West	67	23	10	76	16	08	73	15	12	71	20	09	71	22	07	65	20	15
Republican	35	47	18	48	33	19	55	27	18	53	35	12	47	38	15	43	42	15
Democrat	78	11	11	91	03	06	92	04	04	86	04	10	85	07	08	82	09	09
Independent	61	25	14	70	14	16	71	13	16	72	12	16	67	19	14	64	19	17
Protestant	53	30	17	69	17	14	71	17	12	69	18	13	65	22	13	60	25	15
Catholic	82	11	07	85	07	08	88	05	07	87	06	07	85	07	08	84	09	07
Union	72	18	10															
Nonunion	58	27	15															
Grade School	62	20	18	72	13	15	72	16	12	72	15	13	66	17	17	66	15	19
High School	66	22	12	78	13	09	79	11	10	78	11	11	75	15	10	67	20	13
College	49	42	09	68	21	11	75	14	11	68	23	09	67	27	06	66	27	07
Under 30	70	20	10	80	11	09	84	07	09	77	13	10	84	10	06	75	14	11
30-49	65	21	14	78	11	11	76	13	11	79	09	12	73	16	11	70	19	11
Over 50	56	29	15	67	18	15	72	16	12	67	21	12	62	23	15	60	23	17

KENNEDY: 1963

	April 4-9			May 2-7			May 8-13			May 23-28			June 21-26			July 18-23		
	A%	D%	N%	A%	D%	N%	A%	D%	N%	A%	D%	N%	A%	D%	N%	A%	D%	N%
National	66	21	13	64	25	11	65	23	12	64	24	12	61	26	13	61	27	12
Male	65	24	11	61	28	11	63	27	10	65	28	07	59	31	10	58	32	10
Female	66	19	15	66	22	12	67	20	13	63	21	16	63	23	14	63	23	14
White	63	23	14	61	27	12	63	25	12	60	27	13	57	29	14	57	30	13
Nonwhite	84	08	08	81	10	09	80	09	11	90	06	04	91	05	04	88	07	05
East	67	21	12	69	20	11	71	17	12	72	16	12	75	15	10	71	15	14
Midwest	67	17	16	68	21	11	65	25	10	70	20	10	67	20	13	63	26	11
South	63	23	14	56	30	14	57	28	15	52	37	11	33	51	16	44	43	13
West	64	26	10	61	29	10	67	23	10	60	27	13	74	16	10	64	27	09
Republican	41	44	15	36	49	15	39	49	12	45	40	15	41	43	16	34	49	17
Democrat	84	06	10	80	10	10	81	11	08	79	14	07	74	18	08	77	15	08
Independent	57	25	18	62	27	11	65	17	18	56	28	16	56	27	17	56	32	12
Protestant	60	25	15	58	29	13	60	28	12	59	29	12	53	32	15	52	35	13
Catholic	80	12	08	77	15	08	79	12	09	80	08	12	80	13	07	79	11	10
Union																70	23	07
Nonunion																57	29	14
Grade School	64	19	17	63	22	15	64	22	14	65	21	14	57	25	18	65	23	12
High School	68	20	12	67	22	11	69	20	11	66	24	10	64	25	11	58	28	14
College	60	31	09	57	35	08	58	32	10	57	34	09	62	32	06	59	34	07
Under 30	74	12	14	71	20	09	76	14	10	69	23	08	64	23	13	66	24	10
30-49	71	19	10	65	24	11	67	22	11	67	22	11	66	24	10	63	27	10
Over 50	56	27	17	60	27	13	59	28	13	58	28	14	54	31	15	55	30	15

KENNEDY: 1963

	August 15-20			September 12-17			October 11-16			November 8-13		
	A%	D%	N%	A%	D%	N%	A%	D%	N%	A%	D%	N%
National	62	26	12	56	29	15	58	29	13	58	30	12
Male	59	30	11	54	33	13	56	33	11	57	34	09
Female	66	22	12	58	26	16	60	25	15	60	26	14
White	59	29	12	53	33	14	54	33	13	53	34	13
Nonwhite	90	03	07	82	04	14	84	03	13	90	06	04
East	72	18	10	64	20	16	68	21	11	67	20	13
Midwest	66	23	11	60	26	14	58	26	16	63	28	09
South	44	39	17	40	44	16	45	41	14	45	41	14
West	67	24	09	61	31	08	62	29	09	56	34	10
Republican	45	42	13	37	51	12	30	55	15	31	56	13
Democrat	76	15	09	71	18	11	77	12	11	80	12	08
Independent	54	31	15	53	27	20	58	30	12	52	34	14
Protestant	56	32	12				51	35	14	53	35	12
Catholic	81	12	07				77	14	09	77	15	08
Union												
Nonunion												
Grade School	62	25	13	53	27	20	58	24	18	60	26	14
High School	65	26	09	60	27	13	61	29	10	58	31	11
College	58	28	14	53	40	07	51	37	12	54	37	09
Under 30	73	17	10	63	23	14	69	24	07	68	24	08
30-49	66	24	10	58	27	15	60	28	12	61	29	10
Over 50	55	31	14	51	35	14	52	32	16	53	33	14

JOHNSON: 1963-1964

	December 5-10			December 12-17			January 2-7			January 30-February 5			February 13-18			February 28-March 4		
	A%	D%	N%	A%	D%	N%	A%	D%	N%	A%	D%	N%	A%	D%	N%	A%	D%	N%
National	78	02	20	74	04	22	77	05	18	76	08	16	73	09	18	79	09	12
Male	79	03	18	75	04	21	77	06	17	76	10	14	74	10	16	80	11	09
Female	77	02	21	73	04	23	77	04	19	75	06	19	73	07	20	79	07	14
White	79	03	18	73	05	22	77	06	17	76	08	16	73	09	18	79	10	11
Nonwhite	73	01	26	79	00	21	72	04	24	77	07	16	80	02	18	85	04	11
East	79	01	20	73	02	25	78	05	17	78	05	17	75	06	19	84	07	09
Midwest	78	01	21	79	04	17	77	05	18	78	06	16	77	07	16	81	08	11
South	75	06	19	66	08	26	75	05	19	71	12	17	66	13	21	75	10	15
West	81	01	18	78	02	2ᴼ	75	08	17	76	09	15	76	10	14	75	14	11
Republican	78	03	19	67	05	28	73	08	19	66	13	21	63	17	20	70	20	10
Democrat	82	02	16	77	03	20	82	04	14	82	05	13	84	04	12	86	04	10
Independent	71	03	26	71	08	21	70	07	23	75	10	15	67	09	24	74	10	16
Protestant	78	03	19	71	05	24	78	05	17	73	09	18	72	10	18	77	11	12
Catholic	80	01	19	81	02	17	78	05	17	85	04	11	76	07	17	87	04	09
Union	81	01	18	70	05	25	73	04	23	78	06	16						
Nonunion	77	03	20	75	04	21	78	05	17	75	09	16						
Grade School	71	02	27	69	04	27	76	05	19	76	06	18	69	09	22	77	10	13
High School	81	03	16	75	04	21	76	05	19	75	09	16	77	07	16	81	07	12
College	85	01	14	79	05	16	81	07	12	80	08	12	75	11	14	81	12	07
Under 30	81	04	15	72	03	25	77	06	17	78	09	13	80	08	12	83	09	08
30-49	77	01	22	72	05	23	73	05	22	76	07	17	74	08	18	81	07	12
Over 50	78	03	19	74	04	22	81	05	14	74	09	17	72	09	19	78	10	12

JOHNSON: 1964

	March 13-18 A%	D%	N%	March 27-April 1 A%	D%	N%	April 24-29 A%	D%	N%	May 6-11 A%	D%	N%	May 22-27 A%	D%	N%	June 4-9 A%	D%	N%
National	77	09	14	75	12	13	75	11	14	75	10	15	74	13	13	74	12	14
Male	78	10	12	76	13	11	76	13	11	76	11	13	75	15	10	73	15	12
Female	77	08	15	75	11	14	74	10	16	74	09	17	72	12	16	75	09	16
White	76	10	14	74	13	13	73	12	15	74	11	15	72	15	13	72	13	15
Nonwhite	88	02	10	86	05	09	86	06	08	82	06	12	82	07	11	87	03	10
East	81	06	13	81	08	11	81	09	10	81	05	14	80	10	10	82	06	12
Midwest	77	09	14	77	11	12	77	07	16	81	09	10	77	11	12	74	12	14
South	75	13	12	68	16	16	66	18	16	67	12	21	63	19	18	63	18	19
West	76	08	16	76	13	11	75	11	14	68	17	15	75	15	10	78	12	10
Republican	67	17	16	60	25	15	67	19	14	61	19	20	62	22	16	60	23	17
Democrat	87	03	10	83	06	11	82	06	12	84	06	10	82	08	10	84	06	10
Independent	70	13	17	76	11	13	69	14	17	70	10	20	68	15	17	67	15	18
Protestant	77	10	13	75	13	12	73	12	15	73	12	15	71	15	14	71	14	15
Catholic	82	06	12	79	08	13	80	07	13	84	05	11	81	09	10	82	08	10
Union										80	09	11						
Nonunion										73	11	16						
Grade School	77	07	16	74	11	15	73	08	19	75	08	17	72	11	17	73	10	17
High School	78	09	13	77	10	13	76	12	12	78	08	14	76	13	11	73	13	14
College	78	11	11	77	15	08	77	15	08	69	19	12	71	20	09	78	14	08
Under 30	83	08	09	84	08	08	78	09	13	80	08	12	78	11	11	75	13	12
30-49	77	09	14	76	12	12	76	11	13	75	10	15	75	13	12	78	09	13
Over 50	76	09	15	72	13	15	74	11	15	73	11	16	71	15	14	70	14	16

JOHNSON: 1964-1965

	June 11-16			June 25-30			November 20-25			December 11-16			January 7-12			January 28-February 2		
	A%	D%	N%	A%	D%	N%	A%	D%	N%	A%	D%	N%	A%	D%	N%	A%	D%	N%
National	74	14	12	74	15	11	70	19	11	69	18	13	71	15	14	70	15	15
Male	77	14	09	74	17	09	72	19	09				72	16	12	71	16	13
Female	71	14	15	73	13	14	68	19	13				70	14	16	69	14	17
White	72	16	12	71	17	12	68	21	11				68	17	15	68	16	16
Nonwhite	89	02	09	87	04	09	95	01	04				93	01	06	91	03	06
East	79	09	12	81	10	09	80	12	08				76	10	14	74	09	17
Midwest	75	13	12	78	12	10	72	14	14				74	15	11	73	14	13
South	68	20	12	64	21	15	58	28	14				64	19	17	64	21	15
West	72	15	13	71	17	12	71	23	06				68	20	12	70	15	15
Republican	53	30	17	61	25	14	47	37	16				51	33	16	50	32	18
Democrat	87	06	07	86	07	07	85	09	06				85	06	09	85	04	11
Independent	68	16	16	63	19	18	63	22	15				62	18	20	59	20	21
Protestant	71	17	12	71	17	12	65	23	12				69	16	15	69	17	14
Catholic	83	07	10	82	08	10	82	09	09				75	13	12	74	10	16
Union				81	09	10												
Nonunion				71	17	12												
Grade School	72	12	16	75	12	13	74	15	11				73	11	16	69	12	19
High School	76	13	11	73	16	11	71	19	10				73	15	12	74	14	12
College	74	19	07	74	16	10	65	24	11				63	22	15	66	21	13
Under 30	75	18	07	71	18	11	68	21	11				74	17	09	72	14	14
30-49	78	10	12	75	13	12	73	17	10				71	16	13	70	15	15
Over 50	70	16	14	73	16	11	68	20	12				70	13	17	69	15	16

JOHNSON: 1965

	February 19-24			March 11-16			March 18-23			April 2-7			April 23-28			May 13-18		
	A%	D%	N%	A%	D%	N%	A%	D%	N%	A%	D%	N%	A%	D%	N%	A%	D%	N%
National	68	18	14	68	18	14	69	21	10	67	22	11	64	22	14	70	18	12
Male	69	20	11				69	23	08	67	24	09	67	23	10	72	18	10
Female	68	16	16				70	18	12	66	20	14	61	21	18	69	17	14
White	66	20	14				67	22	11	64	24	12	61	24	15	68	19	13
Nonwhite	87	03	10				85	09	06	88	04	08	87	05	08	88	05	07
East	69	12	19				79	14	07	79	11	10	75	14	11	81	10	09
Midwest	72	18	10				75	16	09	70	18	12	64	18	18	71	18	11
South	66	20	14				50	34	16	53	36	11	49	35	16	56	28	16
West	67	23	10				74	17	09	63	23	14	66	22	12	76	13	11
Republican	48	36	16				57	33	10	50	36	14	46	36	18	53	35	12
Democrat	83	07	10				78	12	10	77	14	09	79	11	10	82	09	09
Independent	60	22	18				64	26	10	62	23	15	55	26	19	65	18	17
Protestant	66	20	14				66	23	11	60	27	13	56	28	16	66	21	13
Catholic	77	11	12				82	12	06	81	08	11	81	08	11	83	10	07
Union	79	11	10													75	12	13
Nonunion	65	20	15													68	20	12
Grade School	66	16	18				69	19	12	64	22	14	63	18	19	73	14	13
High School	71	17	12				69	20	11	69	20	11	64	23	13	70	18	12
College	65	24	11				71	23	06	64	26	10	64	27	09	67	22	11
Under 30	71	17	12				66	24	10	75	19	06	70	18	12	68	20	12
30-49	73	15	12				69	19	12	69	20	11	62	24	14	73	16	11
Over 50	63	21	16				71	20	09	63	24	13	63	22	15	69	18	13

JOHNSON: 1965

	June 4-9			June 24-29			July 16-21			August 5-10			August 27-September 1			September 16-21		
	A%	D%	N%	A%	D%	N%	A%	D%	N%	A%	D%	N%	A%	D%	N%	A%	D%	N%
National	69	19	12	65	21	14	65	20	15	65	22	13	64	25	11	63	24	13
Male	70	21	09	63	25	12	67	22	11	63	26	11	64	26	10	65	24	11
Female	68	17	15	68	17	15	64	18	18	68	19	13	64	23	13	61	23	16
White	67	21	12	63	23	14	62	23	15	62	24	14	60	28	12	60	26	14
Nonwhite	82	07	11	83	06	11	88	03	09	90	05	05	90	04	06	90	03	07
East	77	13	10	70	13	17	77	11	12	72	16	12	77	15	08	77	11	12
Midwest	74	15	11	67	21	12	67	21	12	67	32	01	67	20	13	64	23	13
South	55	30	15	60	28	12	52	30	18	54	32	14	46	41	13	48	36	16
West	69	18	13	66	24	10	64	20	16	70	17	13	64	23	13	62	27	11
Republican	59	29	12	50	35	15	46	39	15	45	40	15	45	46	09	45	40	15
Democrat	80	11	09	77	13	10	80	11	09	80	11	09	79	12	09	78	13	09
Independent	59	24	17	57	26	17	57	23	20	57	29	14	55	29	16	55	28	17
Protestant	65	21	14	63	24	13	60	24	16	61	27	12	60	29	11	58	28	14
Catholic	79	13	08	73	24	13	79	24	10	74	27	13	74	29	14	77	13	10
Union																		
Nonunion																		
Grade School	66	18	16	64	21	15	65	15	20	64	20	16	61	23	16	65	20	15
High School	71	19	10	67	21	12	68	20	12	69	20	11	67	23	10	62	23	15
College	70	19	11	67	21	12	61	28	11	59	32	09	61	31	08	61	31	08
Under 30	71	17	12	67	20	13	75	19	06	74	17	09	69	18	13	71	17	12
30-49	72	17	11	68	20	12	64	22	14	64	23	13	67	23	10	62	26	12
Over 50	65	22	13	63	23	14	65	18	17	63	24	13	59	29	12	60	24	16

JOHNSON: 1965-1966

	October 8-13			October 29-November 2			November 18-23			December 11-16			December 31-January 5			January 21-26		
	A%	D%	N%	A%	D%	N%	A%	D%	N%	A%	D%	N%	A%	D%	N%	A%	D%	N%
National	66	21	13	65	22	13	62	22	16	63	26	11	59	24	17	61	27	12
Male	66	23	11	66	20	14	61	25	14	64	27	09	62	26	12	62	29	09
Female	65	20	15	64	23	13	64	19	17	62	26	12	57	21	22	60	25	15
White				63	23	14	60	24	16	60	29	11	58	25	17	59	28	13
Nonwhite				86	05	09	82	06	12	86	08	06	84	08	08	82	13	05
East	76	13	11	76	11	13	72	13	15	76	16	08	72	09	19	70	19	11
Midwest	66	20	14	69	19	12	61	23	16	64	26	10	59	27	14	60	29	11
South	51	34	15	53	32	15	54	31	15	49	37	14	42	37	21	56	29	15
West	70	19	11	56	30	14	62	23	15	60	30	10	66	20	14	55	33	12
Republican	48	37	15	47	39	14	46	38	16	41	50	09	43	38	19	44	45	11
Democrat	74	16	10	80	10	10	74	12	14	72	17	11	75	12	13	74	16	10
Independent	67	18	15	58	24	18	58	26	16	66	23	11	46	31	23	55	31	14
Protestant	61	24	15	59	27	14	58	26	16	56	32	12				55	32	13
Catholic	77	15	08	78	11	11	71	14	15	77	16	07				73	17	10
Union				70	17	13	71	13	16							64	23	13
Nonunion				63	24	13	60	25	15							61	27	12
Grade School	64	19	17	70	16	14	60	19	21	62	25	13	60	17	23	65	22	13
High School	69	20	11	65	21	14	65	21	14	63	26	11	60	24	16	61	27	12
College	60	28	12	58	33	09	60	30	10	63	29	08	58	31	11	57	36	07
Under 30	69	19	12	69	21	10	70	20	10	67	22	11	66	21	13	66	23	11
30-49	68	20	12	67	20	13	64	21	15	62	29	09	62	22	16	63	25	12
Over 50	61	24	15	62	24	14	56	25	19	62	26	12	54	26	20	59	29	12

JOHNSON: 1966

	February 10-15			March 3-8			March 24-29			April 14-19			May 5-10			May 19-24		
	A%	D%	N%	A%	D%	N%	A%	D%	N%	A%	D%	N%	A%	D%	N%	A%	D%	N%
National	56	34	10	58	28	14	57	28	15	54	33	13	46	34	20	50	33	17
Male	57	35	08	59	31	10	58	28	14	53	34	13	49	35	16	52	34	14
Female	54	34	12	57	25	18	56	29	15	54	33	13	44	32	24	49	32	19
White	52	37	11				54	31	15	51	36	13	44	36	20	49	35	16
Nonwhite	83	09	08				82	06	12	82	05	13	69	08	23	72	05	23
East	64	26	10	63	23	14	68	18	14	64	23	13	52	25	23	58	24	18
Midwest	56	34	10	61	26	13	55	32	13	53	35	12	49	35	16	51	34	15
South	46	41	13	46	34	20	47	37	16	46	40	14	38	40	22	45	36	19
West	56	37	07	60	31	09	55	29	16	48	39	13	44	37	19	47	39	14
Republican	39	54	07	37	49	14	36	50	14	35	53	12	31	52	17	34	52	14
Democrat	70	21	09	74	15	11	74	13	13	70	18	12	61	21	18	61	22	17
Independent	47	41	12	47	33	20	50	34	16	48	37	15	37	40	23	44	37	19
Protestant	53	37	10	53	31	16	51	33	16	49	38	13	40	39	21	47	36	17
Catholic	65	25	10	72	19	09	72	15	13	66	24	10	63	20	17	60	23	17
Union	62	31	07															
Nonunion	54	35	11															
Grade School	57	30	13	59	22	19	59	25	16	54	29	17	50	26	24	48	29	23
High School	55	35	10	59	27	14	58	28	14	55	34	11	45	35	20	52	32	16
College	55	38	07	54	39	07	50	36	14	51	38	11	44	41	15	52	40	08
Under 30	57	34	09	61	25	14	61	27	12	57	28	15	52	30	18	54	31	15
30-49	57	34	09	61	27	12	56	31	13	56	32	12	48	33	19	53	32	15
Over 50	54	35	11	54	29	17	55	28	17	51	36	13	42	36	22	46	35	19

JOHNSON: 1966

	June 16-21			July 8-13			July 29-August 3			August 18-23			September 8-13			October 1-6		
	A%	D%	N%	A%	D%	N%	A%	D%	N%	A%	D%	N%	A%	D%	N%	A%	D%	N%
National	48	39	13	56	30	14	51	38	11	47	39	14	46	39	15	44	42	14
Male	50	41	09	56	33	11	54	39	07	49	39	12	50	38	12	47	40	13
Female	47	36	17	56	28	16	49	38	13	45	39	16	43	40	17	41	44	15
White	47	40	13	52	34	14	48	41	11	44	42	14	43	43	14	42	44	14
Nonwhite	73	19	08	87	03	10	79	13	08	74	09	17	73	08	19	74	16	10
East	58	30	12	67	20	13	60	31	09	56	34	10	56	26	18	53	30	17
Midwest	44	43	13	56	29	15	52	36	12	43	39	18	45	41	14	42	46	12
South	43	42	15	46	42	12	40	46	14	43	43	14	37	48	15	37	48	15
West	48	41	11	50	35	15	52	42	06	45	42	13	45	45	10	44	46	10
Republican	30	61	09	38	49	13	30	63	07	27	62	11	27	61	12	24	65	11
Democrat	66	23	11	70	17	13	65	24	11	65	22	13	58	28	14	59	29	12
Independent	42	40	18	45	39	16	47	42	11	39	45	16	42	41	17	37	46	17
Protestant	42	45	13	51	34	15	45	44	11	41	45	14	41	46	13	42	44	14
Catholic	62	23	15	71	19	10	70	23	07	62	25	13	56	28	16	50	38	12
Union							62	31	07	44	40	16	58	31	11			
Nonunion							48	41	11	49	39	12	42	42	16			
Grade School	50	32	18	55	30	15	54	32	14	42	37	21	52	31	17	49	30	21
High School	49	38	13	56	30	14	51	38	11	50	38	12	45	40	15	44	44	12
College	45	48	07	56	34	10	47	48	05	47	44	09	41	50	09	37	54	09
Under 30	52	37	11	64	30	06	57	36	07	50	39	11	47	40	13	47	40	13
30-49	52	37	11	57	29	14	54	37	09	51	36	13	47	39	14	42	44	14
Over 50	44	40	16	51	34	15	46	40	14	42	42	16	45	40	15	46	40	14

JOHNSON: 1966-1967

	October 21-26			November 10-15			December 8-13			January 7-12			January 26-31			February 16-21		
	A%	D%	N%	A%	D%	N%	A%	D%	N%	A%	D%	N%	A%	D%	N%	A%	D%	N%
National	44	41	15	49	35	16	44	47	09	47	37	16	46	37	17	45	42	13
Male	45	41	14	52	35	13	43	49	08	50	38	12	48	36	16	45	44	11
Female	44	41	15	45	35	20	45	45	10	44	36	20	44	37	19	44	41	15
White	41	44	15	46	38	16	41	51	08	45	39	16	43	39	18	42	45	13
Nonwhite	76	08	16	71	14	15	62	18	20	68	17	15	69	14	17	65	21	14
East	51	33	16	63	23	14	55	37	08	53	30	17	54	27	19	55	32	13
Midwest	43	40	17	46	39	15	41	51	08	50	37	13	42	43	15	42	42	16
South	35	54	11	40	43	17	35	57	08	41	38	21	39	41	20	41	48	11
West	50	32	18	43	37	20	45	40	15	40	48	12	49	36	15	39	51	10
Republican	23	65	12	28	57	15	21	71	08				26	61	13	25	64	11
Democrat	61	24	15	66	18	16	62	29	09				62	20	18	61	26	13
Independent	40	43	17	40	43	17	40	49	11				39	42	19	40	47	13
Protestant	41	44	15	44	39	17	40	50	10	42	41	17	41	42	17	40	46	14
Catholic	56	31	13	61	25	14	55	38	07	59	27	14	58	25	17	56	32	12
Union				57	31	12	50	41	09									
Nonunion				46	36	18	42	49	09									
Grade School	49	33	18	50	29	21	49	41	10	51	32	17	56	24	20	45	37	18
High School	44	41	15	50	33	17	44	45	11	46	36	18	44	39	17	45	43	12
College	38	52	10	42	49	09	35	60	05	45	47	08	36	49	15	46	46	08
Under 30	47	43	10	51	38	11	46	44	10	43	41	16	37	49	14	51	43	06
30-49	44	42	14	50	34	16	41	48	11	43	40	17	45	36	19	46	41	13
Over 50	44	39	17	46	35	19	46	46	08	52	33	15	50	33	17	41	43	16

JOHNSON: 1967

	March 9-14			March 30-April 4			April 19-26			May 11-16			June 2-7			June 22-27		
	A%	D%	N%	A%	D%	N%	A%	D%	N%	A%	D%	N%	A%	D%	N%	A%	D%	N%
National	45	41	14	46	38	16	48	37	15	45	39	16	44	40	16	51	35	14
Male	46	44	10	49	40	11	49	40	11	50	37	13	45	43	12	50	39	11
Female	43	39	18	44	37	19	48	34	18	40	42	18	43	37	20	51	32	17
White	43	43	14	44	41	15	47	38	15	43	42	15	43	41	16	49	37	14
Nonwhite	62	20	18	64	17	19	67	16	17	67	16	17	61	20	19	67	19	14
East	49	33	18	53	30	17	57	27	16	52	32	16	49	34	17	55	29	16
Midwest	45	39	16	40	43	17	47	39	14	44	39	17	45	39	16	51	36	13
South	39	48	13	41	42	17	40	43	17	36	47	17	37	45	18	48	37	15
West	46	48	06	51	39	10	52	40	08	48	43	09	48	40	12	48	42	10
Republican	28	59	13	28	58	14	31	56	13	28	60	12	29	58	13	34	53	13
Democrat	60	29	11	59	25	16	64	23	13	60	23	17	58	26	16	67	21	12
Independent	41	43	16	48	39	13	43	41	16	39	45	16	40	40	20	42	41	17
Protestant	40	46	14	43	43	14	43	42	15	41	44	15	40	43	17	48	37	15
Catholic	52	32	16	56	28	16	62	26	12	57	27	16	53	31	16	58	31	11
Union																		
Nonunion																		
Grade School	42	38	20	42	35	23	49	35	16	41	38	21	41	39	20	48	32	20
High School	46	41	13	49	36	15	48	37	15	46	40	14	46	37	17	52	35	13
College	45	47	08	44	50	06	50	40	10	47	41	12	46	45	09	50	41	09
Under 30	44	47	09	51	43	06	53	37	10	48	41	11	43	42	15	51	37	12
30-49	46	42	12	47	37	16	49	35	16	46	37	17	44	36	20	53	35	12
Over 50	44	38	18	43	38	19	47	38	15	42	42	16	46	41	13	48	35	17

JOHNSON: 1967

	July 13-18			August 3-8			August 24-29			September 14-19			October 6-11			October 27-November 1		
	A%	D%	N%	A%	D%	N%	A%	D%	N%	A%	D%	N%	A%	D%	N%	A%	D%	N%
National	47	39	14	40	48	12	39	48	13	38	48	14	38	50	12	41	49	10
Male	46	42	12	39	50	11	42	46	12	38	50	12	39	53	08	44	49	07
Female	47	37	16	40	45	15	36	50	14	38	46	16	37	48	15	39	49	12
White	45	41	14	37	51	12	37	50	13	35	51	14	36	53	11	39	51	10
Nonwhite	69	15	16	69	17	14	64	22	14	65	14	21	55	26	19	65	24	11
East	52	33	15	45	41	14	47	39	14	44	40	16	43	43	14	52	39	09
Midwest	50	38	12	40	49	11	35	52	13	35	51	14	36	53	11	36	53	11
South	37	47	16	33	51	16	34	53	13	34	51	15	33	56	11	37	55	08
West	48	39	13	41	48	11	40	50	10	40	48	12	38	52	10	38	52	10
Republican	29	58	13	24	65	11	22	67	11	20	70	10	23	70	07	19	73	08
Democrat	63	24	13	53	33	14	53	33	14	55	30	15	53	35	12	63	29	08
Independent	39	44	17	35	52	13	36	52	12	30	54	16	30	56	14	35	52	13
Protestant	42	43	15	37	50	13				34	51	15	34	55	11	36	54	10
Catholic	58	29	13	47	38	15				47	39	14	49	40	11	56	35	09
Union										41	44	15				49	42	09
Nonunion										37	49	14				39	51	10
Grade School	47	35	18	42	40	18	38	43	19	36	42	22	37	46	17	37	49	14
High School	46	38	16	38	48	14	40	48	12	41	45	14	39	50	11	44	48	08
College	47	46	07	39	54	07	37	56	07	32	61	07	37	55	08	38	53	09
Under 30	50	40	10	39	52	09	38	53	09	44	49	07	40	51	09	43	47	10
30-49	45	38	17	39	49	12	41	49	10	37	47	16	39	49	12	45	46	09
Over 50	45	41	14	40	44	16	38	46	16	36	47	17	35	53	12	37	52	11

JOHNSON: 1967-1968

	November 16-21			December 7-12			January 4-9			February 2-7			February 22-27			March 10-15		
	A%	D%	N%	A%	D%	N%	A%	D%	N%	A%	D%	N%	A%	D%	N%	A%	D%	N%
National	42	46	12	46	41	13	48	39	13	41	47	12	41	48	11	36	52	12
Male	45	46	09	46	43	11	49	39	12	38	49	13	40	52	08	37	54	09
Female	40	46	14	46	40	14	48	39	13	43	45	12	43	45	12	35	51	14
White	40	47	13	45	43	12	46	41	13	39	49	12	39	51	10			
Nonwhite	62	31	07	62	16	22	72	16	12	56	24	20	60	24	16			
East	54	34	12	52	37	11	53	34	13	45	41	14	45	44	11	40	46	14
Midwest	38	48	14	45	42	13	46	39	15	41	50	09	39	52	09	31	59	10
South	38	51	11	36	50	14	44	44	12	37	46	17	36	51	13	34	53	13
West	36	54	10	57	31	12	52	39	09	40	51	09	49	45	06	40	51	09
Republican	26	65	09	30	62	08	28	59	13	24	67	09	23	66	11	25	65	10
Democrat	57	32	11	62	25	13	66	23	11	56	31	13	54	36	10	52	36	12
Independent	37	49	14	40	46	14	38	47	15	35	52	13	37	53	10	21	67	12
Protestant	38	50	12	42	44	14	46	42	12	37	50	13	37	52	11	34	55	11
Catholic	52	38	10	60	33	07	55	31	14	52	37	11	52	38	10	44	44	12
Union				55	34	11	56	35	09	46	42	12	45	45	10			
Nonunion				43	44	13	46	40	14	39	48	13	40	50	10			
Grade School	44	42	14	40	43	17	50	35	15	48	36	16	44	42	14	43	45	12
High School	43	46	11	49	39	12	49	39	12	40	48	12	43	48	09	34	53	13
College	37	51	12	47	45	08	44	43	13	33	59	08	35	56	09	30	62	08
Under 30	33	55	12	43	48	09	45	44	11	36	53	11	41	51	08	32	58	10
30-49	43	45	12	48	38	14	49	41	10	40	49	11	39	52	09	34	55	11
Over 50	45	44	11	46	42	12	50	34	16	43	42	15	44	44	12	39	48	13

JOHNSON: 1968

	April 4-9			May 2-7			May 23-28			June 13-18			June 26-July 1			July 18-23		
	A%	D%	N%	A%	D%	N%	A%	D%	N%	A%	D%	N%	A%	D%	N%	A%	D%	N%
National	50	38	12	46	43	11	41	45	14	42	45	13	40	47	13	40	47	13
Male	51	39	10	46	46	08	41	49	10	45	46	09	40	49	11	42	48	10
Female	49	37	14	46	40	14	41	42	17	40	44	16	39	45	16	38	47	15
White	49	39	12	44	46	10	40	47	13	41	47	12	37	50	13	38	49	13
Nonwhite	63	19	18	66	14	20	49	24	27	56	25	19	64	17	19	58	29	13
East	60	30	10	53	37	10	50	34	16	50	39	11	47	42	11	46	39	15
Midwest	47	38	15	46	43	11	40	49	11	45	41	14	35	50	15	39	47	14
South	41	46	13	37	50	13	34	49	17	38	48	14	37	48	15	35	54	11
West	53	39	08	47	43	10	38	51	11	33	56	11	39	51	10	36	53	11
Republican	39	49	12	23	68	09	25	67	08	24	64	12	28	63	09	26	62	12
Democrat	65	24	11	63	27	10	54	30	16	56	32	12	52	35	13	54	35	11
Independent	39	49	12	39	48	13	33	53	14	38	49	13	33	51	16	32	53	15
Protestant	47	41	12	42	46	12	36	50	14	39	48	13	35	50	15	36	52	12
Catholic	59	29	12	56	35	09	55	33	12	53	36	11	51	38	11	48	37	15
Union	55	29	16	56	35	09	48	42	10	52	38	10	42	45	13	43	44	13
Nonunion	48	41	11	42	46	12	38	47	15	40	47	13	39	48	13	39	49	12
Grade School	54	31	15	43	40	17	37	44	19	43	38	19	41	41	18	40	45	15
High School	47	41	12	47	43	10	42	45	13	43	46	11	40	47	13	40	46	14
College	52	40	08	46	47	07	44	48	08	42	51	07	37	54	09	37	56	07
Under 30	48	40	12	48	43	09	44	45	11	35	59	06	36	51	13	37	53	10
30-49	48	41	11	46	41	13	42	44	14	43	43	14	44	44	12	38	50	12
Over 50	53	34	13	45	45	10	38	47	15	45	41	14	38	47	15	42	44	14

JOHNSON: 1968-1969

	August 7-12			September 19-24			November 9-14			December 5-10			January 1-6		
	A%	D%	N%	A%	D%	N%	A%	D%	N%	A%	D%	N%	A%	D%	N%
National	35	52	13	42	51	07	43	44	13	44	43	13	49	37	14
Male	35	55	10	40	55	05	45	46	09	44	48	08	48	41	11
Female	34	49	17	43	47	10	41	42	17	44	39	17	49	34	17
White	32	55	13				42	45	13	42	46	12	47	39	14
Nonwhite	58	22	20				65	23	12	76	12	12	74	11	15
East	39	47	14	49	44	07	51	36	13	50	39	11	53	33	14
Midwest	35	51	14	41	50	09	44	46	10	40	45	15	54	36	10
South	29	58	13	32	60	08	34	50	16	45	42	13	40	41	19
West	36	53	11	44	50	06	43	45	12	40	49	11	44	44	12
Republican	21	68	11	28	66	06	29	60	11	26	62	12	32	54	14
Democrat	48	36	16	58	35	07	59	28	13	60	27	13	63	25	12
Independent	30	57	13	35	55	10	35	52	13	39	50	11	42	43	15
Protestant	33	56	11	38	54	08	37	49	14	40	47	13	45	40	15
Catholic	40	44	16	50	41	09	60	30	10	55	33	12	59	29	12
Union	36	51	13				49	38	13	52	39	09	60	28	12
Nonunion	34	53	13				41	46	13	41	45	14	44	41	15
Grade School	40	43	17	45	47	08	46	36	18	48	35	17	48	33	19
High School	33	54	13	41	50	09	45	44	11	45	43	12	51	35	14
College	32	60	08	38	58	04	35	54	11	36	55	09	44	48	08
Under 30	29	62	09	41	54	05	41	51	08	47	45	08	48	43	09
30-49	36	52	12	41	50	09	41	45	14	44	43	13	49	38	13
Over 50	36	48	16	42	50	08	46	41	13	43	43	14	48	35	17

NIXON: 1969

	January 23-28			February 20-25			March 12-17			March 27-April 1			April 10-15			May 1-6		
	A%	D%	N%	A%	D%	N%	A%	D%	N%	A%	D%	N%	A%	D%	N%	A%	D%	N%
National	59	05	36	60	06	34	65	09	26	63	10	27	61	12	27	62	15	23
Male	60	05	35	59	08	33	69	10	21	64	12	24	62	13	25	61	18	21
Female	59	05	36	60	05	35	62	08	30	61	09	30	60	11	29	63	13	24
White	61	05	34	61	06	33	67	08	25	64	10	26	63	11	26	65	14	21
Nonwhite	44	08	48	42	11	47	49	15	36	41	16	43	41	14	45	33	28	39
East	51	07	42	54	05	41	63	09	28	62	09	29	60	11	29	58	17	25
Midwest	65	04	31	61	07	32	66	08	26	63	09	28	61	11	28	63	15	22
South	60	05	35	62	07	31	67	09	24	63	10	27	64	11	25	65	15	20
West	62	04	34	61	07	32	68	10	22	63	13	24	60	14	26	64	13	23
Republican	80	01	19	76	03	21	84	02	14	84	01	15	84	03	13	83	06	11
Democrat	45	06	49	52	07	41	55	12	33	51	15	34	45	18	37	49	23	28
Independent	59	07	34	56	09	35	65	10	25	60	12	28	61	12	27	60	14	26
Protestant	63	04	33	64	06	30	69	09	22	65	09	26	64	10	26	64	14	22
Catholic	57	05	38	55	06	39	60	07	33	59	11	30	62	12	26	63	14	23
Union	50	06	44	52	09	39	64	08	28	58	10	32	58	13	29	55	22	23
Nonunion	62	05	33	62	06	32	66	09	25	64	10	26	62	11	27	64	13	23
Grade School	52	04	44	52	07	41	60	08	32	53	10	37	58	12	30	56	16	28
High School	59	05	36	61	06	33	66	09	25	64	09	27	60	11	29	62	15	23
College	68	06	26	66	06	28	70	10	20	70	14	16	66	14	20	70	15	15
Under 30	58	10	32	62	10	28	70	09	21	65	16	19	63	15	22	62	19	19
30-49	57	05	38	58	06	36	66	09	25	63	07	30	63	10	27	61	16	23
Over 50	62	03	35	60	05	35	62	09	29	60	10	30	60	12	28	64	12	24

NIXON: 1969

	May 15-20			May 22-27			June 19-24			July 10-15			July 24-29			August 14-19		
	A%	D%	N%	A%	D%	N%	A%	D%	N%	A%	D%	N%	A%	D%	N%	A%	D%	N%
National	65	12	23	62	15	23	63	16	21	58	22	20	65	17	18	62	20	18
Male	67	13	20	64	17	19	66	17	17	60	24	16	64	21	15	65	20	15
Female	63	11	26	60	13	27	60	15	25	55	21	24	66	14	20	60	20	20
White	68	11	21	65	14	21	66	14	20	60	21	19	68	16	16	64	19	17
Nonwhite	39	19	42	33	27	40	44	29	27	36	38	26	43	29	28	44	32	24
East	62	14	24	56	17	27	66	16	18	53	28	19	65	16	19	59	21	20
Midwest	66	13	21	66	15	19	60	15	25	56	24	20	63	19	18	63	17	20
South	66	11	23	64	14	22	62	17	21	59	18	23	67	14	19	66	18	16
West	67	07	26	64	14	22	67	16	17	65	19	16	66	20	14	62	26	12
Republican	83	05	12	84	05	11	83	04	13	79	07	14	86	06	08	80	09	11
Democrat	56	16	28	50	23	27	52	23	25	45	33	22	51	27	22	52	29	19
Independent	64	12	24	61	15	24	61	18	21	57	24	19	66	14	20	63	17	20
Protestant	68	11	21	67	13	20	65	15	20	61	20	19	68	15	17	64	19	17
Catholic	64	10	26	59	15	26	65	15	20	54	24	22	63	18	19	64	18	18
Union	62	14	24	54	18	28	57	18	25	56	24	20	67	16	17			
Nonunion	66	11	23	65	14	21	65	15	20	59	22	19	64	18	18			
Grade School	58	13	29	55	17	28	57	16	27	45	25	30	62	18	20	51	21	28
High School	65	11	24	62	14	24	64	14	22	63	20	17	65	16	19	64	19	17
College	72	13	15	69	15	16	71	18	11	60	26	14	68	20	12	71	21	08
Under 30	68	12	20	64	17	19	66	21	13	65	24	11	64	22	14	67	21	12
30-49	65	11	24	65	13	22	63	14	23	60	20	20	66	16	18	64	20	16
Over 50	64	12	24	59	16	25	62	15	23	53	24	23	65	16	19	59	20	21

NIXON: 1969

	September 11-16			September 17-22			October 2-7			October 17-22			November 12-17			December 12-15		
	A%	D%	N%	A%	D%	N%	A%	D%	N%	A%	D%	N%	A%	D%	N%	A%	D%	N%
National	60	24	16	58	23	19	57	24	19	56	29	15	67	19	14	59	23	18
Male	61	25	14	60	26	14	62	23	15	58	31	11	71	19	10	62	25	13
Female	60	22	18	57	20	23	54	24	22	55	27	18	63	20	17	56	21	23
White	61	23	16	60	22	18	59	23	18	58	28	14	68	19	13	63	19	18
Nonwhite	46	26	28	42	34	24	35	41	24	32	48	20	44	35	21	21	57	22
East	61	22	17	57	24	19	54	26	20	49	35	16	63	20	17	54	27	19
Midwest	59	26	15	59	22	19	57	29	14	59	28	13	71	18	11	63	21	16
South	61	19	20	59	22	19	60	17	23	62	21	17	71	15	14	60	20	20
West	60	29	11	58	26	16	60	25	15	57	31	12	60	27	13	59	24	17
Republican	82	10	08	81	09	10	79	10	11	81	11	08	87	06	07	85	07	08
Democrat	47	34	19	45	33	22	43	36	21	43	40	17	54	29	17	44	34	22
Independent	57	22	21	56	24	20	60	23	17	54	29	17	65	21	14	60	22	18
Protestant	62	22	16	62	21	17	60	21	19	62	25	13	71	15	14	62	21	17
Catholic	60	23	17	54	25	21	56	26	18	50	32	18	65	22	13	57	23	20
Union				53	25	22	49	34	17	46	39	15	61	23	16			
Nonunion				60	23	17	60	21	19	60	25	15	69	18	13			
Grade School	54	27	19	51	25	24	48	24	28	51	28	21	62	16	22	46	24	30
High School	62	21	17	61	21	18	59	23	18	57	28	15	67	20	13	62	22	16
College	64	26	10	61	26	13	65	25	10	61	32	07	71	24	05	66	25	09
Under 30	66	22	12	60	24	16	63	26	11	55	34	11	66	22	12	59	27	14
30-49	59	22	19	58	22	20	56	25	19	53	30	17	67	20	13	59	23	18
Over 50	59	25	16	58	24	18	56	22	22	60	26	14	67	18	15	59	20	21

NIXON: 1970

	January 2-5			January 15-20			January 30-February 2			February 27-March 2			March 18-25			March 20-25		
	A%	D%	N%	A%	D%	N%	A%	D%	N%	A%	D%	N%	A%	D%	N%	A%	D%	N%
National	61	22	17	63	23	14	64	24	12	56	27	17	53	30	17	54	34	12
Male	67	23	10	64	24	12	66	24	10	59	26	15	57	31	12	57	34	09
Female	55	21	24	62	21	17	62	24	14	53	27	20	50	29	21	52	33	15
White	64	20	16	66	21	13	68	21	11	59	24	17	57	28	15	58	32	10
Nonwhite	34	39	27	33	39	28	36	44	20	31	45	24	26	47	27	22	56	22
East	59	26	15	66	22	12	61	28	11	54	25	21	49	35	16	51	38	11
Midwest	61	22	17	61	23	16	64	23	13	52	29	19	51	36	13	53	36	11
South	64	17	19	62	22	16	68	21	11	59	24	17	56	20	24	62	25	13
West	59	24	17	61	25	14	64	24	12	62	28	10	60	28	12	52	28	20
Republican	80	10	10	88	05	07	90	07	03	82	09	09	77	11	12	82	11	07
Democrat	47	32	21	47	34	19	45	38	17	38	42	20	37	46	17	38	47	15
Independent	63	19	18	62	24	14	68	20	12	60	20	20	54	27	19	56	34	10
Protestant	63	19	18	65	21	14	67	21	12	62	22	16	56	27	17	58	30	12
Catholic	61	24	15	62	24	14	63	25	12	51	32	17	50	34	16	52	39	09
Union	54	27	19	55	28	17	57	30	13									
Nonunion	64	20	16	66	21	13	67	21	12									
Grade School	54	21	25	60	23	17	58	27	15	45	29	26	39	33	28	47	33	20
High School	61	22	17	60	24	16	65	22	13	57	26	17	54	30	16	56	34	10
College	69	23	08	74	20	06	68	25	07	67	25	08	66	27	07	58	35	07
Under 30	62	25	13	61	24	15	61	28	11	60	28	12	53	35	12	57	34	09
30-49	61	22	17	63	24	13	63	24	13	57	29	14	54	31	15	53	37	10
Over 50	61	20	19	63	22	15	65	23	12	54	24	22	53	27	20	55	31	14

NIXON: 1970

	April 16-21			April 29-May 4			May 21-26			June 18-23			July 9-14			July 31-August 2		
	A%	D%	N%	A%	D%	N%	A%	D%	N%	A%	D%	N%	A%	D%	N%	A%	D%	N%
National	56	31	13	57	32	11	59	29	12	55	31	14	61	28	11	55	32	13
Male	57	30	13	61	29	10	62	29	09	58	33	09	61	29	10	60	31	09
Female	55	31	14	54	34	12	57	28	15	51	30	19	61	27	12	51	32	17
White	60	28	12	60	29	11	63	26	11	57	29	14	64	25	11	58	29	13
Nonwhite	19	57	24	33	57	10	27	61	12	24	59	17	32	56	12	21	61	18
East	52	35	13	54	35	11	57	32	11	53	34	13	57	31	12	53	37	10
Midwest	57	29	14	51	38	11	57	29	14	53	33	14	58	33	09	55	30	15
South	58	28	14	66	23	11	65	24	11	56	25	19	67	20	13	55	27	18
West	61	30	09	57	30	13	60	30	10	56	35	09	63	29	08	58	30	12
Republican	80	11	09	80	14	06	83	11	06	79	11	10	84	10	06	81	11	08
Democrat	42	43	15	42	45	13	43	43	14	40	44	16	48	40	12	40	45	15
Independent	56	33	11	58	30	12	62	26	12	50	36	14	57	30	13	56	30	14
Protestant	60	27	13	63	27	10	64	25	11	57	29	14	65	24	11	57	29	14
Catholic	55	33	12	48	39	13	56	31	13	55	31	14	57	32	11	53	33	14
Union							51	38	11									
Nonunion							62	26	12									
Grade School	45	35	20	51	35	14	52	30	18	45	31	24	56	29	15	53	31	16
High School	57	31	12	55	32	13	61	28	11	55	33	12	61	27	12	54	31	15
College	67	26	07	67	28	05	62	31	07	64	29	07	64	31	05	58	34	08
Under 30	61	30	09	54	38	08	58	35	07	58	30	12	57	33	10	49	40	11
30-49	54	33	13	58	31	11	62	29	09	56	33	11	65	25	10	56	30	14
Over 50	56	29	15	57	29	14	57	27	16	51	31	18	60	28	12	58	28	14

NIXON: 1970

	August 25–September 1			September 11–14			September 25–28			October 9–14			November 12–17			December 3–8		
	A%	D%	N%	A%	D%	N%	A%	D%	N%	A%	D%	N%	A%	D%	N%	A%	D%	N%
National	55	31	14	57	30	13	51	31	18	58	27	15	57	30	13	52	34	14
Male	57	31	12	57	31	12	52	34	14	61	27	12	61	30	09	56	35	09
Female	54	30	16	57	29	14	51	29	20	55	28	17	54	29	17	47	34	19
White	57	29	14	60	27	13	54	29	17	61	25	14	60	28	12	53	33	14
Nonwhite	31	47	22	27	63	10	23	56	21	25	56	19	29	45	26	33	48	19
East	56	31	13	57	32	11	49	34	17	59	29	12	54	30	16	52	33	15
Midwest	54	32	14	58	29	13	50	32	18	53	33	14	57	28	15	45	43	12
South	57	27	16	58	26	16	50	30	20	64	20	16	59	28	13	59	25	16
West	50	36	14	57	31	12	58	27	15	54	28	18	60	33	07	50	35	15
Republican	80	12	08	85	08	07	82	07	11	82	10	08	85	08	07	79	12	09
Democrat	41	42	17	44	43	13	34	48	18	44	39	17	40	44	16	34	50	16
Independent	52	33	15	50	32	18	49	29	22	57	27	16	58	29	13	51	33	16
Protestant	60	27	13	61	27	12	54	29	17	59	26	15	62	25	13	55	30	15
Catholic	50	33	17	55	30	15	49	31	20	59	27	14	52	34	14	50	35	15
Union										47	39	14						
Nonunion										62	23	15						
Grade School	50	29	21	53	31	16	50	30	20	53	26	21	55	28	17	46	33	21
High School	57	29	14	59	28	13	51	31	18	60	27	13	57	28	15	53	32	15
College	56	36	08	59	31	10	53	33	14	59	31	10	58	35	07	54	40	06
Under 30	55	37	08	52	37	11	52	37	11	52	35	13	58	31	11	50	41	09
30–49	54	33	13	60	27	13	51	32	17	60	28	12	56	30	14	52	33	15
Over 50	56	26	18	58	28	14	52	28	20	59	24	17	58	28	14	53	31	16

NIXON: 1971

	January 8-11			February 19-22			March 11-14			April 2-5			April 23-26			May 14-17		
	A%	D%	N%	A%	D%	N%	A%	D%	N%	A%	D%	N%	A%	D%	N%	A%	D%	N%
National	56	33	11	49	37	14	50	37	13	49	38	13	50	38	12	50	35	15
Male	60	32	08	52	38	10	52	36	12	51	38	11	52	39	09	51	38	11
Female	52	34	14	47	35	18	48	38	14	47	38	15	48	38	14	48	33	19
White	58	32	10	52	35	13	52	34	14	51	37	12	53	36	11	53	33	14
Nonwhite	34	48	18	33	48	19	25	63	12	29	49	22	20	61	19	25	53	22
East	55	34	11	50	35	15	49	39	12	49	39	12	49	38	13	48	35	17
Midwest	53	37	10	48	38	14	46	38	16	48	39	13	50	40	10	47	37	16
South	60	28	12	53	33	14	56	32	12	55	31	14	53	33	14	51	32	17
West	55	34	11	47	43	10	47	41	12	42	46	12	44	45	11	52	38	10
Republican	80	15	05	76	15	09	81	12	07	77	16	07	81	14	05	78	12	10
Democrat	42	44	14	36	50	14	34	51	15	34	52	14	34	52	14	31	51	18
Independent	52	37	11	50	35	15	49	38	13	47	36	17	50	37	13	51	34	15
Protestant	60	30	10	54	33	13	54	33	13	54	34	12	55	33	12	54	31	15
Catholic	52	35	13	46	40	14	45	40	15	44	42	14	47	42	11	46	35	19
Union				48	41	11	42	44	14									
Nonunion				50	35	15	52	35	13									
Grade School	50	34	16	43	39	18	42	41	17	40	38	22	47	34	19	44	32	24
High School	56	33	11	48	37	15	50	36	14	51	37	12	49	40	11	52	34	14
College	62	33	05	59	34	07	57	36	07	52	40	08	55	39	06	51	40	09
Under 30	54	36	10	50	40	10	47	40	13	42	45	13	49	43	08	46	44	10
30-49	53	37	10	50	36	14	50	38	12	52	37	11	53	35	12	51	36	13
Over 50	59	29	12	48	36	16	52	33	15	52	33	15	49	38	13	49	31	20

NIXON: 1971

	June 4-7			June 25-28			July 15-18			August 27-30			October 8-11			October 29–November 2		
	A%	D%	N%	A%	D%	N%	A%	D%	N%	A%	D%	N%	A%	D%	N%	A%	D%	N%
National	48	37	15	48	39	13	50	37	13	49	38	13	52	38	10	49	37	14
Male	50	40	10	48	43	09	49	40	11	48	42	10	53	38	09	51	38	11
Female	47	34	19	48	35	17	51	34	15	49	36	15	51	38	11	48	35	17
White	51	35	14	50	37	13	53	35	12	52	37	11	55	35	10	52	34	14
Nonwhite	27	50	23	25	53	22	30	50	20	22	57	21	21	65	14	20	60	20
East	48	36	16	46	38	16	52	38	10	48	39	13	52	37	11	50	36	14
Midwest	48	39	13	47	39	14	51	35	14	47	43	10	51	38	11	50	36	14
South	53	33	14	52	35	13	54	32	14	51	33	16	53	36	11	53	34	13
West	43	41	16	46	47	07	41	46	13	50	40	10	51	43	06	41	43	16
Republican	79	12	09	73	16	11	82	10	08	75	17	08	80	13	07	75	16	09
Democrat	36	49	15	34	51	15	35	52	13	35	50	15	38	52	10	35	51	14
Independent	43	41	16	47	42	11	42	43	15	50	40	10	46	41	13	48	33	19
Protestant	52	33	15	51	35	14				51	36	13	55	35	10	52	34	14
Catholic	46	39	15	45	41	14				50	37	13	47	43	10	47	39	14
Union				39	48	13	46	43	11	40	45	15	46	44	10	38	47	15
Nonunion				51	36	13	51	35	14	51	37	12	54	36	10	53	33	14
Grade School	50	41	09	48	32	20	51	34	15	44	35	21	43	41	16	41	40	19
High School	50	36	14	49	39	12	50	37	13	49	38	13	53	37	10	48	38	14
College	44	35	21	46	45	09	51	39	10	54	42	04	57	37	06	59	31	10
Under 30	43	41	16	46	43	11	42	44	14	48	41	11	47	45	08	46	43	11
30-49	53	34	13	45	41	14	49	38	13	49	41	10	53	38	09	52	31	17
Over 50	50	33	17	52	33	15	57	31	12	50	35	15	56	31	13	49	37	14

NIXON: 1971-1972

	December 10-13			January 7-10			February 4-7			March 3-5			March 24-27			April 28-May 1		
	A%	D%	N%	A%	D%	N%	A%	D%	N%	A%	D%	N%	A%	D%	N%	A%	D%	N%
National	50	37	13	49	39	12	52	37	11	56	32	12	53	36	11	54	37	09
Male	51	39	10	52	36	12	54	39	07	59	32	09	54	37	09	54	39	07
Female	49	34	17	47	42	11	51	35	14	54	31	15	52	36	12	54	36	10
White	52	35	13	52	38	10	55	35	10	59	29	12	57	33	10	56	36	08
Nonwhite	29	53	18	25	53	22	22	60	18	28	57	15	24	63	13	32	52	16
East	52	35	13	47	39	14	55	33	12	57	30	13	52	35	13	52	40	08
Midwest	46	40	14	48	40	12	50	40	10	58	31	11	51	38	11	51	41	08
South	53	33	14	57	36	07	55	35	10	55	31	14	56	34	10	58	30	12
West	50	39	11	44	44	12	48	42	10	52	36	12	53	40	07	56	38	06
Republican	84	09	07	80	14	06	81	12	07	83	11	06	82	11	07	82	13	05
Democrat	35	51	14	32	55	13	36	53	11	39	45	16	37	50	13	39	51	10
Independent	46	38	16	51	38	11	51	37	12	56	33	11	55	36	09	53	38	09
Protestant	55	32	13	54	35	11				59	29	12	59	31	10	59	31	10
Catholic	47	40	13	48	42	10				54	32	14	48	40	12	48	43	09
Union	39	47	14				43	47	10	50	36	14	47	42	11	41	50	09
Nonunion	54	33	13				55	34	11	58	30	12	55	35	10	58	33	09
Grade School	42	38	20	39	42	19	43	41	16	46	34	20	48	36	16	55	33	12
High School	48	38	14	50	40	10	54	35	11	56	32	12	53	36	11	53	38	09
College	61	33	06	58	34	08	57	38	05	65	29	06	58	37	05	55	38	07
Under 30	47	44	09	45	44	11	49	42	09	53	38	09	47	45	08	51	41	08
30-49	51	36	13	53	36	11	53	38	09	58	30	12	54	35	11	54	37	09
Over 50	51	33	16	50	38	12	54	33	13	56	29	15	55	33	12	55	35	10

NIXON: 1972-1973

	May 26-29			June 16-19			June 23-26			November 11-14			December 8-11			January 12-15		
	A%	D%	N%	A%	D%	N%	A%	D%	N%	A%	D%	N%	A%	D%	N%	A%	D%	N%
National	62	30	08	59	30	11	56	33	11	62	28	10	59	30	11	51	37	12
Male	63	29	08	62	31	07	61	31	08	65	29	06	62	29	09	53	38	09
Female	61	31	08	56	30	14	53	34	13	60	27	13	57	30	13	50	36	14
White	65	28	07	62	28	10	60	29	11	68	23	09	63	26	11	56	33	11
Nonwhite	37	51	12	37	49	14	28	57	15	26	63	11	27	58	15	22	60	18
East	62	28	10	58	27	15	55	30	15	58	31	11	58	33	09	44	44	12
Midwest	56	35	09	57	34	09	55	35	10	61	29	10	61	29	10	54	36	10
South	65	29	06	63	30	07	67	24	09	70	22	08	60	27	13	54	32	14
West	65	27	08	58	30	12	43	47	10	59	31	10	59	29	12	53	36	11
Republican	89	08	03	83	10	07	86	09	05	90	05	05	88	08	04	81	12	07
Democrat	46	42	12	45	43	12	39	48	13	46	43	11	42	45	13	36	52	12
Independent	63	31	06	64	27	09	61	28	11	60	29	11	60	28	12	51	36	13
Protestant	66	27	07	62	28	10	60	29	11	67	25	08	64	24	12	58	30	12
Catholic	60	30	10	61	28	11	57	35	08	57	30	13	58	33	09	44	43	13
Union	54	37	09	50	40	10				50	39	11	51	40	09	44	42	14
Nonunion	64	28	08	62	27	11				66	25	09	62	26	12	54	35	11
Grade School	55	32	13	51	33	16	55	32	13	66	22	12	51	28	21	43	33	24
High School	61	30	09	60	29	11	57	32	11	62	28	10	61	29	10	54	35	11
College	67	29	04	65	30	05	57	34	09	60	33	07	64	32	04	52	43	05
Under 30	60	33	07	55	37	08	48	43	09	56	34	10	55	37	08	42	48	10
30-49	64	29	07	61	29	10	45	41	14	61	31	08	61	27	12	55	36	09
Over 50	61	29	10	61	26	13	60	27	13	67	22	11	60	27	13	55	29	16

NIXON: 1973

	January 26-29			February 16-19			March 30-April 2			April 6-9			April 27-30			May 4-7		
	A%	D%	N%	A%	D%	N%	A%	D%	N%	A%	D%	N%	A%	D%	N%	A%	D%	N%
National	67	25	08	65	25	10	57	34	09	54	36	10	48	40	12	45	42	13
Male	68	27	05	65	27	08	60	32	08	57	34	09	47	45	08	44	47	09
Female	66	23	11	65	24	11	55	36	09	51	38	11	49	36	15	46	38	16
White	70	22	08	69	22	09	61	31	08	58	33	09	51	38	11	50	38	12
Nonwhite	41	47	12	36	48	16	24	60	16	23	62	15	26	55	19	12	73	15
East	64	29	07	64	28	08	55	36	09	49	42	09	43	45	12	41	47	12
Midwest	65	26	09	65	25	10	60	36	04	57	35	08	45	43	12	45	41	14
South	73	19	08	71	18	11	59	28	13	57	32	11	56	30	14	51	37	12
West	64	26	10	59	31	10	56	35	09	51	38	11	47	45	08	42	46	12
Republican	89	07	04	91	07	02	85	09	06	83	11	06	76	17	07	74	15	11
Democrat	51	39	10	47	40	13	40	51	09	38	52	10	33	55	12	24	62	14
Independent	72	22	06	69	22	09	63	29	08	55	34	11	45	42	13	49	41	10
Protestant	69	22	09	69	21	10	64	29	07	59	31	10	56	33	11	51	36	13
Catholic	70	24	06	67	26	07	52	38	10	53	37	10	41	46	13	39	48	13
Union	60	32	08	58	31	11	50	40	10	51	41	08	41	48	11	37	50	13
Nonunion	69	23	08	67	24	09	60	32	08	55	35	10	50	38	12	48	40	12
Grade School	63	26	11	65	24	11	49	37	14	45	43	12	51	31	18	39	42	19
High School	70	21	09	65	26	09	59	33	08	58	32	10	47	40	13	46	43	11
College	64	32	04	65	26	09	62	33	05	52	40	08	47	48	05	47	43	10
Under 30	61	30	09	62	29	09	55	38	07	55	38	07	43	48	09	41	48	11
30-49	67	26	07	65	26	09	61	31	08	55	35	10	52	37	11	46	44	10
Over 50	71	20	09	68	22	10	56	34	10	53	35	12	48	37	15	46	37	17

NIXON: 1973

	May 11-14			June 1-4			June 22-25			July 6-9			August 3-6			August 17-20		
	A%	D%	N%	A%	D%	N%	A%	D%	N%	A%	D%	N%	A%	D%	N%	A%	D%	N%
National	44	45	11	44	44	12	44	45	11	39	49	12	31	58	11	36	54	10
Male	44	46	10	45	45	10	42	48	10	41	50	09	30	61	09	36	56	08
Female	45	45	10	42	43	15	46	42	12	37	49	14	32	55	13	37	52	11
White	49	41	10	48	40	12	48	42	10	42	47	11	33	56	11	39	52	09
Nonwhite	16	69	15	19	67	14	21	64	15	20	67	13	13	73	14	14	76	10
East	38	48	14	45	43	12	40	48	12	35	50	15	30	57	13	35	56	09
Midwest	46	47	07	42	46	12	43	47	10	40	50	10	32	58	10	34	58	08
South	51	39	10	49	39	12	51	37	12	45	42	13	33	52	15	40	48	12
West	41	48	11	36	49	15	41	49	10	35	57	08	28	66	06	38	54	08
Republican	73	18	09	72	15	13	76	17	07	67	22	11	58	30	12	63	28	09
Democrat	28	61	11	26	62	12	27	59	14	24	65	11	19	69	12	20	72	08
Independent	43	47	10	45	43	12	45	45	10	40	48	12	30	60	10	37	54	09
Protestant	48	41	11				50	38	12	44	43	13	36	51	13	41	50	09
Catholic	40	50	10				40	50	10	35	56	09	29	62	09	33	57	10
Union	35	52	13	36	52	12	36	56	08	33	57	10	26	63	11	33	59	08
Nonunion	48	43	09	47	41	12	46	42	12	41	47	12	32	56	12	37	53	10
Grade School	36	48	16	42	38	20	37	46	17	34	46	20	24	57	19	32	54	14
High School	45	45	10	44	44	12	45	44	11	38	51	11	31	58	11	37	53	10
College	51	43	06	45	48	07	48	46	06	46	48	06	36	58	06	38	57	05
Under 30	39	51	10	40	51	09	41	50	09	39	53	08	25	66	09	32	61	07
30-49	46	42	12	43	45	12	49	42	09	38	52	10	33	55	12	35	54	11
Over 50	47	44	09	47	37	16	42	44	14	40	44	16	34	53	13	41	49	10

NIXON: 1973

	September 7-10			September 21-24			October 5-8			October 19-22			November 2-5			November 30-December 3		
	A%	D%	N%	A%	D%	N%	A%	D%	N%	A%	D%	N%	A%	D%	N%	A%	D%	N%
National	34	56	10	33	59	08	30	57	13	27	60	13	27	63	10	31	59	10
Male	34	58	08	35	59	06	28	61	11	31	60	09	26	66	08	32	61	07
Female	34	53	13	31	59	10	31	53	16	24	60	16	28	59	13	30	56	14
White	36	53	11	36	56	08	32	54	14	30	57	13	29	60	11	34	55	11
Nonwhite	12	77	11	10	83	07	09	78	13	11	77	12	12	81	07	13	81	06
East	28	62	10	30	60	10	31	55	14	26	64	10	23	65	12	22	65	13
Midwest	35	53	12	31	62	07	26	64	10	28	60	12	28	63	09	32	61	07
South	40	47	13	36	55	09	35	50	15	31	50	19	34	55	11	41	47	12
West	31	63	06	35	58	07	24	58	18	23	68	09	21	70	09	29	62	09
Republican	63	28	09	65	27	08	57	27	16	54	32	14	56	32	12	55	36	09
Democrat	17	74	09	17	74	09	16	74	10	15	74	11	13	79	08	17	75	08
Independent	34	52	14	32	61	07	29	58	13	27	60	13	25	65	10	30	59	11
Protestant	39	50	11	37	54	09	32	53	15	31	54	15	32	57	11	37	52	11
Catholic	27	62	11	27	66	07	29	59	12	22	67	11	22	68	10	22	70	08
Union	22	68	10	24	67	09	21	68	11	23	63	14	25	65	10	20	68	12
Nonunion	38	51	11	36	56	08	33	53	14	29	58	13	28	62	10	35	55	10
Grade School	30	50	20	34	54	12	30	49	21	24	58	18	29	54	17	25	59	16
High School	35	56	09	32	59	09	28	59	13	29	57	14	27	63	10	31	58	11
College	34	60	06	34	62	04	35	57	08	25	68	07	25	70	05	36	59	05
Under 30	35	56	09	30	63	07	26	62	12	25	63	12	21	72	07	28	63	09
30-49	31	61	08	29	63	08	29	59	12	29	60	11	24	66	10	32	59	09
Over 50	36	49	15	38	53	09	34	50	16	27	57	16	34	54	12	32	55	13

NIXON: 1973-1974

	December 7-10			January 4-7			January 18-21			February 1-4			February 8-11/15-18			February 22-25/March 1-4		
	A%	D%	N%	A%	D%	N%	A%	D%	N%	A%	D%	N%	A%	D%	N%	A%	D%	N%
National	29	60	11	27	63	10	26	64	10	28	59	13	27	63	10	25	64	11
Male	29	62	09	27	64	09	27	66	07	28	63	09	27	65	08	26	66	08
Female	29	58	13	27	62	11	25	62	13	29	55	16	26	62	12	25	61	14
White	31	58	11	29	61	10	28	62	10	31	56	13	29	61	10	27	61	12
Nonwhite	14	71	15	09	80	11	13	77	10	07	79	14	07	82	11	12	81	07
East	22	68	10	22	70	08	22	71	07	24	65	11	20	70	10	20	70	10
Midwest	27	65	08	29	61	10	27	62	11	30	58	12	30	62	08	26	63	11
South	35	50	15	33	55	12	34	54	12	35	48	17	31	56	13	31	54	15
West	31	56	13	21	70	09	21	71	08	22	67	11	24	67	09	22	70	08
Republican	53	37	10	53	35	12	53	37	10	59	30	11	54	35	11	55	30	15
Democrat	17	71	12	11	82	07	12	80	08	16	74	10	12	81	07	14	77	09
Independent	26	63	11	26	63	11	28	60	12	25	60	15	26	62	12	24	64	12
Protestant	33	55	12	31	57	12	30	60	10	34	54	12	32	58	10	30	58	12
Catholic	22	68	10	22	73	05	22	69	09	19	68	13	18	71	11	20	69	11
Union	20	73	07	17	75	08	17	75	08	20	71	09	22	69	09	20	71	09
Nonunion	31	57	12	30	59	11	29	60	11	32	54	14	28	62	10	27	61	12
Grade School	33	50	17	30	55	15	25	57	18	31	54	15	24	58	18	29	53	18
High School	26	62	12	26	66	08	27	64	09	29	59	12	26	65	09	22	67	11
College	31	63	06	25	66	09	26	69	05	26	62	12	31	63	06	28	64	08
Under 30	22	68	10	20	73	07	24	68	08	24	64	12	25	69	06	21	73	06
30-49	27	61	12	25	66	09	26	65	09	28	61	11	25	63	12	24	68	08
Over 50	35	54	11	32	55	13	29	59	12	32	53	15	30	59	11	30	52	18

NIXON: 1974

	March 8-11/15-18			March 29-April 1			April 12-15			April 19-22/26-29			May 3-6			May 10-13		
	A%	D%	N%	A%	D%	N%	A%	D%	N%	A%	D%	N%	A%	D%	N%	A%	D%	N%
National	26	62	12	26	65	09	25	62	13	26	60	14	25	58	17	25	61	14
Male	27	64	09	26	68	06	27	65	08	26	63	11	24	61	15	24	65	11
Female	25	61	14	25	63	12	23	59	18	26	57	17	27	55	18	26	58	16
White	29	60	11	28	63	09	28	59	13	29	57	14	27	56	17	27	60	13
Nonwhite	08	80	12	10	80	10	07	78	15	06	77	17	12	71	17	14	68	18
East	24	66	10	19	72	09	22	63	15	22	63	15	21	63	16	23	63	14
Midwest	27	61	12	27	66	07	25	62	13	28	59	13	24	57	19	22	64	14
South	29	58	13	31	56	13	29	59	12	30	56	14	33	48	19	32	54	14
West	24	66	10	27	67	06	23	64	13	26	60	14	23	66	11	22	66	12
Republican	53	38	09	56	35	09	53	33	14	53	31	16	50	29	21	48	37	15
Democrat	14	76	10	11	81	08	11	78	11	14	76	10	15	70	15	14	75	11
Independent	25	64	11	27	63	10	24	63	13	27	58	15	26	61	13	23	63	14
Protestant	29	59	12	31	59	10	30	56	14	30	56	14	33	52	15	28	57	15
Catholic	24	64	12	21	71	08	19	69	12	21	63	16	16	68	16	20	69	11
Union	18	73	09	21	74	05	20	68	12	19	68	13	19	67	14	20	69	11
Nonunion	29	59	12	28	62	10	27	60	13	29	57	14	28	55	17	27	59	14
Grade School	21	58	21	29	58	13	23	58	19	24	53	23	21	58	21	24	52	24
High School	26	63	11	24	67	09	24	63	13	28	58	14	25	57	18	25	61	14
College	30	64	06	26	68	06	30	63	07	24	68	08	31	59	10	25	70	05
Under 30	24	68	08	25	67	08	17	71	12	24	64	12	23	61	16	24	65	11
30-49	25	64	11	24	68	08	27	61	12	25	64	11	26	58	16	22	66	12
Over 50	28	58	14	28	61	11	29	56	15	29	54	17	27	55	18	29	54	17

NIXON: 1974

	May 17-20			May 31-June 3			June 21-24			June 28-July 1			July 12-15			August 2-5		
	A%	D%	N%	A%	D%	N%	A%	D%	N%	A%	D%	N%	A%	D%	N%	A%	D%	N%
National	26	61	13	28	61	11	26	61	13	28	58	14	24	63	13	24	66	10
Male	26	64	10	29	62	09	28	61	11	31	57	12	27	64	09	23	69	08
Female	26	58	16	27	60	13	25	61	14	25	59	16	21	62	17	24	63	13
White	28	59	13	30	59	11	29	59	12	31	56	13	26	61	13	26	64	10
Nonwhite	16	72	12	15	73	12	08	75	17	10	72	18	08	73	19	10	76	14
East	22	66	12	24	68	08	21	65	14	26	58	16	20	68	12	20	69	11
Midwest	26	63	11	28	60	12	24	66	10	28	60	12	25	64	11	21	67	12
South	33	51	16	33	53	14	32	50	18	32	51	17	29	55	16	30	58	12
West	23	67	10	25	64	11	29	62	09	23	65	12	19	65	16	25	72	03
Republican	54	33	13	53	35	12	48	40	12	55	32	13	50	37	13	50	38	12
Democrat	12	76	12	16	75	09	15	73	12	13	73	14	11	77	12	13	77	10
Independent	27	61	12	27	61	12	27	61	12	27	59	14	24	61	15	22	69	09
Protestant	31	57	12	34	53	13	29	57	14	33	54	13	28	58	14	28	60	12
Catholic	22	65	13	21	69	10	24	64	12	19	66	15	17	69	14	18	73	09
Union	20	69	11	22	69	09	18	69	13	21	63	16	18	70	12	16	76	08
Nonunion	29	58	13	29	59	12	29	58	13	30	56	14	25	60	15	26	63	11
Grade School	28	55	17	30	48	22	25	55	20	38	47	15	20	59	21	22	58	20
High School	24	64	12	29	61	10	25	62	13	25	61	14	24	63	13	23	68	09
College	31	59	10	22	71	07	31	64	05	26	61	13	26	66	08	26	69	05
Under 30	17	71	12	22	72	06	26	66	08	21	65	14	20	69	11	19	74	07
30-49	28	60	12	27	62	11	27	61	12	24	61	15	25	62	13	23	68	09
Over 50	32	55	13	32	52	16	26	58	16	35	51	14	25	59	16	27	59	14

FORD: 1974

	August 16-19			September 6-9			September 27-30			October 11-14			October 18-21			November 8-11		
	A%	D%	N%	A%	D%	N%	A%	D%	N%	A%	D%	N%	A%	D%	N%	A%	D%	N%
National	71	03	26	66	13	21	50	28	22	52	29	19	54	28	18	47	33	20
Male	70	04	26	67	14	19	49	31	20	51	31	18	53	32	15	46	38	16
Female	71	03	26	66	12	22	51	26	23	53	27	20	54	26	20	48	29	23
White	74	03	23	67	12	21	52	28	20	55	27	18	56	28	16	50	32	18
Nonwhite	51	06	43	62	19	19	40	32	28	34	38	28	37	36	27	29	41	30
East	67	03	30	63	14	23	52	27	21	47	35	18	52	30	18	42	38	20
Midwest	76	02	22	71	11	18	55	27	18	57	24	19	55	26	19	50	33	17
South	68	04	28	71	10	19	46	30	24	52	27	21	53	29	18	51	27	22
West	72	06	22	57	17	26	45	31	24	54	28	18	54	31	15	47	35	18
Republican	77	02	21	77	05	18	65	16	19	73	12	15	73	10	17	72	13	15
Democrat	68	04	28	61	18	21	43	37	20	42	38	20	44	37	19	37	42	21
Independent	70	04	26	66	12	22	52	24	24	53	27	20	56	29	15	47	35	18
Protestant	71	03	26	68	12	20	51	29	20	56	24	20	58	26	16	52	29	19
Catholic	73	03	24	65	13	22	54	23	23	51	29	20	52	28	20	42	40	18
Union	66	03	31	61	18	21	42	37	21	46	37	17	50	35	15	40	39	21
Nonunion	71	04	25	68	11	21	52	26	22	54	26	20	55	26	19	50	31	19
Grade School	66	03	31	64	12	24	44	33	23	48	30	22	46	28	26	43	32	25
High School	68	04	28	65	13	22	48	28	24	52	28	20	55	28	17	46	32	22
College	80	03	17	72	12	16	58	25	17	56	29	15	57	31	12	53	36	11
Under 30	67	04	29	70	14	16	56	25	19	53	28	19	54	33	13	51	34	15
30-49	69	03	28	65	11	24	48	28	24	52	30	18	54	27	19	46	33	21
Over 50	74	04	22	64	14	22	48	31	21	52	28	20	53	27	20	46	33	21

FORD: 1974-1975

	November 15-18			December 6-9			January 10-13			January 28-February 3			February 28-March 2			March 7-10		
	A%	D%	N%	A%	D%	N%	A%	D%	N%	A%	D%	N%	A%	D%	N%	A%	D%	N%
National	48	32	20	42	41	17	37	39	24	39	43	18	39	45	16	38	45	17
Male	47	38	15	37	49	14	37	44	19	37	48	15	35	52	13	39	49	12
Female	49	26	25	47	34	19	38	34	28	39	39	22	42	39	19	38	41	21
White	50	31	19	45	40	15	40	37	23	41	41	18	42	43	15	42	42	16
Nonwhite	31	41	28	21	51	28	25	46	29	24	55	21	21	56	23	21	57	22
East	44	35	21	43	41	16	36	38	26	36	48	16	37	47	16	35	49	16
Midwest	49	33	18	45	40	15	26	42	22	43	39	18	41	43	16	42	44	14
South	47	28	25	37	42	21	43	34	23	36	43	21	39	43	18	37	42	21
West	55	30	15	43	42	15	33	41	26	39	43	18	34	49	17	41	43	16
Republican	67	14	19	60	25	15	57	24	19	63	24	13	60	24	16	65	22	13
Democrat	41	42	17	32	53	15	31	44	25	28	55	17	29	57	14	28	56	16
Independent	48	30	22	43	39	18	35	41	24	38	41	21	38	46	16	36	46	18
Protestant	51	30	19	45	39	16	41	35	24	41	41	18	42	42	16	44	39	17
Catholic	46	35	19	43	44	13	34	39	27	38	45	17	35	51	14	35	49	16
Union	41	38	21	42	42	16	33	43	24	38	45	17	33	51	16	39	44	17
Nonunion	50	30	20	42	41	17	40	37	23	39	42	19	40	43	17	38	45	17
Grade School	34	40	26	38	47	15	31	36	33	26	48	26	28	50	22	35	43	22
High School	50	30	20	42	39	19	36	39	25	39	43	18	39	45	16	35	47	18
College	55	28	17	45	42	13	44	40	16	47	39	14	47	41	12	49	41	10
Under 30	55	28	17	44	40	16	40	41	19	39	43	18	43	42	15	37	49	14
30-49	47	32	21	41	42	17	36	37	27	40	43	17	38	45	17	40	42	18
Over 50	44	35	21	42	41	17	37	38	25	37	44	19	36	47	17	39	44	17

FORD: 1975

	March 28-31			April 4-7			April 18-21			May 2-5			May 30-June 2			June 27-30		
	A%	D%	N%	A%	D%	N%	A%	D%	N%	A%	D%	N%	A%	D%	N%	A%	D%	N%
National	37	43	20	44	37	19	39	46	15	40	43	17	51	33	16	52	33	15
Male	36	49	15	43	40	17	39	50	11	38	48	14	54	35	11	51	36	13
Female	38	38	24	44	34	22	39	43	18	41	39	20	48	31	21	52	32	16
White	40	41	19	47	36	17	42	46	12	42	42	16	54	30	16	56	30	14
Nonwhite	19	55	26	25	42	33	25	49	26	24	52	24	30	50	20	22	59	19
East	31	47	22	41	40	19	38	50	12	40	42	18	48	36	16	54	30	16
Midwest	36	46	18	46	36	18	40	45	15	41	41	18	50	36	14	50	38	12
South	41	36	23	44	35	21	38	43	19	38	44	18	53	30	17	52	31	17
West	41	44	15	43	37	20	40	47	13	40	47	13	54	27	19	51	36	13
Republican	60	23	17	63	21	16	61	28	11	64	24	12	68	20	12	70	17	13
Democrat	29	54	17	34	46	20	29	57	14	28	56	16	40	41	19	41	45	14
Independent	35	43	22	43	40	17	41	43	16	41	40	19	57	30	13	54	30	16
Protestant	40	40	20	47	33	20	41	44	15	44	40	16	51	32	17	54	31	15
Catholic	38	45	17	41	41	18	38	47	15	36	44	20	52	33	15	49	36	15
Union	31	51	18	39	42	19	36	50	14	36	47	17	46	37	17	44	42	14
Nonunion	39	41	20	45	35	20	40	45	15	41	42	17	53	31	16	55	30	15
Grade School	26	45	29	44	29	27	31	46	23	30	47	23	36	39	25	44	34	22
High School	38	42	20	40	39	21	38	47	15	39	43	18	51	33	16	50	35	15
College	43	45	12	50	39	11	49	43	08	47	41	12	62	27	11	61	29	10
Under 30	39	44	17	42	38	20	41	45	14	39	46	15	55	34	11	49	36	15
30-49	38	41	21	42	40	18	38	47	15	39	43	18	54	32	14	54	31	15
Over 50	34	45	21	46	34	20	38	47	15	40	42	18	46	32	22	51	35	14

FORD: 1975

	August 1-4			August 15-18			September 12-15			October 3-6			October 17-20			October 31-November 3		
	A%	D%	N%	A%	D%	N%	A%	D%	N%	A%	D%	N%	A%	D%	N%	A%	D%	N%
National	45	37	18	46	37	17	45	38	17	47	37	16	47	40	13	44	44	12
Male	43	43	14	45	41	14	44	43	13	47	42	11	46	43	11	45	47	08
Female	47	31	22	46	34	20	46	34	20	47	32	21	47	38	15	44	40	16
White	46	36	18	48	36	16	47	37	16	50	35	15	49	39	12	46	42	12
Nonwhite	35	44	21	28	47	25	25	52	23	23	52	25	22	50	28	27	54	19
East	43	38	19	42	41	17	44	42	14	45	37	18	45	42	13	37	50	13
Midwest	45	38	17	47	36	17	49	38	13	51	39	10	49	40	11	43	44	13
South	47	32	21	48	33	19	40	33	27	45	40	15	45	40	15	47	39	14
West	45	40	15	46	40	14	47	40	13	48	39	13	48	39	13	51	41	08
Republican	65	18	17	67	21	12	63	23	14	71	18	11	74	19	07	70	21	09
Democrat	37	44	19	32	48	20	36	47	17	34	48	18	33	54	13	29	59	12
Independent	45	39	16	49	34	17	48	35	17	50	35	15	49	36	15	48	39	13
Protestant	48	34	18	46	37	17	45	36	19	50	35	15	42	45	13	47	40	13
Catholic	45	36	19	48	34	18	49	37	14	49	36	15	49	39	12	42	46	12
Union	43	42	15	35	49	16	38	49	13	42	48	10	43	43	14	39	49	12
Nonunion	46	35	19	50	33	17	47	35	18	48	35	17	48	40	12	46	42	12
Grade School	35	41	24	33	40	27	28	46	26	35	39	26	36	43	21	29	54	17
High School	44	36	20	44	38	18	44	39	17	45	38	17	47	40	13	45	43	12
College	56	33	11	59	33	08	58	30	12	58	34	08	51	39	10	51	39	10
Under 30	47	35	18	51	32	17	51	33	16	51	34	15	51	37	12	48	41	11
30-49	47	36	17	47	39	14	45	39	16	48	37	15	49	39	12	50	38	12
OVER 50	42	38	20	41	40	19	40	41	19	44	38	18	41	44	15	36	50	14

FORD: 1975-1976

	November 21-24			December 5-8			December 12-15			January 2-5			January 23-26			January 30-February 2		
	A%	D%	N%	A%	D%	N%	A%	D%	N%	A%	D%	N%	A%	D%	N%	A%	D%	N%
National	41	46	13	46	37	17	39	46	15	46	42	12	45	45	10	46	40	14
Male	43	48	09	46	42	12	37	50	13	47	46	07	46	47	07	44	43	13
Female	39	45	16	46	33	21	41	42	17	44	39	17	44	42	14	48	37	15
White	43	45	12	48	37	15	41	45	14	47	41	12	47	43	10	48	39	13
Nonwhite	29	56	15	26	44	30	23	47	30	33	50	17	31	53	16	32	43	25
East	38	50	12	44	40	16	35	50	15	40	48	12	40	49	11	41	43	16
Midwest	47	41	12	49	36	15	43	45	12	47	41	12	47	44	09	53	36	11
South	43	41	16	45	34	21	39	43	18	47	38	15	47	41	12	46	36	18
West	33	56	11	44	40	16	41	43	16	51	40	09	46	46	08	45	46	09
Republican	60	29	11	67	20	13	59	30	11	66	24	10	63	30	07	67	23	10
Democrat	30	57	13	33	47	20	30	53	17	35	53	12	35	54	11	35	50	15
Independent	42	56	02	46	39	15	38	48	14	50	37	13	47	43	10	47	38	15
Protestant	45	42	13	49	34	17	41	43	16	48	40	12	48	41	11	50	37	13
Catholic	38	50	12	44	41	15	36	50	14	44	42	14	40	49	11	43	42	15
Union	37	51	12	42	41	17	23	65	12	36	51	13	34	53	13	38	48	14
Nonunion	42	45	13	47	36	17	42	42	16	49	39	12	50	41	09	49	37	14
Grade School	36	53	11	35	41	24	36	43	21	36	47	17	40	49	11	45	39	16
High School	40	46	14	46	35	19	39	46	15	45	42	13	46	42	12	45	41	14
College	46	44	10	52	39	09	42	45	13	53	38	09	46	47	07	50	38	12
Under 30	49	41	10	48	35	17	42	42	16	53	36	11	47	43	10	45	40	15
30-49	41	46	13	50	34	16	40	44	16	44	44	12	43	45	12	49	38	13
Over 50	35	51	14	41	41	18	37	49	14	41	45	14	46	45	09	45	41	14

FORD: 1976

	February 27–March 1			March 19–22			April 9–12			May 20–23			June 11–14			December 10–13		
	A%	D%	N%	A%	D%	N%	A%	D%	N%	A%	D%	N%	A%	D%	N%	A%	D%	N%
National	48	38	14	50	36	14	48	41	11	47	38	15	45	40	15	53	32	15
Male	52	37	11	49	40	11	48	41	11	45	42	13	46	41	13	53	35	12
Female	46	38	16	51	33	16	48	40	12	49	34	17	45	39	16	54	28	18
White	51	36	13	53	34	13	50	39	11	49	36	15	48	38	14	58	28	14
Nonwhite	23	59	18	33	51	16	36	51	13	36	49	15	27	57	16	27	49	24
East	42	43	15	51	38	11	44	46	10	42	42	16	38	48	14	49	34	17
Midwest	54	35	11	51	37	12	48	38	14	52	35	13	49	37	14	58	28	14
South	47	35	18	49	34	17	51	38	11	49	36	15	49	35	16	54	28	18
West	51	38	11	52	33	15	51	39	10	43	39	18	46	39	15	51	38	11
Republican	69	19	12	73	16	11	72	21	07	64	24	12	68	23	09	80	12	08
Democrat	37	51	12	36	49	15	35	51	14	36	49	15	35	50	15	40	44	16
Independent	52	32	16	55	32	13	49	41	10	51	33	16	46	38	16	54	27	19
Protestant	49	37	14	54	33	13	52	36	12	51	35	14	48	38	14	54	30	16
Catholic	51	37	12	47	40	13	46	45	09	45	39	16	46	42	12	56	30	14
Union	40	47	13	45	44	11	42	48	10	42	38	20	40	48	12	46	36	18
Nonunion	52	34	14	52	34	14	50	38	12	49	38	13	48	37	15	55	30	15
Grade School	41	43	16	36	47	17	43	40	17	39	44	17	39	39	22	45	35	20
High School	48	37	15	50	35	15	46	42	12	48	35	17	44	42	14	52	30	18
College	53	36	11	60	31	09	55	39	06	50	39	11	52	37	11	59	33	08
Under 30	49	35	16	55	33	12	54	39	07	50	35	15	45	43	12	56	28	16
30–49	46	41	13	50	36	14	50	39	11	46	37	17	47	38	15	47	37	16
Over 50	50	36	14	47	38	15	44	43	13	46	41	13	45	39	16	56	30	14

CARTER: 1977

	February 4-7			February 18-21			March 4-7			March 18-21			March 25-28			April 1-4		
	A%	D%	N%	A%	D%	N%	A%	D%	N%	A%	D%	N%	A%	D%	N%	A%	D%	N%
National	66	08	26	71	09	20	70	09	21	75	09	16	72	10	18	67	14	19
Male	67	08	25	72	09	19	70	11	19	75	10	15	71	10	19	67	14	19
Female	64	09	27	70	08	22	71	07	22	74	08	18	72	10	18	67	15	18
White	66	08	26	71	09	20	69	10	21	73	10	17	71	11	18	67	15	18
Nonwhite	62	08	30	75	05	20	79	04	17	85	03	12	78	06	16	71	10	19
East	63	06	31	71	07	22	73	08	19	73	08	19	72	10	18	70	11	19
Midwest	66	09	25	69	10	21	71	11	18	72	11	17	74	09	17	67	14	19
South	74	07	19	78	06	16	70	09	21	79	07	14	70	11	19	66	17	17
West	57	12	31	63	11	26	65	09	26	74	09	17	71	09	20	67	15	18
Republican	49	18	33	58	16	26	53	21	26	60	19	21	56	24	20	54	25	21
Democrat	77	03	20	79	04	17	80	05	15	84	03	13	81	05	14	78	06	16
Independent	60	09	31	69	09	22	69	07	24	73	10	17	70	10	20	63	18	19
Protestant	67	09	24	72	09	19	69	11	20	74	09	17	71	11	18	64	17	19
Catholic	63	07	30	71	08	21	70	07	23	78	08	14	74	09	17	74	09	17
Union	71	08	21	68	09	23	77	07	16	77	08	15	77	06	17	72	11	17
Nonunion	64	08	28	72	08	20	68	10	22	74	09	17	70	11	19	66	15	19
Grade School	63	04	33	69	09	22	68	08	24	66	09	25	69	09	22	65	11	24
High School	64	09	27	70	08	22	72	09	19	76	07	17	71	10	19	65	15	20
College	70	09	21	74	09	17	68	11	21	77	12	11	75	11	14	73	14	13
Under 30	70	08	22	75	07	18	77	07	16	77	09	14	77	09	14	73	12	15
30-49	65	08	27	73	08	19	70	10	20	77	07	16	71	10	19	71	11	18
Over 50	63	08	29	67	10	23	65	10	25	71	11	18	68	12	20	61	18	21

CARTER: 1977

	April 15-18			April 29-May 2			May 6-9			May 20-23			June 3-6			June 17-20		
	A%	D%	N%	A%	D%	N%	A%	D%	N%	A%	D%	N%	A%	D%	N%	A%	D%	N%
National	63	18	19	63	18	19	66	19	15	64	19	17	63	19	18	63	18	19
Male	63	20	17	64	18	18	65	21	14	63	22	15	65	19	16	63	18	19
Female	63	15	22	63	18	19	66	17	17	65	16	19	61	19	20	63	20	17
White	62	19	19	62	20	18	66	19	15	65	19	16	62	20	18	63	18	19
Nonwhite	71	10	19	72	07	21	60	17	23	56	17	27	70	10	20	64	16	20
East	62	18	20	68	14	18	66	18	16	66	12	22	64	17	19	63	17	20
Midwest	64	20	16	59	21	20	59	23	18	64	20	16	63	21	16	60	19	21
South	63	17	20	68	16	16	72	16	12	63	21	16	63	22	15	62	20	18
West	64	14	22	56	24	20	64	19	17	61	23	16	60	17	23	70	16	14
Republican	46	34	20	48	33	19	54	28	18	46	35	19	45	36	19	52	31	17
Democrat	73	11	16	73	09	18	75	12	13	71	12	17	73	12	15	73	11	16
Independent	60	18	22	62	20	18	62	23	15	66	18	16	59	20	21	59	21	20
Protestant	63	19	18	61	20	19	64	20	16	63	20	17	63	21	16	63	19	18
Catholic	65	15	20	65	16	19	69	18	13	67	15	18	62	17	21	63	17	20
Union	67	15	18	70	14	16	68	17	15	62	19	19	66	18	16	65	15	20
Nonunion	62	18	20	62	19	19	65	19	16	63	24	13	62	19	19	63	19	18
Grade School	62	17	21	60	12	28	62	17	21	64	14	22	56	22	22	54	17	29
High School	61	19	20	60	21	19	63	20	17	60	22	18	61	20	19	64	18	18
College	68	15	17	71	17	12	74	18	08	70	15	15	70	16	14	68	18	14
Under 30	70	13	17	70	18	12	69	19	12	68	17	15	68	15	17	66	17	17
30-49	62	16	22	62	16	22	66	19	15	63	22	15	65	21	14	65	18	17
Over 50	59	22	19	61	19	20	63	19	18	61	17	22	56	22	22	59	19	22

CARTER: 1977

	July 8-11			July 22-25			August 5-8			August 19-22			September 9-12			September 30-October 3		
	A%	D%	N%	A%	D%	N%	A%	D%	N%	A%	D%	N%	A%	D%	N%	A%	D%	N%
National	62	22	16	67	17	16	60	23	17	66	16	18	54	29	17	59	24	17
Male	61	23	16	70	17	13	61	25	14	66	20	14	57	29	14	60	24	16
Female	63	21	16	64	17	19	59	21	20	66	12	22	51	29	20	59	23	18
White	61	24	15	66	18	16	59	24	17	66	17	17	53	31	16	59	25	16
Nonwhite	68	09	23	73	09	18	68	16	16	68	11	21	58	18	24	60	13	27
East	64	21	15	73	13	14	65	20	15	66	17	17	56	23	21	60	24	16
Midwest	59	24	17	63	21	16	59	23	18	68	13	19	53	31	16	59	27	14
South	64	22	14	65	17	18	60	23	17	67	15	18	53	31	16	61	21	18
West	61	22	17	65	19	16	55	26	19	63	19	18	53	32	15	57	22	21
Republican	43	37	20	47	34	19	46	38	16	52	27	21	36	50	14	41	45	14
Democrat	73	14	13	77	10	13	70	14	16	76	10	14	64	19	17	69	15	16
Independent	59	25	16	65	18	17	57	25	18	65	16	19	51	32	17	57	25	18
Protestant	60	24	16	64	20	16	59	23	18	64	16	20	53	30	17	57	25	18
Catholic	64	21	15	72	13	15	66	21	13	73	13	14	56	27	17	60	23	17
Union	60	21	19	73	15	12	63	22	15	66	16	18	55	30	15	55	28	17
Nonunion	63	22	15	65	18	17	59	23	18	66	15	19	53	29	18	61	22	17
Grade School	60	22	18	59	18	23	49	26	25	57	17	26	49	29	22	55	21	24
High School	58	23	19	67	17	16	60	22	18	66	15	19	51	31	18	59	23	18
College	71	20	09	70	19	11	65	24	11	71	18	11	61	28	11	62	26	12
Under 30	66	22	12	73	12	15	66	18	16	73	13	14	62	23	15	63	21	16
30-49	61	21	18	67	19	14	61	25	14	65	17	18	54	30	16	63	20	17
Over 50	60	23	17	61	20	19	54	25	21	62	17	21	46	34	20	54	28	18

CARTER: 1977

	October 14-17			October 21-24			October 28-31			November 4-7			November 18-21			December 9-12		
	A%	D%	N%	A%	D%	N%	A%	D%	N%	A%	D%	N%	A%	D%	N%	A%	D%	N%
National	55	29	16	54	30	16	51	31	18	55	30	15	56	30	14	57	27	16
Male	56	31	13	55	31	14	52	34	14	54	33	13	55	33	12	57	29	14
Female	54	27	19	54	28	18	51	27	22	55	28	17	57	26	17	56	26	18
White	54	30	16	54	31	15	51	31	18	54	32	14	54	32	14	56	28	16
Nonwhite	61	20	19	55	19	26	58	21	21	63	15	22	70	12	18	64	20	16
East	57	23	20	53	30	17	55	24	21	56	28	16	57	30	13	54	32	14
Midwest	54	28	18	52	30	18	48	33	19	57	28	15	53	29	18	55	27	18
South	54	32	14	56	30	14	55	30	15	55	30	15	59	29	12	60	25	15
West	53	35	12	57	26	17	45	36	19	50	36	14	53	32	15	58	26	16
Republican	36	51	13	35	49	16	33	56	11	43	48	09	35	54	11	43	44	13
Democrat	64	22	14	66	20	14	65	19	16	65	20	15	69	18	13	67	19	14
Independent	55	26	19	52	32	16	46	31	23	50	34	16	55	29	16	53	28	19
Protestant										55	30	15	55	31	14	56	30	14
Catholic										57	30	13	60	27	13	61	21	18
Union	57	27	16	54	32	14	53	27	20	57	28	15	56	28	16	56	29	15
Nonunion	54	30	16	54	29	17	51	31	18	54	31	15	56	30	14	57	27	16
Grade School	52	26	22	49	25	26	46	27	27	49	28	23	58	25	17	55	25	20
High School	54	29	17	54	30	16	52	29	19	54	30	16	55	29	16	56	27	17
College	59	30	11	58	30	12	53	35	12	59	31	10	56	33	11	58	30	12
Under 30	61	23	16	57	31	12	61	22	17	62	23	15	61	26	13	60	22	18
30-49	54	28	18	55	26	19	50	33	17	55	30	15	57	30	13	60	25	15
Over 50	51	34	15	52	31	17	45	34	21	49	36	15	52	32	16	51	34	15

CARTER: 1978

	January 6-9			January 20-23			February 11-14			February 24-27			March 2-5			March 10-13		
	A%	D%	N%	A%	D%	N%	A%	D%	N%	A%	D%	N%	A%	D%	N%	A%	D%	N%
National	55	27	18	52	28	20	47	34	19	50	33	17	49	33	18	50	35	15
Male	56	30	14	53	31	16	49	36	15	51	36	13	49	39	12	49	37	14
Female	54	24	22	51	26	23	45	33	22	49	31	20	48	28	24	51	32	17
White	53	29	18	51	30	19	45	37	18	50	35	15	47	35	18	48	37	15
Nonwhite	63	16	21	54	20	26	55	21	24	56	21	23	59	23	18	63	16	21
East	57	24	19	50	32	18	50	29	21	51	36	13	57	27	16	53	34	13
Midwest	58	26	16	53	28	19	38	44	18	47	33	20	41	37	22	45	37	18
South	56	26	18	54	24	22	52	32	16	55	28	17	50	31	19	55	30	15
West	46	34	20	49	31	20	46	32	22	47	38	15	43	41	16	44	39	17
Republican	34	52	14	34	46	20	28	57	15	32	54	14	32	49	19	31	58	11
Democrat	65	17	18	60	20	20	55	27	18	63	22	15	64	21	15	63	24	13
Independent	53	28	19	53	29	18	49	32	19	48	35	17	41	40	19	46	33	21
Protestant	59	27	14	50	30	20	48	34	18	50	35	15	46	35	19	48	35	17
Catholic	51	26	23	57	25	18	47	34	19	54	31	15	54	29	17	55	35	10
Union	64	21	15	55	26	19	52	32	16	54	32	14	52	29	19	49	36	15
Nonunion	52	29	19	51	29	20	45	35	20	49	34	17	48	34	18	49	34	17
Grade School	53	20	27	60	20	20	49	26	25	49	22	29	50	26	24	51	29	20
High School	56	24	20	49	31	20	44	36	20	54	32	14	48	33	19	49	34	17
College	53	37	10	53	29	18	50	35	15	45	42	13	49	37	14	49	39	12
Under 30	61	23	16	56	26	18	48	31	21	56	31	13	52	29	19	55	29	16
30-49	55	25	20	50	29	21	51	33	16	48	37	15	50	33	17	49	36	15
Over 50	50	31	19	51	30	19	42	38	20	48	32	20	45	36	19	46	38	16

CARTER: 1978

	March 31–April 3			April 14–17			April 28–May 1			May 5–8			May 19–22			June 2–5		
	A%	D%	N%	A%	D%	N%	A%	D%	N%	A%	D%	N%	A%	D%	N%	A%	D%	N%
National	48	39	13	40	44	16	41	42	17	41	43	16	43	43	14	44	41	15
Male	46	43	11	41	47	12	41	47	12	42	46	12	43	46	11	45	42	13
Female	49	36	15	40	41	19	41	38	21	41	40	19	42	41	17	42	40	18
White	47	41	12	39	46	15	41	44	15	40	44	16	41	46	13	43	42	15
Nonwhite	55	24	21	52	24	24	46	23	31	54	29	17	54	23	23	52	28	20
East	48	41	11	41	42	17	40	39	21	42	42	16	44	41	15	43	42	15
Midwest	48	38	14	39	44	17	40	44	16	41	41	18	39	47	14	42	39	19
South	49	35	16	40	45	15	47	36	17	43	42	15	48	36	16	45	39	16
West	44	45	11	41	45	14	35	51	14	39	49	12	37	53	10	45	43	12
Republican	31	60	09	25	63	12	21	66	13	27	61	12	24	65	11	28	57	15
Democrat	60	27	13	51	35	14	56	27	17	51	34	15	55	32	13	54	32	14
Independent	44	42	14	36	44	20	35	47	18	36	47	17	40	45	15	40	44	16
Protestant	46	41	13	41	44	15				41	44	15	42	44	14	44	41	15
Catholic	52	35	13	39	44	17				43	42	15	47	39	14	45	41	14
Union	54	37	09	44	43	13	39	45	16	42	41	17	44	44	12	47	39	14
Nonunion	46	40	14	40	44	16	42	41	17	41	44	15	42	43	15	43	41	16
Grade School	52	23	25	44	38	18	44	33	23	43	34	23	51	31	18	47	30	23
High School	46	41	13	39	43	18	39	42	19	43	42	15	41	43	16	42	42	16
College	48	44	08	40	50	10	43	46	11	38	50	12	39	51	10	46	43	11
Under 30	55	34	11	44	43	13	47	34	19	46	39	15	49	37	14	53	33	14
30–49	46	41	13	39	43	18	41	42	17	43	43	14	40	45	15	38	46	16
Over 50	44	41	15	39	45	16	36	48	16	37	46	17	40	47	13	42	42	16

CARTER: 1978

	June 16-19			July 8-11			July 21-24			August 4-7			August 11-14			August 18-21		
	A%	D%	N%	A%	D%	N%	A%	D%	N%	A%	D%	N%	A%	D%	N%	A%	D%	N%
National	42	42	16	40	41	19	39	44	17	39	44	17	40	43	17	43	41	16
Male	42	44	14	42	43	15	39	47	14	38	47	15	42	45	13	41	45	14
Female	43	40	17	39	40	21	38	42	20	40	41	19	39	41	20	44	37	19
White	40	45	15	39	44	17	37	46	17	38	46	16	38	46	16	42	42	16
Nonwhite	64	21	15	47	26	27	53	26	21	48	23	29	52	26	22	54	27	19
East	41	46	13	40	42	18	43	40	17	41	44	15	37	46	17	39	43	18
Midwest	39	40	21	38	46	16	39	48	13	34	46	20	39	43	18	44	41	15
South	48	38	14	40	38	22	40	44	16	44	38	18	47	38	15	45	37	18
West	40	47	13	44	39	17	30	45	25	37	50	13	35	48	17	42	43	15
Republican	23	66	11	20	64	16	23	62	15	25	64	11	26	61	13	28	59	13
Democrat	55	30	15	52	28	20	50	35	15	49	33	18	51	33	16	52	30	18
Independent	39	44	17	36	48	16	35	46	19	35	47	18	34	48	18	41	47	12
Protestant	42	44	14	40	41	19	39	44	17	39	44	17	39	45	16	42	43	15
Catholic	42	40	18	44	37	19	39	45	16	44	41	15	43	40	17	45	37	18
Union	44	42	14	42	39	19	36	48	16	38	42	20	40	40	20	47	38	15
Nonunion	42	42	16	40	42	18	39	43	18	39	45	16	40	44	16	42	41	17
Grade School	43	38	19	51	26	23	39	41	20	43	30	27	46	33	21	49	28	23
High School	43	40	17	40	40	20	38	43	19	40	42	18	41	41	18	42	40	18
College	41	49	10	35	51	14	40	48	12	36	54	10	35	53	12	40	49	11
Under 30	49	35	16	46	37	17	45	39	16	43	39	18	43	36	21	48	33	19
30-49	41	45	14	38	45	17	33	49	18	44	44	12	39	47	14	41	44	15
Over 50	38	47	15	41	39	20	38	44	18	32	48	20	39	45	16	41	45	14

CARTER: 1978

	September 8-11			September 15-18			September 22-25			October 27-30			November 10-13			December 1-4		
	A%	D%	N%	A%	D%	N%	A%	D%	N%	A%	D%	N%	A%	D%	N%	A%	D%	N%
National	42	42	16	45	40	15	48	34	18	49	36	15	52	36	12	50	34	16
Male	46	41	13	45	41	14	46	37	17	47	41	12	55	35	10	50	35	15
Female	39	42	19	44	39	17	49	32	19	51	32	17	49	37	14	51	32	17
White	40	44	16	44	42	14	47	36	17	48	38	14	51	38	11	49	36	15
Nonwhite	56	27	17	49	28	23	59	16	25	56	25	19	61	25	14	61	17	22
East	38	44	18	40	45	15	46	34	20	52	36	12	52	38	10	53	32	15
Midwest	44	38	18	49	33	18	44	40	16	48	36	16	53	37	10	46	39	15
South	46	38	16	43	40	17	53	28	19	48	35	17	54	35	11	52	30	18
West	39	49	12	46	43	11	49	35	16	49	40	11	50	35	15	51	33	16
Republican	26	66	08	23	67	10	31	53	16	33	55	12	31	61	08	33	55	12
Democrat	52	32	16	54	29	17	60	24	16	62	24	14	63	26	11	62	24	14
Independent	37	44	19	47	38	15	43	37	20	42	41	17	52	35	13	48	33	19
Protestant	41	43	16	44	41	15	47	35	18	48	37	15	54	36	10	50	35	15
Catholic	44	37	19	49	37	14	51	32	17	54	31	15	55	33	12	54	30	16
Union	44	43	13	49	39	12	52	30	18	45	39	16	54	34	12	52	34	14
Nonunion	42	41	17	43	41	16	47	35	18	50	36	14	52	37	11	50	33	17
Grade School	51	33	16	45	37	18	47	25	28	55	26	19	57	30	13	49	31	20
High School	40	41	19	46	37	17	49	34	17	48	37	15	52	34	14	52	32	16
College	41	48	11	42	47	11	46	39	15	48	41	11	50	44	06	49	37	14
Under 30	41	41	18	53	31	16	49	34	17	51	37	12	53	33	14	54	27	19
30-49	40	45	15	42	43	15	45	36	19	47	36	17	52	37	11	52	37	11
Over 50	44	39	17	41	44	15	49	33	18	50	36	14	52	38	10	46	39	15

CARTER: 1978-1979

	December 8-11			January 5-8			January 19-22			February 2-5			February 23-26			March 2-5		
	A%	D%	N%	A%	D%	N%	A%	D%	N%	A%	D%	N%	A%	D%	N%	A%	D%	N%
National	51	34	15	50	36	14	43	41	16	42	42	16	37	46	17	39	48	13
Male	49	38	13	49	40	11	43	44	13	44	43	13	37	48	15	40	49	11
Female	54	29	17	51	33	16	44	38	18	41	41	18	37	45	18	39	47	14
White	49	35	16	49	38	13	43	42	15	42	43	15	37	47	16	38	50	12
Nonwhite	64	22	14	62	22	16	48	31	21	45	36	19	41	35	24	52	31	17
East	49	31	20	50	35	15	47	40	13	44	40	16	35	50	15	38	50	12
Midwest	54	34	12	49	38	13	38	43	19	39	44	17	40	43	17	40	47	13
South	52	35	13	57	31	12	46	38	16	47	39	14	37	47	16	43	44	13
West	49	32	19	44	40	16	42	44	14	37	36	27	37	45	18	36	52	12
Republican	32	58	10	33	58	09	24	65	11	24	67	09	22	67	11	27	64	09
Democrat	62	23	15	59	26	15	55	30	15	55	29	16	47	38	15	48	40	12
Independent	50	32	18	50	37	13	43	42	15	39	44	17	34	47	19	35	51	14
Protestant	53	35	12	49	39	12	41	43	16	43	41	16	37	48	15	40	49	11
Catholic	51	29	20	53	31	16	45	40	15	46	43	11	41	41	18	40	45	15
Union	49	34	17	50	34	16	44	41	15	36	47	17	38	44	18	42	48	10
Nonunion	52	33	15	50	37	13	43	41	16	44	41	15	37	47	16	39	48	13
Grade School	61	19	20	49	29	22	44	32	24	39	37	24	38	38	24	40	40	20
High School	50	35	15	49	37	14	43	39	18	41	42	17	36	47	17	40	47	13
College	48	39	13	52	38	10	43	49	08	45	45	10	39	49	12	37	54	09
Under 30	53	32	15	54	34	12	49	38	13	46	35	19	41	44	15	43	46	11
30-49	49	35	16	53	33	14	44	41	15	41	43	16	36	46	18	40	48	12
Over 50	51	33	16	45	40	15	38	44	18	41	45	14	36	48	16	37	49	14

CARTER: 1979

	March 16-19			March 23-26			April 6-9			May 4-7			May 18-21			June 1-4		
	A%	D%	N%	A%	D%	N%	A%	D%	N%	A%	D%	N%	A%	D%	N%	A%	D%	N%
National	47	39	14	42	44	14	40	46	14	37	49	14	32	53	15	29	56	15
Male	47	43	10	43	46	11	39	50	11	35	54	11	31	55	14	27	62	11
Female	46	37	17	42	41	17	42	42	16	39	44	17	33	50	17	31	51	18
White	45	42	13	42	45	13	39	48	13	37	51	12	32	54	14	28	57	15
Nonwhite	60	22	18	51	32	17	53	31	16	43	32	25	35	43	22	35	46	19
East	51	35	14	41	47	12	41	44	15	40	47	13	31	53	16	28	59	13
Midwest	44	43	13	44	41	15	41	48	11	35	51	14	32	53	15	29	56	15
South	47	40	13	45	41	14	43	43	14	43	42	15	38	48	14	33	52	15
West	43	42	15	39	47	14	35	50	15	28	61	11	26	57	17	25	57	18
Republican	30	60	10	29	58	13	22	66	12	28	61	11	24	65	11	20	68	12
Democrat	56	30	14	53	33	14	52	34	14	47	39	14	37	48	15	36	49	15
Independent	45	42	13	37	50	13	38	51	11	32	56	12	31	53	16	26	58	16
Protestant	47	41	12	43	43	14	41	46	13	34	50	16	34	51	15	29	56	15
Catholic	46	38	16	43	46	11	40	45	15	44	46	10	30	55	15	30	55	15
Union	46	41	13	43	46	11	41	46	13	37	50	13	29	55	16	27	60	13
Nonunion	47	39	14	43	43	14	40	46	14	37	49	14	33	52	15	29	55	16
Grade School	52	29	19	43	40	17	34	47	19	40	38	22	34	38	28	29	47	24
High School	45	41	14	39	46	15	39	45	16	35	49	16	31	54	15	28	57	15
College	47	43	10	49	42	09	47	46	07	39	54	07	34	57	09	31	59	10
Under 30	53	33	14	49	37	14	44	42	14	45	42	13	38	49	13	32	56	12
30-49	41	44	15	41	46	13	41	47	12	36	52	12	28	58	14	29	55	16
Over 50	47	40	13	40	46	14	37	47	16	32	51	17	32	50	18	26	57	17

CARTER: 1979

	June 22-25			June 29-July 2			July 13-16			August 3-6			August 10-13			August 17-20		
	A%	D%	N%	A%	D%	N%	A%	D%	N%	A%	D%	N%	A%	D%	N%	A%	D%	N%
National	29	57	14	28	59	13	29	58	13	32	53	15	33	55	12	32	54	14
Male	27	62	11	28	62	10	27	62	11	32	56	12	33	58	09	34	56	10
Female	31	52	17	28	57	15	31	54	15	32	51	17	34	52	14	31	52	17
White	28	59	13	26	62	12	29	58	13	30	56	14	33	57	10	31	56	13
Nonwhite	35	46	19	43	40	17	30	55	15	43	37	20	40	37	23	45	38	17
East	28	62	10	25	66	09	25	59	16	29	58	13	28	61	11	25	64	11
Midwest	28	58	14	25	61	14	29	56	15	30	53	17	29	58	13	32	52	16
South	31	54	15	32	54	14	31	56	13	37	49	14	44	47	09	40	46	14
West	31	52	17	33	54	13	32	53	15	31	53	16	31	55	14	32	54	14
Republican	19	68	13	19	72	09	18	73	09	18	71	11	22	70	08	22	68	10
Democrat	41	46	13	34	52	14	37	50	13	41	46	13	43	46	11	42	46	12
Independent	20	66	14	28	60	12	27	57	16	29	56	15	30	58	12	27	59	14
Protestant	29	56	15	29	59	12	29	58	13	33	53	14	35	52	13	32	52	16
Catholic	32	56	12	28	58	14	28	58	14	31	55	14	31	59	10	31	58	11
Union	30	59	11	27	62	11	24	65	11	31	55	14	30	57	13	29	56	15
Nonunion	29	56	15	29	58	13	30	56	14	32	53	15	35	54	11	33	54	13
Grade School	36	40	24	36	53	11	34	49	17	31	50	19	38	45	17	39	41	20
High School	26	61	13	28	58	14	27	57	16	33	51	16	32	56	12	32	54	14
College	31	59	10	25	65	10	31	63	06	31	60	09	32	59	09	31	60	09
Under 30	26	60	14	34	54	12	31	54	15	32	53	15	34	54	12	37	50	13
30-49	30	59	11	24	65	11	27	63	10	30	54	16	32	56	12	31	56	13
Over 50	31	52	17	28	57	15	29	55	16	33	54	13	34	55	11	31	55	14

CARTER: 1979

	September 7-10			September 28-October 1			October 5-8			October 12-15			November 2-5			November 16-19		
	A%	D%	N%	A%	D%	N%	A%	D%	N%	A%	D%	N%	A%	D%	N%	A%	D%	N%
National	30	55	15	33	54	13	29	58	13	31	55	14	32	55	13	38	49	13
Male	29	59	12	33	56	11	30	60	10	33	57	10	30	61	09	37	53	10
Female	30	52	18	32	52	16	28	57	15	30	53	17	34	50	16	38	47	15
White	30	57	13	31	56	13	28	60	12	30	57	13	32	57	11	36	52	12
Nonwhite	32	44	24	46	38	16	33	51	16	45	39	16	36	43	21	48	35	17
East	28	62	10	30	61	09	27	64	09	31	55	14	25	64	11	39	51	10
Midwest	32	53	15	31	51	18	27	60	13	33	50	17	33	55	12	36	50	14
South	30	50	20	37	49	14	35	50	15	34	55	11	38	48	14	42	44	14
West	27	59	14	32	53	15	23	62	15	26	61	13	30	57	13	32	54	14
Republican	15	76	09	18	70	12	20	73	07	24	70	06	18	75	07	27	64	09
Democrat	37	49	14	41	46	13	34	52	14	40	46	14	40	46	14	47	40	13
Independent	30	53	17	29	58	13	28	59	13	26	58	16	31	56	13	29	58	13
Protestant	31	57	12	34	53	13	29	59	12	33	54	13	34	54	12	39	47	14
Catholic	30	56	14	33	55	12	29	57	14	29	66	05	29	59	12	37	51	12
Union	28	59	13	30	56	14	29	59	12	33	53	14	34	57	09	40	50	10
Nonunion	30	55	15	33	54	13	29	58	13	31	55	14	31	55	14	37	49	14
Grade School	36	43	21	40	40	20	28	52	20	32	48	20	40	40	20	35	43	22
High School	27	56	17	32	54	14	29	57	14	31	53	16	31	56	13	39	48	13
College	31	61	08	30	61	09	28	65	07	32	62	06	30	61	09	36	56	08
Under 30	28	56	16	34	52	14	28	58	14	37	50	13	35	53	12	38	50	12
30-49	32	55	13	32	55	13	31	60	09	28	58	14	27	61	12	36	53	11
Over 50	29	56	15	32	55	13	27	57	16	29	56	15	35	52	13	39	46	15

CARTER: 1979-1980

	November 30-December 3			December 7-10			January 5-8			January 25-28			February 1-4			February 29-March 3		
	A%	D%	N%	A%	D%	N%	A%	D%	N%	A%	D%	N%	A%	D%	N%	A%	D%	N%
National	51	37	12	54	35	11	56	33	11	58	32	10	55	36	09	52	38	10
Male	49	41	10	53	39	08	56	36	08	57	35	08	53	39	08	52	39	09
Female	54	33	13	55	32	13	56	31	13	58	30	12	57	33	10	52	37	11
White	51	39	10	54	36	10	56	34	10	57	33	10	55	37	08	51	40	09
Nonwhite	53	26	21	55	32	13	61	27	12	60	30	10	60	28	12	57	27	16
East	48	41	11	50	39	11	57	32	11	56	32	12	54	38	08	50	39	11
Midwest	55	31	14	56	33	11	54	34	12	59	32	09	55	35	10	50	39	11
South	58	32	10	60	30	10	62	28	10	60	32	08	64	29	07	54	37	09
West	43	47	10	50	40	10	51	42	07	55	36	09	44	45	11	53	38	09
Republican	39	54	07	42	45	13	40	51	09	41	47	12	43	50	07	39	52	09
Democrat	62	27	11	62	29	09	65	26	09	67	26	07	65	26	09	62	31	07
Independent	48	41	11	55	36	09	53	36	11	56	33	11	48	43	09	48	39	13
Protestant	52	37	11	54	34	12	57	33	10	59	31	10	56	36	08	52	37	11
Catholic	53	37	10	56	36	08	54	36	10	59	32	09	55	34	11	54	39	07
Union	54	35	11	55	34	11	51	34	15	59	33	08	55	34	11	53	35	12
Nonunion	51	37	12	54	35	11	58	33	09	57	32	11	55	36	09	52	39	09
Grade School	56	30	14	62	24	14	57	25	18	60	27	13	58	31	11	55	32	13
High School	51	35	14	51	37	12	56	33	11	58	31	11	53	37	10	51	38	11
College	50	43	07	56	38	06	56	38	06	56	38	06	58	36	06	51	41	08
Under 30	56	34	10	51	38	11	56	35	09	58	33	09	54	38	08	55	36	09
30-49	48	40	12	54	36	10	54	36	10	55	34	11	56	35	09	50	40	10
Over 50	52	36	12	57	32	11	58	30	12	59	31	10	56	35	09	52	38	10

CARTER: 1980

	March 7-10			March 27-30			April 11-14			May 2-5			May 16-19			May 30-June 2		
	A%	D%	N%	A%	D%	N%	A%	D%	N%	A%	D%	N%	A%	D%	N%	A%	D%	N%
National	43	45	12	39	51	10	39	50	11	43	47	10	38	51	11	38	52	10
Male	44	47	09	39	53	08	37	53	10	41	51	08	35	55	10	36	54	10
Female	42	43	15	39	49	12	41	47	12	44	44	12	41	47	12	41	48	11
White	42	47	11	38	53	09	40	51	09	42	49	09	39	52	09	37	54	09
Nonwhite	51	29	20	49	37	14	36	44	20	48	36	16	34	46	20	45	38	17
East	40	49	11	35	56	09	39	52	09	37	56	07	39	52	09	34	57	09
Midwest	45	42	13	40	52	08	39	50	11	45	46	09	41	50	09	41	49	10
South	47	40	13	49	42	09	40	47	13	51	39	10	43	43	14	42	45	13
West	37	50	13	29	55	16	39	52	09	34	49	17	26	62	12	35	56	09
Republican	25	63	12	23	68	09	28	64	08	25	63	12	31	63	06	22	68	10
Democrat	54	35	11	50	40	10	48	41	11	55	37	08	47	41	12	51	41	08
Independent	39	49	12	35	56	09	36	54	10	36	53	11	33	58	09	32	55	13
Protestant	45	43	12	42	48	10	37	51	12	44	45	11	37	51	12	39	50	11
Catholic	40	49	11	36	54	10	45	47	08	44	49	07	43	48	09	41	53	06
Union	48	44	08	39	55	06	39	51	10	46	43	11	41	50	09	34	55	11
Nonunion	41	45	14	39	50	11	39	50	11	41	49	10	37	51	12	40	50	10
Grade School	48	39	13	38	48	14	43	41	16	50	39	11	33	48	19	43	41	16
High School	43	44	13	40	50	10	38	50	12	43	45	12	41	48	11	39	52	09
College	40	50	10	39	53	08	39	55	06	38	55	07	36	58	06	35	56	09
Under 30	46	42	12	42	48	10	44	48	08	45	46	09	45	46	09	42	48	10
30-49	42	46	12	37	55	08	34	56	10	39	51	10	34	56	10	35	55	10
Over 50	42	45	13	39	49	12	41	46	13	44	45	11	37	49	14	39	50	11

CARTER: 1980

	June 13-16			June 27-30			July 11-14			August 15-18			September 12-15			November 21-24		
	A%	D%	N%	A%	D%	N%	A%	D%	N%	A%	D%	N%	A%	D%	N%	A%	D%	N%
National	32	56	12	31	58	11	33	55	12	32	55	13	37	55	08	31	56	13
Male	30	61	09	31	61	08	29	61	10	31	58	11	35	59	06	28	61	11
Female	35	51	14	30	56	14	36	49	15	33	52	15	39	51	10	34	51	15
White	32	57	11	30	60	10	31	57	12	30	58	12	33	60	07	28	60	12
Nonwhite	33	52	15	37	45	18	40	44	16	46	34	20	66	23	11	55	27	18
East	26	63	11	29	62	09	30	58	12	28	64	08	37	57	06	31	57	12
Midwest	33	55	12	29	60	11	32	57	11	30	53	17	36	53	11	27	60	13
South	41	47	12	35	54	11	39	50	11	42	47	11	40	54	06	37	49	14
West	28	61	11	31	56	13	28	55	17	25	56	19	35	56	09	27	61	12
Republican	15	75	10	20	76	04	15	76	09	14	78	08	12	83	05	12	82	06
Democrat	47	46	07	42	47	11	48	42	10	48	40	12	61	32	07	50	37	13
Independent	31	56	13	25	65	10	25	60	15	20	65	15	22	68	10	23	64	13
Protestant	32	56	12	32	58	10	36	52	12	35	52	13	38	54	08	32	55	13
Catholic	37	52	11	31	57	12	29	60	11	31	58	11	40	52	08	30	59	11
Union	30	60	10	28	66	06	32	56	12	31	58	11	38	56	06	29	58	13
Nonunion	33	55	12	32	56	12	33	54	13	32	54	14	37	54	09	32	55	13
Grade School	35	46	19	38	49	13	34	48	18	41	41	18	48	39	13	38	41	21
High School	34	54	12	29	59	12	36	52	12	31	55	14	37	55	08	34	52	14
College	29	64	07	30	62	08	26	64	10	30	62	08	32	63	05	22	70	08
Under 30	33	53	14	32	56	12	38	51	11	34	51	15	39	53	08	32	54	14
30-49	34	56	10	29	60	11	29	58	13	29	61	10	36	57	07	27	61	12
Over 50	30	58	12	31	59	10	32	55	13	34	52	14	38	54	08	34	53	13

CARTER: 1980

	December 5-8		
	A%	D%	N%
National	34	55	11
Male	30	61	09
Female	38	50	12
White	31	59	10
Nonwhite	55	30	15
East	28	61	11
Midwest	35	51	14
South	38	53	09
West	36	57	07
Republican	14	81	05
Democrat	49	38	13
Independent	30	60	10
Protestant	36	53	11
Catholic	34	57	09
Union	32	55	13
Nonunion	35	55	10
Grade School	38	45	17
High School	36	52	12
College	29	66	05
Under 30	43	48	09
30-49	29	59	12
Over 50	32	57	11

REAGAN: 1981

	January 30–February 2			February 13–16			March 13–16			April 3–6			April 10–13			May 8–11		
	A%	D%	N%	A%	D%	N%	A%	D%	N%	A%	D%	N%	A%	D%	N%	A%	D%	N%
National	51	13	36	55	18	27	60	24	16	67	18	15	67	19	14	68	21	11
Male	54	13	33	58	17	25	65	22	13	70	16	14	71	16	13	70	20	10
Female	48	14	38	53	18	29	55	26	19	63	21	16	64	22	14	65	22	13
White	54	12	34	61	15	24	65	21	14	73	12	15	74	14	12	73	16	11
Nonwhite	25	27	48	18	40	42	22	49	29	25	59	16	23	51	26	31	51	18
East	49	12	39	53	17	30	55	24	21	63	22	15	63	22	15	64	21	15
Midwest	52	13	35	55	18	27	61	22	17	65	19	16	74	11	15	70	22	08
South	52	13	35	57	22	21	63	23	14	72	13	15	65	22	13	69	21	10
West	50	17	33	58	14	28	58	29	13	66	20	14	66	24	10	68	19	13
Republican	74	04	22	78	06	16	87	05	08	87	05	08	91	03	06	92	04	04
Democrat	38	20	42	39	28	33	41	39	20	52	29	19	46	34	20	51	35	14
Independent	53	12	35	57	16	27	61	22	17	69	16	15	75	14	11	70	17	13
Protestant	52	15	33	58	18	24	62	24	14	69	17	14	67	20	13	69	21	10
Catholic	52	11	37	57	13	30	58	22	20	69	16	15	70	16	14	69	19	12
Union	50	13	37	55	20	25	60	26	14	62	24	14	63	21	16	66	23	11
Nonunion	51	14	35	56	17	27	59	24	17	68	17	15	68	19	13	68	20	12
Grade School	30	15	55	37	24	39	40	39	21	50	27	23	54	31	15	55	25	20
High School	56	12	32	56	17	27	60	22	18	69	16	15	66	19	15	68	20	12
College	54	15	31	64	16	20	68	21	11	71	18	11	76	13	11	72	21	07
Under 30	50	20	30	55	24	21	56	28	16	63	23	14	64	24	12	65	27	08
30–49	54	10	36	56	16	28	63	22	15	70	18	12	68	15	17	72	18	10
Over 50	49	12	39	55	15	30	58	24	18	67	15	18	68	19	13	65	19	16

REAGAN: 1981

	June 5-8			June 19-22			June 26-29			July 17-20			July 24-27			July 31-August 3		
	A%	D%	N%	A%	D%	N%	A%	D%	N%	A%	D%	N%	A%	D%	N%	A%	D%	N%
National	59	28	13	59	29	12	58	30	12	60	29	11	56	30	14	60	28	12
Male	61	27	12	66	23	11	63	28	09	63	28	09	63	28	09	62	27	11
Female	57	29	14	52	34	14	53	32	15	55	32	13	49	33	18	56	30	14
White	65	23	12	65	23	12	64	24	12	64	25	11	61	26	13	66	23	11
Nonwhite	20	60	20	19	66	15	21	66	13	22	67	11	27	56	17	20	58	22
East	60	27	13	56	29	15	53	24	23	59	28	13	52	33	15	58	30	12
Midwest	61	27	12	58	30	12	58	32	10	62	29	09	60	27	13	58	29	13
South	57	28	15	62	26	12	60	25	15	60	28	12	52	32	16	57	30	13
West	57	33	10	60	29	11	61	30	09	64	26	10	60	30	10	68	23	09
Republican	87	06	07	85	08	07	88	05	07	85	08	07	80	11	09	87	07	06
Democrat	44	45	11	41	43	16	41	47	12	41	45	14	38	44	18	45	42	13
Independent	58	26	16	62	27	11	56	30	14	60	31	09	60	29	11	58	27	15
Protestant	61	28	11	60	28	12	61	28	11	62	29	09	56	31	13	59	28	13
Catholic	58	26	16	61	26	13	55	32	13	59	29	12	58	27	15	63	26	11
Union	56	35	09	57	31	12	53	38	09	58	33	09	52	33	15	54	31	15
Nonunion	60	26	14	59	28	13	59	28	13	60	29	11	57	30	13	61	27	12
Grade School	40	37	23	38	42	20	42	40	18	45	37	18	35	42	23	48	33	19
High School	60	28	12	58	28	14	57	30	13	58	31	11	57	29	14	60	28	12
College	67	24	09	70	23	07	67	25	08	69	23	08	65	27	08	64	27	09
Under 30	59	31	10	59	29	12	59	29	12	56	32	12	60	29	11	57	32	11
30-49	62	26	12	64	26	10	59	32	09	64	29	07	58	29	13	59	29	12
Over 50	56	28	16	54	30	16	56	29	15	59	28	13	51	32	17	62	25	13

REAGAN: 1981

	August 14-17			August 18-21			October 2-5			October 30–November 2			November 13-16			November 20-23		
	A%	D%	N%	A%	D%	N%	A%	D%	N%	A%	D%	N%	A%	D%	N%	A%	D%	N%
National	60	29	11	52	37	11	56	35	09	53	35	12	49	40	11	54	37	09
Male	66	27	07	60	31	09	61	32	07	60	31	09	53	39	08	60	34	06
Female	54	32	14	44	43	13	51	37	12	47	39	14	46	41	13	50	39	11
White	66	23	11	58	31	11	62	30	08	61	30	09	55	35	10	59	32	09
Nonwhite	18	70	12	10	77	13	12	71	17	19	59	22	15	71	14	26	64	10
East	57	31	12	49	42	09	56	36	08	51	36	13	45	45	10	50	40	10
Midwest	63	26	11	54	32	14	57	33	10	60	30	10	51	37	12	53	40	07
South	59	30	11	51	39	10	57	32	11	49	39	12	47	41	12	56	32	12
West	59	33	08	54	35	11	51	41	08	55	34	11	53	38	09	62	34	04
Republican	85	08	07	82	11	07	87	08	05	88	06	06	81	14	05	85	12	03
Democrat	42	45	13	33	56	11	36	56	08	31	55	14	30	57	13	37	54	09
Independent	60	30	10	55	31	14	55	31	14	58	31	11	48	42	10	56	33	11
Protestant	59	30	11	53	36	11	56	34	10	54	35	11				57	34	09
Catholic	63	25	12	53	37	10	58	33	09	58	28	14				53	36	11
Union	47	38	15	49	41	10	47	40	13	52	37	11				51	42	07
Nonunion	63	27	10	53	36	11	58	33	09	54	34	12				56	35	09
Grade School	44	37	19	32	51	17	39	48	13	36	48	16	34	47	19	46	41	13
High School	59	30	11	52	37	11	56	33	11	52	35	13	47	41	12	53	38	09
College	69	25	06	61	31	08	63	31	06	64	29	07	59	36	05	63	32	05
Under 30	60	32	08	50	40	10	56	36	08	53	36	11	50	41	09	50	39	11
30-49	61	28	11	56	33	11	58	33	09	56	33	11	49	41	10	59	35	06
Over 50	59	29	12	50	38	12	54	36	10	51	37	12	48	39	13	54	37	09

REAGAN: 1981-1982

	December 11-14			January 8-11			January 22-25			February 5-8			March 12-15			April 2-5		
	A%	D%	N%	A%	D%	N%	A%	D%	N%	A%	D%	N%	A%	D%	N%	A%	D%	N%
National	49	41	10	49	40	11	47	42	11	47	43	10	46	45	09	45	46	09
Male	51	42	07	53	37	10	49	41	10	51	41	08	52	40	08	50	43	07
Female	46	41	13	45	43	12	46	42	12	42	46	12	41	49	10	41	49	10
White	55	35	10	55	35	10	52	37	11	52	38	10	51	40	09	50	42	08
Nonwhite	17	74	09	13	71	16	16	74	10	11	76	13	13	76	11	17	71	12
East	45	45	10	43	46	11	46	42	12	44	44	12	46	45	09	41	51	08
Midwest	51	39	10	51	38	11	50	40	10	45	45	10	48	44	08	45	48	07
South	48	42	10	50	38	12	47	42	11	48	40	12	47	42	11	46	44	10
West	51	39	10	54	36	10	47	41	12	50	45	05	44	49	07	49	40	11
Republican	81	13	06	80	13	07	82	13	05	83	12	05	84	10	06	80	14	06
Democrat	29	62	09	30	60	10	29	61	10	26	65	09	26	66	08	23	70	07
Independent	50	38	12	50	35	15	47	37	16	51	35	14	47	43	10	51	37	12
Protestant	53	38	09	53	38	09	48	42	10	47	42	11	48	43	09	47	45	08
Catholic	43	45	12	47	40	13	50	37	13	45	44	11	46	45	09	46	45	09
Union	47	44	09	39	48	13	43	47	10	41	51	08	40	52	08	37	55	08
Nonunion	49	41	10	52	37	11	48	40	12	48	41	11	49	42	09	47	44	09
Grade School	37	46	17	43	45	12	29	51	20	24	59	17	30	54	16	32	55	13
High School	50	41	09	47	39	14	49	40	11	47	42	11	46	44	10	43	48	09
College	52	40	08	56	39	05	53	39	08	56	38	06	54	42	04	55	39	06
Under 30	49	43	08	45	42	13	46	40	14	51	40	09	45	46	09	52	39	09
30-49	48	41	11	48	40	12	49	44	07	49	43	08	50	43	07	43	49	08
Over 50	49	41	10	53	38	09	47	40	13	42	46	12	44	46	10	42	49	09

REAGAN: 1982

	April 23-26 A%	D%	N%	April 30-May 3 A%	D%	N%	May 14-17 A%	D%	N%	June 11-14 A%	D%	N%	June 25-28 A%	D%	N%	July 23-26 A%	D%	N%
National	43	47	10	44	46	10	45	44	11	45	45	10	44	46	10	42	46	12
Male	49	41	10	50	42	08	47	43	10	51	39	10	48	45	07	48	45	07
Female	38	53	09	40	49	11	43	45	12	39	52	09	40	47	13	38	47	15
White	48	42	10	49	42	09	51	37	12	50	41	09	49	41	10	46	43	11
Nonwhite	14	76	10	17	72	11	14	79	07	12	77	11	16	72	12	20	67	13
East	37	53	10	39	52	09	44	44	12	39	51	10	40	48	12	40	49	11
Midwest	44	45	11	44	46	10	51	40	09	45	46	09	47	44	09	42	48	10
South	45	43	12	49	42	09	37	50	13	47	43	10	44	45	11	40	47	13
West	48	46	06	46	44	10	49	43	08	49	41	10	48	45	07	49	39	12
Republican	83	11	06	81	14	05	80	14	06	77	17	06	79	13	08	74	18	08
Democrat	20	71	09	24	67	09	22	66	12	25	65	10	24	68	08	25	64	11
Independent	45	43	12	45	42	13	51	36	13	45	44	11	46	41	13	43	46	11
Protestant				46	45	09	46	43	11	47	44	09	47	43	10	44	44	12
Catholic				44	46	10	45	43	12	45	44	11	43	45	12	40	48	12
Union				34	56	10	36	52	12	33	58	09	37	54	09	35	58	07
Nonunion				47	43	10	47	42	11	48	42	10	46	43	11	44	43	13
Grade School	32	54	14	30	57	13	31	56	13	39	48	13	46	39	15	28	50	22
High School	41	48	11	41	48	11	45	44	11	41	49	10	40	50	10	43	47	10
College	53	42	05	57	36	07	52	39	09	53	39	08	51	42	07	49	42	09
Under 30	43	46	11	44	45	11	41	48	11	43	47	10	40	49	11	47	42	11
30-49	44	48	08	48	44	08	47	41	12	46	44	10	47	45	08	41	49	10
Over 50	43	46	11	41	48	11	46	44	10	46	46	08	45	43	12	41	46	13

REAGAN: 1982

	July 30–August 2			August 13–16			August 27–30			September 17–20			October 15–18			November 5–8		
	A%	D%	N%	A%	D%	N%	A%	D%	N%	A%	D%	N%	A%	D%	N%	A%	D%	N%
National	41	47	12	41	49	10	42	46	12	42	48	10	42	48	10	43	47	10
Male	45	44	11	44	48	08	47	44	09	47	43	10	46	44	10	45	45	10
Female	37	50	13	38	50	12	37	48	15	37	53	10	38	51	11	41	49	10
White	45	43	12	45	44	11	47	40	13	47	43	10	47	42	11	48	42	10
Nonwhite	14	73	13	13	76	11	09	79	12	13	75	12	12	77	11	15	76	09
East	40	49	11	42	48	10	39	49	12	43	50	07	35	55	10	40	50	10
Midwest	45	45	10	42	48	10	44	42	14	43	46	11	40	47	13	45	45	10
South	38	46	16	38	49	13	42	45	13	40	48	12	42	48	10	40	48	12
West	40	48	12	41	50	09	44	47	09	44	47	09	55	38	07	47	43	10
Republican	75	18	07	75	18	07	77	15	08	77	17	06	79	14	07	82	14	04
Democrat	21	67	12	23	69	08	19	68	13	21	69	10	19	71	10	22	70	08
Independent	44	42	14	38	49	13	48	40	12	44	44	12	45	41	14	40	46	14
Protestant	43	45	12	42	48	10	43	43	14	46	46	08	46	44	10	44	46	10
Catholic	46	44	10	41	48	11	41	48	11	42	46	12	37	54	09	43	47	10
Union	32	55	13	32	62	06	34	56	10	36	53	11	37	52	11	36	54	10
Nonunion	43	45	12	43	46	11	44	43	13	44	46	10	43	47	10	44	45	11
Grade School	35	52	13	33	50	17	28	53	19	34	56	10	32	52	16	28	58	14
High School	38	49	13	40	49	11	40	47	13	39	49	12	39	49	12	43	45	12
College	49	40	11	47	46	07	53	40	07	51	43	06	52	43	05	50	45	05
Under 30	42	46	12	40	48	12	44	43	13	41	47	12	36	51	13	38	48	14
30–49	42	45	13	42	50	08	41	48	11	46	44	10	47	47	06	45	46	09
Over 50	40	48	12	39	49	12	41	46	13	39	52	09	41	47	12	44	48	08

REAGAN: 1982-1983

	November 19-22			December 10-13			January 14-17			January 21-24			January 28-31			February 25-28		
	A%	D%	N%	A%	D%	N%	A%	D%	N%	A%	D%	N%	A%	D%	N%	A%	D%	N%
National	43	47	10	41	50	09	37	54	09	37	53	10	35	56	09	40	50	10
Male	48	44	08	47	46	07	42	50	08	39	53	08	39	55	06	43	49	08
Female	39	49	12	36	54	10	32	58	10	35	53	12	32	57	11	37	51	12
White	47	43	10	46	45	09	41	50	09	42	49	09	39	53	08	45	45	10
Nonwhite	20	67	13	09	85	06	17	75	08	09	77	14	13	78	09	14	78	08
East	42	51	07	36	57	07	35	55	10	37	55	08	29	65	06	40	53	07
Midwest	42	47	11	46	44	10	41	50	09	39	52	09	35	56	09	35	53	12
South	41	46	13	38	52	10	35	57	08	35	51	14	38	52	10	41	48	11
West	49	43	08	46	48	06	35	55	10	38	55	07	40	50	10	47	45	08
Republican	81	11	08	76	17	07	68	22	10	67	26	07	69	23	08	79	14	07
Democrat	22	70	08	21	71	08	18	76	06	19	72	09	19	76	05	17	75	08
Independent	46	42	12	42	49	09	42	49	09	41	48	11	34	55	11	46	42	12
Protestant	46	45	09	42	49	09	39	52	09	40	50	10	36	53	11	43	48	09
Catholic	43	47	10	41	50	09	38	54	08	36	55	09	37	57	06	39	52	09
Union	33	58	09	37	55	08	27	64	09	36	57	07	25	67	08	39	56	05
Nonunion	46	44	10	42	49	09	39	52	09	37	52	11	38	53	09	41	48	11
Grade School	32	55	13	25	61	14	21	64	15	22	62	16	16	66	18	25	53	22
High School	43	47	10	40	51	09	37	54	09	35	54	11	36	55	09	38	53	09
College	49	43	08	51	44	05	45	49	06	49	45	06	43	53	04	51	43	06
Under 30	44	46	10	44	49	07	40	50	10	43	48	09	40	53	07	40	50	10
30-49	41	49	10	39	52	09	39	55	06	33	56	11	34	58	08	44	50	06
Over 50	45	45	10	40	51	09	33	57	10	36	54	10	33	56	11	37	51	12

REAGAN: 1983

	March 11-14			April 15-18			April 29–May 2			May 13-16			May 20-23			June 10-13		
	A%	D%	N%	A%	D%	N%	A%	D%	N%	A%	D%	N%	A%	D%	N%	A%	D%	N%
National	41	49	10	41	49	10	43	46	11	43	45	12	46	43	11	43	45	12
Male	47	47	06	42	49	09	48	42	10	50	40	10	49	41	10	47	45	08
Female	35	52	13	39	50	11	38	50	12	36	50	14	43	44	13	40	46	14
White	45	46	09	45	45	10	48	42	10	47	41	12	49	39	12	48	41	11
Nonwhite	13	71	16	13	76	11	18	68	14	17	71	12	21	67	12	15	69	16
East	38	53	09	38	52	10	39	52	09	39	49	12	45	44	11	36	52	12
Midwest	44	46	10	39	51	10	40	50	10	41	47	12	44	43	13	48	43	09
South	38	52	10	40	47	13	42	44	14	46	43	11	45	46	09	46	41	13
West	46	44	10	46	48	06	56	37	07	50	38	12	50	36	14	43	46	11
Republican	78	17	05	77	17	06	78	15	07	79	13	08	78	14	08	79	14	07
Democrat	23	66	11	23	68	09	25	65	10	22	67	11	26	63	11	21	68	11
Independent	41	48	11	43	45	12	46	41	13	47	41	12	49	37	14	51	35	14
Protestant	45	45	10	42	48	10	46	44	10	45	43	12	48	41	11	45	43	12
Catholic	38	51	11	43	48	09	43	47	10	42	45	13	46	42	12	44	44	12
Union	37	52	11	32	60	08	41	49	10	36	53	11	45	44	11	39	53	08
Nonunion	42	48	10	42	47	11	43	46	11	45	43	12	46	42	12	45	43	12
Grade School	34	49	17	28	54	18	33	52	15	33	52	15	34	48	18	28	54	18
High School	38	52	10	39	51	10	40	49	11	40	47	13	46	42	12	43	45	12
College	50	43	07	50	43	07	53	39	08	54	38	08	50	41	09	52	41	07
Under 30	37	55	08	39	50	11	39	49	12	41	47	12	44	43	13	45	42	13
30-49	46	45	09	43	47	10	45	44	11	44	45	11	48	41	11	46	44	10
Over 50	39	49	12	39	51	10	43	47	10	44	43	13	45	44	11	40	48	12

REAGAN: 1983

	June 24-27			July 22-25			July 29-August 1			August 5-8			August 12-15			August 19-22		
	A%	D%	N%	A%	D%	N%	A%	D%	N%	A%	D%	N%	A%	D%	N%	A%	D%	N%
National	47	44	09	42	47	11	44	42	14	44	46	10	43	45	12	43	46	11
Male	52	42	06	51	41	08	49	39	12	50	43	07	48	41	11	47	43	10
Female	42	46	12	34	52	14	40	44	16	38	50	12	38	49	13	39	49	12
White	51	40	09	48	41	11	50	37	13	50	41	09	49	40	11	48	42	10
Nonwhite	22	64	14	14	74	12	13	71	16	12	74	14	13	69	18	11	72	17
East	48	43	09	39	50	11	38	48	14	39	49	12	41	47	12	36	51	13
Midwest	45	45	10	43	48	09	48	40	12	48	43	09	43	46	11	42	46	12
South	48	41	11	41	45	14	43	41	16	40	48	12	42	45	13	46	42	12
West	46	48	06	47	43	10	49	39	12	50	45	05	48	41	11	46	47	07
Republican	82	12	06	78	15	07	78	11	11	78	16	06	81	14	05	78	14	08
Democrat	28	64	08	19	70	11	24	63	13	22	69	09	21	66	13	21	69	10
Independent	50	38	12	48	41	11	47	37	16	50	39	11	42	43	15	47	42	11
Protestant	48	43	09	43	45	12	45	42	13	45	46	09	45	43	12	44	44	12
Catholic	49	41	10	44	46	10	48	38	14	46	44	10	46	43	11	43	48	09
Union	40	52	08	34	56	10	37	52	11	39	51	10	36	52	12	35	53	12
Nonunion	49	42	09	45	44	11	46	39	15	45	45	10	45	43	12	44	45	11
Grade School	38	47	15	27	56	17	26	55	19	30	54	16	34	50	16	24	55	21
High School	45	46	09	39	49	12	45	41	14	41	50	09	42	45	13	40	48	12
College	56	39	05	55	39	06	52	39	09	55	37	08	49	43	08	56	39	05
Under 30	44	45	11	42	47	11	52	37	11	47	44	09	45	42	13	42	47	11
30-49	48	44	08	45	48	07	43	44	13	41	49	10	41	48	11	44	46	10
Over 50	48	43	09	40	46	14	40	44	16	44	46	10	44	44	12	41	46	13

REAGAN: 1983

	September 9-12			September 16-19			October 7-10			October 21-24			November 18-21			December 9-12		
	A%	D%	N%	A%	D%	N%	A%	D%	N%	A%	D%	N%	A%	D%	N%	A%	D%	N%
National	47	42	11	47	43	10	45	44	11	49	41	10	53	37	10	54	38	08
Male	53	39	08	54	39	07	50	40	10	55	38	07	58	33	09	59	33	08
Female	42	45	13	42	44	14	41	47	12	45	43	12	48	41	11	48	42	10
White	51	38	11	53	37	10	50	40	10	54	36	10	58	32	10	58	34	08
Nonwhite	19	69	12	15	71	14	18	67	15	20	69	11	14	71	15	21	68	11
East	42	48	10	45	43	12	38	48	14	45	46	09	50	38	12	50	40	10
Midwest	48	41	11	49	43	08	44	47	09	52	40	08	51	40	09	60	33	07
South	48	37	15	51	38	11	50	39	11	50	38	12	58	34	08	53	39	08
West	52	44	04	48	44	08	50	40	10	50	40	10	50	36	14	52	39	09
Republican	84	12	04	80	14	06	78	15	07	82	12	06	91	07	02	83	10	07
Democrat	26	65	09	25	65	10	26	64	10	28	61	11	33	57	10	33	60	07
Independent	49	35	16	50	37	13	48	41	11	52	38	10	51	36	13	58	34	08
Protestant	50	42	08	52	39	09	48	41	11	53	37	10	56	34	10	56	37	07
Catholic	48	38	14	44	43	13	45	43	12	51	40	09	48	38	14	54	35	11
Union	43	50	07	41	50	09	37	54	09	47	46	07	58	34	08	42	50	08
Nonunion	48	40	12	49	40	11	47	41	12	50	39	11	50	36	14	56	35	09
Grade School	43	45	12				37	48	15	38	44	18	41	41	18	42	47	11
High School	42	45	13				40	46	14	48	41	11	52	38	10	52	38	10
College	57	36	07				53	40	07	54	40	06	58	34	08	58	36	06
Under 30	45	41	14	46	43	11	41	45	14	51	39	10	51	39	10	51	39	10
30-49	48	43	09	51	42	07	44	48	08	51	41	08	55	36	09	56	38	06
Over 50	48	41	11	46	41	13	49	38	13	46	42	12	53	35	12	53	37	10

REAGAN: 1984

	January 13-16			January 27-30			February 10-13			March 16-19			April 6-9			May 3-5		
	A%	D%	N%	A%	D%	N%	A%	D%	N%	A%	D%	N%	A%	D%	N%	A%	D%	N%
National	52	38	10	55	37	08	55	36	09	54	39	07	54	36	10	52	37	11
Male	57	36	07	60	34	06	60	33	07	58	37	05	57	36	07	54	37	09
Female	48	40	12	50	40	10	51	38	11	50	40	10	52	36	12	50	38	12
White	57	33	10	59	33	08	60	32	08	59	33	08	59	31	10	55	33	12
Nonwhite	15	73	12	20	71	09	25	64	11	15	79	06	15	77	08	26	67	07
East	49	41	10	58	34	08	52	40	08	51	42	07	48	45	07	49	41	10
Midwest	54	36	10	51	40	09	55	36	09	49	41	10	50	37	13	48	40	12
South	55	32	13	56	35	09	61	29	10	57	34	09	59	31	10	57	32	11
West	50	44	06	55	38	07	53	40	07	57	40	03	58	34	08	52	36	12
Republican	84	10	06	91	07	02	86	11	03	87	08	05	87	08	05	85	08	07
Democrat	31	60	09	31	59	10	33	60	07	32	61	07	29	61	10	29	60	11
Independent	53	34	13	59	32	09	56	32	12	56	36	08	61	28	11	52	35	13
Protestant	54	36	10	57	35	08	58	34	08	56	38	06	56	34	10			
Catholic	57	35	08	55	35	10	54	37	09	55	37	08	55	36	09			
Union	48	44	08	51	43	06	57	38	05	44	48	08	45	45	10	48	43	09
Nonunion	54	36	10	56	35	09	55	35	10	56	37	07	57	34	09	53	36	11
Grade School	38	47	15	42	44	14	39	48	13	40	47	13	40	42	18	30	55	15
High School	50	38	12	53	39	08	53	37	10	51	40	09	52	38	10	52	35	13
College	59	35	06	60	33	07	64	31	05	61	35	04	62	32	06	56	36	08
Under 30	53	35	12	59	33	08	52	40	08	55	39	06	58	35	07	59	32	09
30-49	55	37	08	55	37	08	58	33	09	56	37	07	58	34	08	54	36	10
Over 50	50	40	10	52	39	09	57	34	09	50	41	09	48	40	12	44	43	13

REAGAN: 1984

	May 18-21			June 6-8			June 22-25			June 29-July 2			July 6-9			July 13-16		
	A%	D%	N%	A%	D%	N%	A%	D%	N%	A%	D%	N%	A%	D%	N%	A%	D%	N%
National	54	38	08	55	33	12	54	36	10	53	37	10	54	35	11	55	35	10
Male	58	36	06	63	27	10	60	32	08	56	35	09	59	32	09	63	29	08
Female	50	39	11	49	37	14	49	40	11	50	39	11	49	39	12	49	39	12
White	58	34	08	59	29	12	59	31	10	58	32	10	59	31	10	60	30	10
Nonwhite	18	71	11	31	59	10	19	70	11	16	73	11	18	68	14	21	69	10
East	52	42	06	54	34	12	50	39	11	51	37	12	46	40	14	51	39	10
Midwest	51	38	11	51	37	12	55	35	10	50	40	10	57	36	07	60	32	08
South	54	37	09	57	30	13	56	34	10	56	33	11	53	35	12	58	30	12
West	59	35	06	51	39	10	55	37	08	56	37	07	61	29	10	51	38	11
Republican	85	10	05	90	06	04	89	08	03	88	07	05	87	08	05	87	09	04
Democrat	32	61	07	27	56	17	25	63	12	28	63	09	28	63	09	34	55	11
Independent	58	30	12	64	26	10	59	30	11	58	29	13	58	28	14	56	31	13
Protestant	53	37	10				58	32	10	55	36	09	56	36	08	58	32	10
Catholic	60	34	06				49	38	13	51	38	11	53	34	13	56	35	09
Union	45	50	05	46	41	13	47	40	13	46	43	11	38	47	15	47	44	09
Nonunion	56	35	09	57	31	12	56	35	09	55	35	10	58	32	10	58	32	10
Grade School	37	47	16	37	31	32	36	49	15	34	46	20	39	45	16	40	46	14
High School	51	40	09	50	34	16	51	36	13	51	38	11	52	35	13	52	37	11
College	62	33	05	64	30	06	63	32	05	62	32	06	60	33	07	64	29	07
Under 30	53	39	08	60	34	06	54	36	10	54	35	11	54	32	14	59	33	08
30-49	55	37	08	54	32	14	57	34	09	58	32	10	53	37	10	59	33	08
Over 50	53	38	09	59	32	09	51	38	11	49	41	10	55	36	09	49	38	13

REAGAN: 1984

	July 27-30			August 10-13			September 7-10			September 21-24			September 28-October 1			October 26-29		
	A%	D%	N%	A%	D%	N%	A%	D%	N%	A%	D%	N%	A%	D%	N%	A%	D%	N%
National	52	37	11	54	38	08	57	36	07	57	36	07	54	35	11	58	33	09
Male	53	38	09	60	34	06	60	34	06	59	35	06	57	33	10	60	32	08
Female	51	36	13	48	42	10	54	37	09	55	37	08	51	37	12	57	33	10
White	57	32	11	58	34	08	62	31	07	62	32	06	59	31	10	64	28	08
Nonwhite	17	71	12	14	75	11	18	73	09	18	70	12	18	69	13	24	64	12
East	50	35	15	48	44	08	54	38	08	51	42	07	44	41	15	52	37	11
Midwest	50	36	14	55	35	10	56	35	09	59	33	08	56	34	10	52	34	14
South	53	36	11	55	36	09	57	34	09	58	36	06	58	32	10	64	29	07
West	52	43	05	58	37	05	61	35	04	58	35	07	57	36	07	66	30	04
Republican	87	07	06	90	06	04	92	04	04	92	05	03	93	05	02	92	05	03
Democrat	24	66	10	23	69	08	22	69	09	25	66	09	23	65	12	26	64	10
Independent	54	32	14	57	30	13	63	28	09	57	34	09	49	34	17	62	25	13
Protestant	55	36	09	56	36	08	61	33	06	60	35	05	57	34	09	58	34	08
Catholic	51	35	14	54	36	10	54	37	09	56	34	10	50	36	14	62	28	10
Union	44	44	12	41	50	09	52	41	07	49	45	06	42	48	10	44	46	10
Nonunion	54	35	11	57	35	08	58	34	08	58	35	07	56	33	11	62	29	09
Grade School	44	39	17	38	49	13	40	49	11	45	43	12	42	43	15	46	46	08
High School	49	39	12	48	42	10	58	33	09	52	41	07	51	36	13	55	34	11
College	57	34	09	65	31	04	60	35	05	63	30	07	58	34	08	64	30	06
Under 30	50	38	12	53	37	10	60	33	07	55	35	10	56	32	12	54	36	10
30-49	54	35	11	57	37	06	60	34	06	59	36	05	55	37	08	52	40	08
Over 50	50	39	11	52	40	08	51	40	09	56	38	06	52	36	12	62	29	09

REAGAN: 1984-1985

	November 9-12			November 30–December 3			December 7-10			January 11-14			January 25-28			February 15-18		
	A%	D%	N%	A%	D%	N%	A%	D%	N%	A%	D%	N%	A%	D%	N%	A%	D%	N%
National	61	31	08	62	30	08	59	32	09	62	29	09	64	28	08	60	31	09
Male	64	29	07	67	27	06	64	29	07	67	26	07	64	30	06	61	31	08
Female	58	33	09	56	34	10	55	34	11	57	32	11	63	27	10	58	31	11
White	66	26	08	68	25	07	65	26	09	67	24	09	69	24	07	62	29	09
Nonwhite	26	64	10	22	64	14	23	67	10	32	58	10	31	58	11	38	50	12
East	55	38	07	56	34	10	57	34	09	57	30	13	59	30	11	53	37	10
Midwest	56	35	09	64	29	07	58	29	13	64	28	08	69	25	06	59	30	11
South	68	24	08	65	25	10	61	28	11	64	28	08	62	31	07	65	25	10
West	64	27	09	61	35	04	61	35	04	63	31	06	66	27	07	60	35	05
Republican	93	04	03	94	04	02	89	08	03	88	07	05	90	06	04	88	07	05
Democrat	33	60	07	30	60	10	33	57	10	39	54	07	39	52	09	35	56	09
Independent	60	25	15	67	24	09	61	27	12	61	25	14	64	27	09	60	27	13
Protestant	63	29	08	62	30	08	61	30	09	65	27	08	64	28	08	61	30	09
Catholic	61	31	08	66	27	07	62	29	09	58	31	11	67	26	07	60	30	10
Union	57	34	09	54	38	08	54	38	08	57	34	09	61	34	05	50	40	10
Nonunion	62	30	08	64	28	08	60	30	10	63	28	09	64	27	09	62	29	09
Grade School	38	48	14	54	33	13	43	44	13	45	38	17	44	38	18	44	41	15
High School	58	31	11	58	31	11	56	33	11	61	28	11	63	30	07	59	30	11
College	65	30	05	67	29	04	64	29	07	67	28	05	69	25	06	63	31	06
Under 30	66	26	08	67	27	06	59	30	11	70	24	06	69	24	07	65	29	06
30-49	63	30	07	62	29	09	61	32	07	59	32	09	62	31	07	59	32	09
Over 50	57	34	09	58	33	09	58	32	10	59	30	11	61	29	10	55	33	12

REAGAN: 1985

	March 8-11			April 12-15			May 17-20			June 7-10			July 12-15			August 13-15		
	A%	D%	N%	A%	D%	N%	A%	D%	N%	A%	D%	N%	A%	D%	N%	A%	D%	N%
National	56	37	07	52	37	11	55	37	08	58	32	10	63	28	09	65	26	09
Male	58	34	08	58	34	08	57	35	08	62	31	07	65	27	08	69	24	07
Female	53	40	07	47	40	13	53	38	09	53	35	12	60	30	10	62	28	10
White	60	33	07	57	33	10	60	32	08	62	29	09	66	25	09	69	23	08
Nonwhite	28	61	11	23	63	14	21	68	11	26	60	14	36	53	11	38	45	17
East	53	41	06	49	37	14	50	41	09	52	36	12	63	27	10	63	26	11
Midwest	56	39	05	48	41	11	54	40	06	59	32	09	62	30	08	67	27	06
South	57	33	10	56	35	09	57	33	10	62	26	12	64	26	10	72	17	11
West	57	36	07	56	36	08	59	32	09	56	39	05	62	31	07	56	37	07
Republican	88	08	04	83	10	07	87	09	04	87	08	05	87	09	04	90	06	04
Democrat	28	66	06	25	65	10	24	66	10	35	54	11	39	50	11	39	50	11
Independent	55	35	10	55	33	12	55	34	11	58	30	12	64	25	11	68	22	10
Protestant	58	36	06	52	38	10	58	34	08	58	33	09	64	29	07	69	23	08
Catholic	53	39	08	59	30	11	55	37	08	61	28	11	63	26	11	64	27	09
Union	51	41	08	47	42	11	39	52	09	50	40	10	54	37	09	55	33	12
Nonunion	57	36	07	53	36	11	59	33	08	59	31	10	65	26	09	68	24	08
Grade School	40	45	15	30	54	16	37	51	12	40	43	17	45	39	16	44	41	15
High School	52	40	08	49	39	12	51	39	10	54	35	11	60	30	10	65	25	10
College	63	32	05	60	32	08	63	31	06	66	28	06	69	24	07	68	26	06
Under 30	58	32	10	54	36	10	60	33	07	61	29	10	63	25	12	72	21	07
30-49	57	37	06	56	35	09	56	35	09	60	32	08	65	27	08	67	27	06
Over 50	52	40	08	47	40	13	50	41	09	52	36	12	60	33	07	59	28	13

REAGAN: 1985

	August 16-19			September 13-16			October 11-14			November 1-4			November 11-18			December 6-9		
	A%	D%	N%	A%	D%	N%	A%	D%	N%	A%	D%	N%	A%	D%	N%	A%	D%	N%
National	57	32	11	60	30	10	63	29	08	62	28	10	65	24	11	63	29	08
Male	63	29	08	65	28	07	67	26	07	67	25	08	68	24	08	65	28	07
Female	52	34	14	56	32	12	58	32	10	58	30	12	64	23	13	61	30	09
White	61	29	10	64	27	09	66	26	08	65	25	10	70	20	10	67	25	08
Nonwhite	28	53	19	34	55	11	33	55	12	33	53	14	38	49	13	34	57	09
East	57	29	14	62	27	11	67	27	06	62	30	08	69	21	10	60	32	08
Midwest	54	37	09	54	36	10	55	35	10	65	28	07	62	30	08	67	26	07
South	56	32	12	60	30	10	63	29	08	63	27	10	66	22	12	64	30	06
West	63	29	08	66	27	07	66	25	09	57	25	18	66	22	12	61	27	12
Republican	89	05	06	85	10	05	90	06	04	90	05	05	90	05	05	85	10	05
Democrat	34	56	10	41	48	11	39	50	11	43	46	11	41	46	13	43	50	07
Independent	54	30	16	60	30	10	63	28	09	57	29	14	66	20	14	67	22	11
Protestant	58	30	12	60	31	09	63	29	08	63	28	09	66	25	09	63	30	07
Catholic	59	33	08	69	23	08	66	27	07	62	24	14	66	21	13	67	25	08
Union	50	39	11	57	34	09	57	37	06	57	33	10				59	35	06
Nonunion	58	31	11	61	29	10	64	27	09	63	26	11				63	28	09
Grade School	42	38	20	37	38	25	46	44	10	48	37	15	43	33	24	52	40	08
High School	54	34	12	61	30	09	62	29	09	60	27	13	64	25	11	60	30	10
College	65	27	08	64	30	06	67	27	06	67	26	07	70	21	09	70	24	06
Under 30	59	31	10	65	24	11	59	31	10	66	24	10	73	19	08	67	24	09
30-49	60	31	09	61	32	07	66	27	07	63	27	10	68	21	11	59	33	08
Over 50	53	34	13	57	32	11	61	31	08	57	31	12	58	29	13	63	29	08

REAGAN: 1986

	January 10-13			March 4-10			April 11-14			May 16-19			June 6-9			June 9-16		
	A%	D%	N%	A%	D%	N%	A%	D%	N%	A%	D%	N%	A%	D%	N%	A%	D%	N%
National	64	27	09	63	26	11	62	29	09	68	23	09	61	29	10	64	26	10
Male	68	24	08	67	25	08	66	26	08	74	21	05	66	25	09	72	22	06
Female	59	30	11	60	26	14	57	32	11	62	25	13	56	34	10	57	29	14
White	67	25	08	67	23	10	66	25	09	72	19	09	64	27	09	67	24	09
Nonwhite	34	49	17	35	46	19	30	56	14	38	51	11	33	50	17	45	40	15
East	59	30	11	61	25	14	67	23	10	69	24	07	61	30	09	62	27	11
Midwest	67	24	09	61	31	08	58	33	09	67	21	12	57	34	09	64	30	06
South	63	28	09	65	20	15	61	26	13	68	21	11	63	26	11	67	23	10
West	66	27	07	65	28	07	62	34	04	67	27	06	61	28	11	63	25	12
Republican	91	05	04	88	07	05	86	10	04	88	07	05	86	09	05	87	08	05
Democrat	42	48	10	40	46	14	43	47	10	51	37	12	40	49	11	45	44	11
Independent	62	25	13	60	26	14	63	25	12	69	22	09	64	27	09	65	23	12
Protestant	65	27	08	63	26	11	62	28	10	66	24	10	61	29	10			
Catholic	64	26	10	66	24	10	67	28	05	74	19	07	63	27	10			
Union	57	33	10				62	34	04	60	31	09	51	40	09			
Nonunion	65	26	09				62	27	11	70	21	09	63	27	10			
Grade School	52	28	20	50	27	23	49	27	24	44	33	23	43	36	21	39	52	09
High School	61	30	09	61	28	11	60	30	10	68	21	11	59	30	11	64	24	12
College	69	24	07	68	22	10	67	27	06	73	23	04	67	27	06	69	24	07
Under 30	66	27	07	68	23	09	62	27	11	74	18	08	64	27	09	71	19	10
30-49	64	28	08	67	22	11	65	29	06	71	23	06	65	26	09	66	26	08
Over 50	61	27	12	56	31	13	58	31	11	62	24	14	52	34	14	58	31	11

REAGAN: 1986

	July 11-14			August 8-11			September 12-15			September 13-17			October 24-27			December 4-5		
	A%	D%	N%	A%	D%	N%	A%	D%	N%	A%	D%	N%	A%	D%	N%	A%	D%	N%
National	63	28	09	61	27	12	61	25	14	63	26	11	63	29	08	47	44	09
Male	69	26	05	62	29	09	61	26	13	68	25	07	64	29	07	53	41	06
Female	58	30	12	59	26	15	59	25	16	59	27	14	61	29	10	43	46	11
White	66	25	09	65	24	11	65	22	13	67	24	09	65	27	08	50	41	09
Nonwhite	42	48	10	30	49	21	33	45	22	39	36	25	42	51	07	31	63	06
East	66	27	07	62	26	12	64	22	14	65	25	10	64	30	06	45	49	06
Midwest	61	30	09	65	24	11	60	26	14	57	28	15	60	29	11	48	43	09
South	64	26	10	61	27	12	59	26	15	65	25	10	61	30	09	47	41	12
West	64	28	08	55	33	12	58	27	15	66	27	07	66	27	07	50	42	08
Republican	88	06	06	86	08	06	86	06	08	92	06	02	86	10	04	74	17	09
Democrat	44	47	09	44	42	14	43	44	13	37	48	15	45	47	08	24	68	08
Independent	65	25	10	58	27	15	60	23	17	63	25	12	62	28	10	45	44	11
Protestant	64	27	09	62	26	12	60	25	15	63	26	11	62	30	08			
Catholic	66	26	08	69	20	11	60	26	14	64	25	11	68	23	09			
Union	58	35	07	51	37	12	52	33	15				59	34	07			
Nonunion	65	26	09	63	25	12	63	23	14				63	28	09			
Grade School	50	35	15	41	30	29	38	23	39	46	43	11	54	30	16			
High School	61	28	11	62	26	12	58	28	14	62	25	13	62	28	10			
College	70	25	05	64	28	08	68	23	09	67	25	08	65	31	04			
Under 30	70	21	09	70	18	12	67	21	12	70	20	10	65	24	11	53	39	08
30-49	65	27	08	65	26	09	62	26	12	66	24	10	61	33	06	52	41	07
Over 50	58	32	10	49	36	15	53	28	19	55	32	13	62	30	08	37	51	12

REAGAN: 1986-1987

	December 5-8			January 16-19			March 6-9			March 14-18			April 10-13			June 5-8		
	A%	D%	N%	A%	D%	N%	A%	D%	N%	A%	D%	N%	A%	D%	N%	A%	D%	N%
National	48	43	09	48	43	09	43	46	11	47	44	09	48	43	09	47	44	09
Male	50	43	07	52	41	07	46	44	10	50	42	08	53	40	07	49	43	08
Female	45	44	11	45	45	10	40	47	13	44	46	10	44	46	10	44	45	11
White	51	40	09	53	38	09	46	43	11	50	41	09	52	40	08	50	41	09
Nonwhite	22	69	09	19	74	07	19	70	11	26	66	08	25	63	12	21	66	13
East	42	47	11	49	41	10	41	46	13	45	43	12	44	44	12	43	51	06
Midwest	45	47	08	47	45	08	38	49	13	46	48	06	48	47	05	50	39	11
South	55	36	09	48	44	08	49	42	09	49	40	11	54	37	09	50	40	10
West	46	45	09	50	41	09	41	47	12	47	46	07	45	48	07	44	47	09
Republican	78	17	05	80	14	06	73	21	06	74	17	09	76	16	08	76	19	05
Democrat	25	67	08	23	69	08	24	65	11	22	70	08	23	69	08	25	66	09
Independent	50	40	10	49	40	11	41	43	16	46	44	10	50	41	09	48	40	12
Protestant	51	41	08	51	41	08	45	45	10	48	44	08	50	42	08	49	42	09
Catholic	45	45	10	46	45	09	44	46	10	48	41	11	48	43	09	44	47	09
Union	41	47	12	43	50	07	38	50	12				41	54	05	40	52	08
Nonunion	49	42	09	50	41	09	44	45	11				50	41	09	48	43	09
Grade School	41	45	14	32	50	18	41	38	21	33	55	12	47	37	16	40	48	12
High School	45	45	10	49	42	09	38	47	15	46	43	11	47	44	09	45	44	11
College	52	41	07	51	42	07	48	46	06	50	43	07	49	44	07	50	43	07
Under 30	50	39	11	51	39	10	44	43	13	55	38	07	51	39	10	48	41	11
30-49	48	44	08	52	41	07	44	44	12	48	43	09	48	45	07	51	41	08
Over 50	46	44	10	43	47	10	40	50	10	41	48	11	47	44	09	42	49	09

REAGAN: 1987

	June 8-14			July 10-13			August 7-10			August 24-September 2			October 23-26			December 4-7		
	A%	D%	N%	A%	D%	N%	A%	D%	N%	A%	D%	N%	A%	D%	N%	A%	D%	N%
National	53	40	07	49	43	08	45	41	14	49	42	09	51	41	08	49	41	10
Male	57	38	05	54	39	07	51	38	11	58	33	09	56	38	06	54	39	07
Female	50	41	09	44	47	09	40	44	16	41	50	09	46	43	11	44	43	13
White	58	36	06	53	39	08	50	37	13	51	40	09	54	38	08	52	38	10
Nonwhite	26	67	07	15	72	13	18	68	14	31	60	09	20	66	14	26	63	11
East	53	37	10	50	43	07	45	43	12	43	49	08	50	44	06	43	44	13
Midwest	54	40	06	50	42	08	45	41	14	47	43	10	49	43	08	52	40	08
South	59	38	03	50	40	10	48	38	14	54	36	10	51	35	14	49	40	11
West	47	45	08	45	48	07	43	42	15	50	42	08	53	41	06	51	40	09
Republican	82	13	05	78	16	06	75	17	08	78	13	09	79	15	06	79	14	07
Democrat	29	65	06	28	65	07	26	61	13	21	73	06	30	61	09	26	64	10
Independent	53	38	09	48	39	13	45	37	18	51	39	10	50	40	10	49	37	14
Protestant	53	41	06	48	42	10	46	41	13	53	38	09	52	39	09	51	40	09
Catholic	56	37	07	52	42	06	45	40	15	42	49	09	52	40	08	48	39	13
Union				43	50	07	38	49	13				46	44	10	39	49	12
Nonunion				50	41	09	47	40	13				52	40	08	51	39	10
Grade School	33	61	06	37	52	11	34	48	18	40	51	09	43	42	15	45	41	14
High School	55	37	08	45	45	10	42	41	17	45	44	11	49	40	11	47	39	14
College	55	40	05	55	39	06	51	40	09	54	40	06	54	41	05	51	43	06
Under 30	61	35	04	54	37	09	50	36	14	51	38	11	56	32	12	53	36	11
30-49	57	36	07	50	41	09	46	42	12	52	41	07	52	42	06	49	41	10
Over 50	45	47	08	43	49	08	41	44	15	43	47	10	45	46	09	45	45	10

REAGAN: 1988

	January 22-25			March 4-7			March 8-12			April 8-11			May 2-8			May 13-22		
	A%	D%	N%	A%	D%	N%	A%	D%	N%	A%	D%	N%	A%	D%	N%	A%	D%	N%
National	49	40	11	50	42	08	51	37	12	50	39	11	50	38	12	48	43	09
Male	53	37	10	56	39	05	58	34	08	56	35	09	58	33	09	52	40	08
Female	45	42	13	43	45	12	45	40	15	44	43	13	43	42	15	44	46	10
White	52	37	11	54	37	09	54	34	12	54	36	10	53	35	12	52	39	09
Nonwhite	27	59	14	20	71	09	34	56	10	25	57	18	30	60	10	23	66	11
East	49	42	09	47	44	09	46	38	16	48	43	09	53	39	08	44	48	08
Midwest	46	44	10	48	45	07	51	37	12	53	38	09	45	41	14	46	44	10
South	52	34	14	54	37	09	57	34	09	52	34	14	56	34	10	53	36	11
West	49	40	11	47	45	08	50	40	10	46	44	10	43	40	17	46	48	06
Republican	79	14	07	83	15	02	81	12	07	78	16	06	86	08	06	77	17	06
Democrat	30	60	10	31	61	08	28	64	08	30	59	11	25	64	11	25	68	07
Independent	48	36	16	47	41	12	51	35	14	53	34	13	49	36	15	49	37	14
Protestant	49	41	10	54	38	08	57	31	12	51	38	11	52	37	11	48	42	10
Catholic	54	33	13	45	45	10	51	39	10	54	37	09	53	35	12	49	43	08
Union	49	41	10	43	53	04				39	51	10				41	51	08
Nonunion	49	39	12	51	40	09				53	36	11				49	41	10
Grade School	38	43	19	44	33	18	41	21	38	41	44	15	43	51	06	38	49	13
High School	48	40	12	46	43	11	53	37	10	51	37	12	48	38	14	47	43	10
College	52	38	10	54	41	05	52	38	10	50	41	09	53	36	11	50	43	07
Under 30	53	31	16	53	37	10	56	34	10	57	30	13	54	33	13	57	35	08
30-49	50	41	09	49	46	05	49	40	11	48	41	11	50	38	12	44	46	10
Over 50	45	44	11	48	41	11	50	36	14	47	43	10	47	42	11	45	46	09

REAGAN: 1988

	June 10-13			June 24-27			July 1-7			July 15-18			August 19-22			September 25-October 1		
	A%	D%	N%	A%	D%	N%	A%	D%	N%	A%	D%	N%	A%	D%	N%	A%	D%	N%
National	51	39	10	48	40	12	51	35	14	54	36	10	53	37	10	54	37	09
Male	53	38	09	51	38	11	59	32	09	57	32	11	59	35	06	59	35	06
Female	50	39	11	45	42	13	43	38	19	50	40	10	48	38	14	49	39	12
White	55	35	10	51	38	11	53	33	14	59	31	10	57	34	09	58	33	09
Nonwhite	24	64	12	23	60	17	33	53	14	19	72	09	24	57	19	25	59	16
East	51	42	07	46	38	16	49	38	13	55	39	06	56	36	08	51	40	09
Midwest	54	34	12	53	39	08	48	36	16	55	35	10	48	41	11	54	37	09
South	53	36	11	47	39	14	54	32	14	56	31	13	57	32	11	58	32	10
West	44	45	11	46	45	09	49	37	14	48	41	11	50	39	11	49	42	09
Republican	82	11	07	77	15	08	78	14	08	85	11	04	86	10	04	87	08	05
Democrat	31	59	10	29	60	11	29	57	14	34	57	09	33	58	09	24	65	11
Independent	53	35	12	50	36	14	49	33	18	51	33	16	53	32	15	55	35	10
Protestant	53	37	10	44	43	13	51	35	14	55	36	09	54	37	09	56	34	10
Catholic	50	40	10	56	32	12	51	34	15	57	31	12	57	33	10	57	35	08
Union	43	48	09	36	46	18				55	38	07	45	48	07			
Nonunion	53	37	10	50	39	11				54	35	11	55	34	11			
Grade School	40	43	17	54	38	08	44	33	23	45	35	20	41	38	21	35	52	13
High School	51	38	11	45	41	14	49	36	15	54	34	12	52	37	11	53	35	12
College	53	39	08	50	40	10	53	35	12	54	39	07	57	35	08	58	37	05
Under 30	50	37	13	54	33	13	59	26	15	56	32	12	63	28	09	62	32	06
30-49	53	38	09	47	40	13	51	35	14	56	37	07	50	40	10	56	36	08
Over 50	50	41	09	45	44	11	44	42	14	50	38	12	50	39	11	47	39	14

REAGAN: 1988

	October 21-24			November 11-14			December 27-29		
	A%	D%	N%	A%	D%	N%	A%	D%	N%
National	51	38	11	57	35	08	63	29	08
Male	56	35	09	62	32	06	67	26	07
Female	45	42	13	51	39	10	59	32	09
White	54	35	11	61	31	08	67	26	07
Nonwhite	29	59	12	25	63	12	34	50	16
East	55	35	10	55	37	08	64	27	09
Midwest	50	38	12	57	31	12	60	32	08
South	53	36	11	57	37	06	67	27	06
West	43	47	10	57	37	06	58	31	11
Republican	86	09	05	84	12	04	93	05	02
Democrat	25	64	11	31	61	08	38	51	11
Independent	55	30	15	60	29	11	58	31	11
Protestant	55	34	11	58	35	07	64	29	07
Catholic	45	45	10	58	34	08	64	25	11
Union	38	54	08	49	42	09			
Nonunion	54	35	11	58	34	08			
Grade School	46	43	11	47	39	14	58	30	12
High School	50	36	14	56	34	10	60	27	13
College	52	41	07	59	36	05	67	31	02
Under 30	49	36	15	57	35	08	71	22	07
30-49	54	36	10	56	36	08	63	30	07
Over 50	48	43	09	57	34	09	56	33	11

PART TWO
Analysis

1 / PREDISPOSITIONS

Scholarly research on presidential approval typically attempts to explain approval levels in the public by focusing on changes in them. Although it is important to examine shifts in approval levels, focusing on them exclusively leads us to overlook factors that explain much of the public's long-term level of approval of the president. Thus, a useful place to begin an examination of presidential approval is with the public's predispositions toward the president. These are generally not subject to sharp changes, and they mediate the impact of more volatile influences.

Party Identification

The single most important influence on the attitudes of Americans regarding the president is their political party identification. Party identification serves as one of the fundamental orienting mechanisms in American politics. Most Americans develop an attachment to one of the major political parties by the time they reach adulthood (see table 1.1),[1] and it affects how they evaluate the rest of the political landscape.

A large body of research has shown that people have a need for cognitive balance, for consistency in their views.[2] Because of its prominence as a guide to politics, party identification affects how individuals view what the president stands for and how well he is performing his job. Those of the president's party tend to attribute their policy positions to him[3] and may change their issue stands to bring them into line with his.[4] They have an incentive to see the chief executive in a favorable light. Conversely, citizens of the opposition party have less need to perceive consistency between their views and those of the president and less need to evaluate him favorably. Indeed, their party identification highlights differences with the president.

Thus, evaluation of the president's performance should reflect the

TABLE 1.1   Partisan Identification (%)

Year	Democrats	Republicans	Independents
1952	47	27	23
1956	44	29	23
1960	45	29	23
1964	52	25	23
1968	45	24	29
1972	40	23	35
1976	40	23	36
1980	41	22	35
1984	37	27	34
1988	35	28	36

Source: SRC/CPS National Election Studies

underlying partisan loyalties of the public.[5] Members of the president's party are predisposed to approve of his performance and members of the opposition party are predisposed to be less approving. Independents—those without explicit partisan attachments—should fall between Democrats and Republicans in their levels of approval of the president. Although many of those who identify with the president's party are prone to support his performance because of basic policy agreement with him,[6] more is at work than simply a congruence of views. Party identification influences as well as reflects political evaluations.

A study of changes in the public's assessment of one of the world's most popular men, Dwight Eisenhower, after he declared himself a Republican in 1952, illustrates the impact of partisan attachments on the evaluation of political leaders. The authors concluded:

> There is no reason to believe that admiration for him had followed any lines of political or social cleavage. Therefore it is noteworthy that our first measurements of public response to Eisenhower drawn after his commitment to the Republican party showed a popular image quite strongly correlated with the individual's own partisan attachment. The stronger the loyalty the voter felt for the Republican Party, the more unconditional his respect for Eisenhower. Democrats were much less enthusiastic, and where sense of identification with the Democratic party was strong enough, evaluated Eisenhower negatively. . . .
>
> Had Eisenhower chosen instead the Democratic party, we may assume the relationship would have rotated in the opposing direction: strong Republicans would have decided they disliked Eisenhower.[7]

The time-series data clearly reflect the importance of partisan identification as an influence on public evaluations of the president's job per-

TABLE 1.2 Average Yearly Presidential Approval of Partisan Groups (%)

Year	PP	Democrats		Republicans		Independents	
		AP	DA	AP	DA	AP	DA
1953	R	56	24	87	4	68	14
1954	R	50	35	88	6	69	17
1955	R	56	26	90	4	74	12
1956	R	56	29	93	3	76	12
1957	R	47	35	86	7	66	18
1958	R	37	46	82	9	56	27
1959	R	48	35	88	6	66	18
1960	R	44	40	87	7	64	21
1961	D	87	4	58	22	72	10
1962	D	86	6	49	35	69	17
1963	D	79	10	44	40	61	23
1964	D	84	6	62	21	67	14
1965	D	79	11	49	37	60	24
1966	D	67	21	32	56	44	40
1967	D	59	27	26	62	38	46
1968	D	57	31	26	63	35	53
1969	D	49	24	82	6	60	17[a]
1970	R	41	43	82	10	57	28
1971	R	35	51	79	13	48	38
1972	R	40	48	84	10	57	33
1973	R	26	63	70	21	42	47
1974	R	24	63	58	27	35	50
1975	R	32	51	65	22	44	40
1976	R	36	50	69	21	50	36
1977	D	73	12	46	36	60	21
1978	D	57	28	28	59	42	40
1979	D	46	41	24	66	34	52
1980	D	53	37	25	67	35	54
1981	R	40	44	85	8	59	26
1982	R	23	67	79	14	46	42
1983	R	24	67	78	15	47	41
1984	R	28	62	89	7	58	30
1985	R	36	54	88	7	60	28
1986	R	40	49	86	9	61	28
1987	R	25	66	77	15	48	40
1988	R	30	61	83	12	52	34

PP = President's party
AP = Approval
DA = Disapproval
[a] Does not include the January 1969 poll on Lyndon Johnson.

formance. Democrats, Republicans, and Independents evaluate the president differently. Table 1.2 shows the average annual level of approval and disapproval of the president for each of these groups in the 1953–88 time period.[8] The average absolute difference between Democrats and Republicans is 39 percentage points, a very substantial figure. Independents fall in between, averaging 18 percentage points difference from Democrats and 21 percentage points from Republicans. Members of the president's party are always more likely to approve than disapprove of his performance, usually by very large margins, whereas in 22 of the 36 years under study here the identifiers with the opposition party are more likely to disapprove than to approve the president's handling of his job.

Presidents typically receive high support from their fellow partisans, and this support is usually stable over time. Republican presidents do especially well, averaging 81 percent approval from fellow Republicans. Eisenhower never fell below a yearly average of 82 percent approval from Republicans, while Reagan's lowest yearly average was 77 percent. In Nixon's first term 79 percent was his lowest average among his party cohorts. Only in the troubled second term did Nixon and then Ford fall to more modest levels of approval, and even then they received on the average the support of two out of three Republicans.

Examining the columns for disapproval also illuminates the influence of party affiliation on evaluations of the president. Not only do identifiers with the president's party have a strong tendency to approve of his performance in office, but they also are unlikely to disapprove of it. For example, in no year did even 10 percent of fellow partisans disapprove of Eisenhower's performance. Ronald Reagan faced only slightly higher disapproval rates among Republicans, while Nixon enjoyed similarly low levels of intraparty opposition until the Watergate story broke. Even then, only about one out of five Republicans failed to approve of Nixon's or Ford's handling of the presidency.

Democratic presidents face a more challenging task in obtaining approval from those who identify with their party; they average 67 percent approval from Democrats. The base of the Democratic party has traditionally been larger and more diverse than that of the Republican party, including most liberals and many moderates and conservatives. Yet it is difficult to please everyone at once. The Kennedy-Johnson administrations did well with Democrats until Vietnam became a major point of contention in 1966. Then approval levels of President Johnson declined considerably among Democratic party identifiers. Jimmy Carter never enjoyed the high levels of party support of his Democratic predecessors, and he actually fell to below 50 percent approval among Democrats in 1979.

Democratic presidents also encounter greater obstacles in trying to minimize the disapproval of fellow partisans. Democrats are more likely than Republicans to disapprove of one of their own in the White House. Jimmy Carter averaged 30 percent disapproval among Democrats in his term, and Lyndon Johnson averaged almost one in four Democrats in disapproval in his elected term of 1965–68. Nevertheless, many more Democrats approve than disapprove of Democratic presidents.

We can also see the impact of partisanship on evaluations of the president by examining presidential approval at a specific point in time. In the first week of August of 1974, shortly before he resigned, Richard Nixon's overall support stood at 24 percent—the lowest point of any president in our study. Approval among Democrats had diminished to a meager 13 percent, and among Independents Nixon received only a 22 percent approval rating. Yet even at this point in the Watergate crisis, 50 percent of Republicans gave the president their approval.

Five years later, in July 1979, Jimmy Carter, a Democrat, saw his approval level fall to 29 percent overall. Republican approval stood at only 18 percent. Democrats, on the other hand, were more than twice as likely to support Carter, according him 37 percent approval. Independents were in the middle at 27 percent.

The absolute levels of presidential approval not only differ for each group of partisans; they also may shift by different magnitudes or in opposite directions. In other words, Democrats, Republicans, and Independents do not always react the same to the president or to the events and conditions by which they evaluate him. What Democrats see as positive, Republicans may view as quite negative and vice versa. When we regress presidential approval among Democrats on that among Republicans over time,[9] we obtain an R^2 of .58. In other words, presidential approval among Republicans and Democrats has 58 percent common variance. Although the movement over time of the two groups is related, Democratic movement and Republican movement are conceptually distinct variables.

Despite the influence of party identification, it clearly functions as only a partially effective perceptual screen. Perceptions that are inconsistent with party identification escape its mediating effects and influence individuals. The data in table 1.2 indicate, for example, that many members of the opposition party support the president. On the average, a Republican president receives a 39 percent approval rating from Democrats, and a Democratic president receives a similar 39 percent approval rating from Republicans. Obviously, factors other than party affiliation influence citizens' evaluations of the president.

It is also possible that the strength of party identification as a source of predispositions has diminished in recent years. The results of research on whether parties are less salient to people and thus provide less of a psychological anchor for political attitudes are mixed.[10] We do know that, as table 1.1 shows, the percentage of the population identifying with one of the two major parties has decreased since the 1950s. The impact of this change has been more apparent than real, because many Independents really lean toward one of the parties and act in ways similar to partisans.[11] Nevertheless, the relative size of the Independent category has grown, and the percentage of strong partisans in the population has decreased.[12] Thus a somewhat smaller percentage of the population is strongly predisposed to support or withhold support from the president because of party affiliation.

If the impact of party identification on evaluations of the president has diminished over time, presidential approval should be more volatile, subject to the effects of more transitory influences. As one can see by examining the size of the standard deviations of presidential approval reported in table 1.3, this prediction is partially borne out by the increased volatility of the polls in the 1960s and 1970s. This instability has not increased steadily over time, however; it decreased substantially in the 1980s, when it almost returned to the level of the 1950s. (Because we are using aggregate data, however, we do not know if the stability masks changes in the attitudes of individuals.)

TABLE 1.3   Volatility of Presidential Approval

Administration	Standard Deviation of Approval
Eisenhower	6.9
Kennedy-Johnson	13.5
Nixon-Ford	12.2
Carter	12.2
Reagan	7.7

The introduction of many new people into the electorate in the 1960s and 1970s when the post-World War II baby boom generation reached adulthood, coupled with the unique political traumas of those years may have caused a temporary decrease in the impact of party on presidential approval. Yet partisanship has proved to be resilient,[13] and party identification remains an important intermediary between the president and the public. It significantly affects how the public perceives and reacts to the chief executive and the events and conditions by which they assess him.

There is more to the explanation of presidential approval, however. Changes in the party identification of individuals are made slowly, if at all. Yet much sharper changes in presidential approval occur. In addition, some people may change their party identification in response to their evaluations of the actions or policies of presidents, reversing the direction of causality that underlies the previous analysis.[14] Party identification is an influencing, not a controlling, predisposition. Therefore, it is necessary to examine other factors that affect public attitudes toward the president.

Positivity Bias

Americans tend to express favorable opinions of people. They have a general disposition to prefer, to learn, and to expect positive relationships more than negative relationships and to perceive stimuli as positive rather than negative. This orientation provides the foundation for the predisposing factor called the positivity bias. One noted social scientist has defined it as the tendency "to show evaluation of public figures and institutions in a generally positive direction."[15]

The causes of the positivity bias are not well known,[16] but it seems to have the greatest potential for influence in ambiguous situations, such as the beginning of a president's term. New occupants of the White House are unknown to the public in the role of chief executive and therefore may receive the benefit of the doubt in public evaluations.

Although the positivity bias should encourage public approval throughout a president's tenure, it is likely to be especially important at the beginning of a new president's term, when he lacks a record. One way to see the impact of positivity bias is to compare the electoral percentage by which a president won election with his approval levels in the first Gallup Poll after his inauguration. In table 1.4 we find such a comparison (President Ford is excluded because he never won an election to the presidency). The figures show clearly that a substantially larger percentage of the people are willing to give new presidents, with the exceptions of Ronald Reagan and George Bush, approval at the beginning of their terms than were willing to vote for them two months earlier. Obviously, favoring the candidate who loses an election does not preclude supporting the person who wins the election once he takes office.

Ronald Reagan's relatively low initial approval levels may seem puzzling, but there is additional evidence that he also benefited from both the ambiguity surrounding new presidents and the positivity bias. In table 1.5 we find that although Ronald Reagan was one of the best-known people in the country in 1981, had sought his party's nomination for president three times, and had just finished a year-long election campaign, 43 percent of the people did not feel they knew enough about him to have an opinion, favorable or unfavorable. This percentage had steadily increased over the previous year, when only 20 percent of the people had no opinion. It

TABLE 1.4 Comparison of Electoral Percentage and Postinaugural Approval (%)

President	First Election	
	Popular Vote in Election	*Approval in First Postinaugural Polls*
Eisenhower	55	68
Kennedy	50	72
Johnson	61	70
Nixon	43	59
Carter	50	66
Reagan	51	51
Bush	53	51
	Reelection	
Eisenhower	57	72
Nixon	61	67
Reagan	59	64

appears that the public in January 1981 was waiting to evaluate Reagan on new criteria. On the other hand, the public may have been reluctant to support the new president, who was an unusually unpopular winning candidate.[17] In any event, Reagan benefited from this increased ambiguity. As the table shows, the percentage of people holding an "unfavorable" opinion of him steadily decreased to a mere 11 percent at the time of his inauguration. Moving people from negative to neutral opinions increases the prospect that they will eventually support the president, and in Reagan's case this is exactly what happened.

George Bush did especially poorly in his first postinaugural poll, receiving only 51 percent approval. As in Reagan's case, this low rate was the result of a reluctance of the public to reach an opinion about his performance. Forty-three percent of the people refrained from evaluating

TABLE 1.5 Favorability of Opinion on Ronald Reagan, January 1980–January 1981 (%)

Opinion of Reagan	January 1980	August 1980	November 1980	January 1981
Favorable	42	46	41	46
Unfavorable	38	27	21	11
No opinion	20	27	38	43

Source: News release, CBS News/*New York Times* Poll (February 2, 1981), 2.

Bush in January 1989. By March, however, only 24 percent abstained, and his approval rating was up to a comfortable 63 percent.

When presidents win reelection, they do not necessarily receive the same boost from the positivity bias that they benefited from in their initial elections. After four years they are no longer ambiguous stimuli to the public. Because only three men have won two presidential elections in recent history—Dwight Eisenhower, Richard Nixon, and Ronald Reagan— one must exercise caution in reaching generalizations. As the figures in the bottom half of table 1.4 show, Eisenhower at reelection did much better in his first postinaugural approval poll than in his election. Even supporters of Adlai Stevenson liked Ike. Nixon and Reagan also won landslide victories in their reelection bids. In these cases, however, they did only slightly better in their first postinaugural polls than in their elections. There is less potential for exceeding your electoral percentage when you win a large percentage of the vote.

A related factor may affect presidents' public approval levels early in their terms. When people have little basis on which to evaluate the president, they may turn to other sources for cues. A new chief executive is generally treated favorably in the press. Moreover, excitement and symbolism are inherent in the peaceful transfer of power, inaugural festivities, and "new beginnings." All of this creates a positive environment for the initial evaluations of presidents and buttresses any tendency toward the positivity bias.

Several studies have found evidence of what some authors term a fait accompli or bandwagon effect. Many people, especially those voting for the loser, tend to view the winner more favorably after an election than they did before the election. The depolarization of politics following an election and the positivity bias itself probably help to create an environment conducive to attitude change.[18]

As presidents perform their duties, they become better known to citizens, who have more bases for judgments about them. Moreover, the public may be more likely to perceive implications of presidential policies regarding their own lives as time passes. If people view the implications unfavorably, they may be more receptive and attentive to negative information about the president.[19] Thus, the positivity bias and related factors appear to give most presidents a boost in the polls early in their terms. Whether the "honeymoon" lasts depends on other factors, however.

The Persistence of Approval

We have seen that presidents typically begin their tenures in office with the benefit of substantial public support. How long does this period of grace last? Conventional wisdom says, "Not very long." The thrust of the argument is that soon presidents will have to make hard choices that will inevitably alienate segments of the population and the president's supportive "coalition of minorities" begins to unravel.[20]

On its face this view seems compelling. Presidents themselves testify in its behalf. In a revealing response to a reporter's question concerning whether a president can expect to rate very highly with the American people, Jimmy Carter answered:

> In this present political environment, it is almost impossible. There are times of euphoria that sweep the nation immediately after an election or after an inauguration day or maybe after a notable success, like the Camp David Accords, when there is a surge of popularity for a president. But most of the decisions that have to be made by a President are inherently not popular ones. They are contentious. There is not a single vote to be derived from the evolution of a national energy policy. It is down all the way because the highly motivated consumer groups, for instance, or environmentalists, and so forth, can never be satisfied with any acceptable proposal that has a chance to be approved by the Congress, and the oil companies, and all those who are from producing states can never be satisfied with a compromise that's acceptable to Congress and is able to be passed.
>
> And for the President to espouse a balanced program naturally arouses the condemnation, certainly the opposition, criticism at least, of those highly-motivated opinion-shapers.
>
> In addition, there are times when you have to take a stand that you know is unpopular. A typical case . . . is the Panama Canal Treaties. When we got to the conclusion of the Panama Canal negotiations after 14 years of negotiating, knowing that this is in the best interest of our country, there was a public opinion poll run . . . that showed only 8 percent of the American people favored a new Panama Canal Treaty. But my predecessors, ever since President Johnson, all the knowledgeable people in the State Department, mine and the previous Administrations, knew that we had to have a new Panama Canal Treaty. And for me to espouse that, to work with a great deal of commitment to get two-thirds vote in the Senate, was patently a losing proposition. . . .
>
> And you are constantly involved in contention and debate.[21]

Before accepting the inevitability of substantially declining approval levels, however, it is useful to turn to the data. They show that presidential honeymoons with the public are not always short-lived. President Eisenhower began his tenure with a 68 percent approval rating. By January 1954 it had risen to 71 percent. A year later it was still at 70 percent, and after three years in office, Eisenhower enjoyed a 76 percent approval rating.

At his second inauguration he stood at 73 percent approval in the polls. In other words, he ended his first term with an approval rating 5 percentage points above where he began it. The second term showed more slippage, ending at 59 percent. Nevertheless, a 10 percentage point decline in approval over eight years in office is not very substantial and provides weak support for the argument that hard choices induce disapproval.

Of course, Eisenhower might simply be an exception. In contrast to the elderly, conservative Republican war hero was the young dynamic leader of the New Frontier, John Kennedy. He began his term with 72 percent approval and saw it rise to 79 percent a year later. In January 1963 his 74 percent rating was still 2 percentage points higher than when he took office. By the time of his assassination in November, his approval had fallen to 58 percent, still a comfortable majority and only 14 percentage points below where he began.

Lyndon Johnson's experience was different. He began his administration with a 78 percent approval rating in the wake of the death of John Kennedy, and this rose to 79 percent in February 1964. At his inauguration in 1965 his approval still stood at 71 percent, but it gradually declined throughout the rest of his term, somewhat parallel to the escalation of the war in Vietnam.

President Nixon's approval ratings did not vary greatly early in his first term. The 59 percent approval he had at the beginning rose to 67 percent in November 1969 and stood at 63 percent after a year in office. After two years in the White House he had a 56 percent approval rating, only 3 percentage points below where he began. A year later he had lost another 3 percentage points, but his approval rating shot up to 67 percent at the time of his second inauguration, 8 percentage points above his standing four years earlier. After Watergate broke, however, his approval levels fell steadily until his resignation in August 1974.

Gerald Ford took office with the goodwill of the American people following the upheaval of Watergate. His first approval rating was 71 percent, but his public support plummeted 21 points in September, following his pardon of Richard Nixon. Nevertheless, by August 1975 he had lost only 4 additional percentage points, and he finished his term at 53 percent, 3 percentage points above his September 1974 figure.

The first Gallup Poll following Jimmy Carter's inauguration showed him with a 66 percent approval rating. This rose to 75 percent two months later, but he fell to 52 percent after a year in office and to 43 percent at the midpoint of his term. By the end of his term he had only 34 percent approval.

Ronald Reagan's tenure in office found him riding a roller coaster in his relations with the public. He began rather low in the polls at 51 percent approval. By May he had risen to 68 percent, but he declined to 49 percent by November. From there his approval level steadily decreased to 35 percent in January 1983. It then increased to 55 percent after three years in office, and at the time of his second inauguration he stood at 64 percent approval, 13 percentage points above his initial level. Even in October 1986 the president enjoyed a 63 percent approval rating. Then the Iran-contra affair broke, and he hovered around the 50 percent level (which is where he began) for most of the next two years. At the very end of his term, however, Reagan's approval level increased and once again exceeded 60 percent.

What these shifts in presidents' approval ratings show is that declines occur, but they are neither inevitable nor swift. Eisenhower maintained his standing with the public very well for two complete terms. Reagan experienced considerable volatility in his relations with the public, but his record does not indicate that public support, once lost, cannot be revived and maintained.

Kennedy held his public support for two years, as did Ford, after an initial sharp decline one month into his term. Nixon's approval levels were also quite resilient for his entire first term. Johnson's and Carter's approval losses were more rapid. In Johnson's case, the initial ratings were inflated owing to the unique emotional climate at the time he assumed office. The same was true, of course, for Ford.

Thus, "honeymoons" are not necessarily fleeting phenomena in which new occupants of the White House receive a short breathing period from the public. Instead, constituents seem to be willing to give a new chief executive the benefit of the doubt for some time. In January 1982 more than 70 percent of the public felt it unfair to judge President Reagan's economic program, passed in mid-1981, until at least the end of 1982.[22] It is up to each president to exploit the goodwill provided by the public's predisposition and to use it as a foundation on which to build solid support for his administration.

Long-Term Decline

Presidential approval may rise or fall over the long run—across presidencies—as well as within presidential terms. The period of 1953–88 has been punctuated by turmoil and intense political conflict. Such shocks to the political system may undermine the public's confidence in the presidency as an institution. Examining presidential approval across the terms of presidents is necessary for determining whether systemic changes in approval levels have taken place.

As table 1.6 shows, from 1953 through 1965, with the single exception of 1958, at least 60 percent of the public approved the president on the average. Support of two out of three Americans was not unusual. Starting in 1966, however, approval levels changed dramatically. Since then presidents have received the approval of even a bare majority of the public less than half of the time.

TABLE 1.6   Average Yearly Presidential Approval (%)

Year	Approval
1953	68
1954	66
1955	71
1956	73
1957	64
1958	55
1959	64
1960	61
1961	76
1962	72
1963	65
1964	74
1965	66
1966	51
1967	44
1968	42
1969	61
1970	57
1971	50
1972	56
1973	42
1974	35
1975	43
1976	48
1977	62
1978	46
1979	37
1980	41
1981	58
1982	44
1983	44
1984	55
1985	60
1986	61
1987	48
1988	52

What happened? It is not possible to provide a definitive answer to such a sweeping question, but it is reasonable to argue that the Vietnam War, a highly divisive policy following an era of peace and consensus on the cold war, had a destructive effect on President Johnson's approval levels. Although Richard Nixon rebounded somewhat from his predecessor's modest standing in the polls in 1966–68, he did not rise to pre-1966 levels, and Watergate sent his approval levels to new lows.

Just how much residual effect the factors of Vietnam and Watergate have had on the approval levels of subsequent presidents is impossible to determine with certainty. We do know that President Ford's pardon of Richard Nixon tied Ford irrevocably to Watergate and that his public support plunged immediately after the pardon was announced. Moreover, there is survey evidence that for many people Watergate reduced confidence in the office of the president.[23]

Presidents Carter and Reagan did not enjoy uniformly high levels of approval. President Reagan began his term lower in the polls than any modern president and, like his predecessor, had less than 50 percent approval by his second year in office. Oddly, it was only for a two-year period beginning near the end of his first term that he sustained high levels of approval.

Thus, although it is possible that the generally low levels of public support for most recent presidents is purely a product of their individual actions and characteristics, it is difficult not to conclude that the events of the late 1960s and early 1970s have weakened the predispositions of many Americans to support the president. This conclusion is consistent with findings of a decline in the enthusiasm of voters for winning presidential candidates over the same period.[24]

The Role of Personality

One factor commonly associated with approval is personality. In common usage the term "personality" refers to personal characteristics such as warmth, charm, and humor that may influence responses to an individual on a personal level. It is not unusual for observers to conclude that the public evaluates presidents more on style than on substance, especially in an era in which the media and sophisticated public relations campaigns play a prominent role in presidential politics. In other words, some argue that the public evaluates the president by how much they may like him as a person.

If personality affects presidential approval at all, it is not likely to be a dynamic influence. The president's personality does not change during his tenure in office, and, as Neustadt argues, the impressions the public holds of the president's personality form early and change slowly.[25]

Although the public may "like" the president, it still may not approve of the way he is handling his job. In a July 1978 poll Jimmy Carter's job approval rating was only 39 percent, yet 76 percent of the public felt he was a "likeable person."[26]

Ronald Reagan provides a good test case of the role of personality in presidential approval. Some, especially the president's detractors, ascribed Reagan's standing in the polls primarily to his personal charm and telegenic good looks, his stage presence and professional skills as a television performer ("the great communicator"), the White House's extensive "packaging" of the president's public appearances, or to a Teflon coating that immunized him from accountability for problems of governing and public policy. On the other hand, Richard Wirthlin, the president's principal pollster, argues that the president's standing in the polls was not the result of his "nice" personality.[27]

Prior to the Reagan administration, to obtain a measure of personal likability rather than performance the Gallup Poll periodically asked respondents whether they had a "favorable" or "unfavorable" opinion of the president. Since that time it has relied primarily upon a question that asks respondents whether they approve or disapprove of the president "as a person." In a split ballot test in 1982, Gallup found exactly the same percentage approving Reagan as a person as having a favorable opinion of him. Since the two questions elicited identical responses, the results can be used to compare presidents.

A comparison of the results of asking the same people whether they approved of President Reagan's handling of his job and whether they approved of him as a person can be found in table 1.7. Reagan was liked personally throughout his tenure by large majorities, ranging from 67 to 81 percent. On the other hand, the proportion approving his performance in office was consistently lower. The average difference between approval of Reagan as a person and approval of his performance as president was 21 percentage points, representing over a fifth of the public.

Other data support the conclusion that Reagan's approval levels were not dependent on his personality. A study of six ABC News/*Washington Post* national surveys in the period 1982–84 found that on the average 39 percent of the people liked both Reagan and his policies, but an average of 29 percent of the people liked him but disapproved of his policies. People falling into the latter category overwhelmingly planned to vote against the president in the 1984 election.[28] A *Los Angeles Times* national survey in November 1983 also found that 29 percent of the public liked the president personally but disliked most of his policies.[29]

Equally important, contrary to conventional wisdom, Reagan was not particularly well liked by the American people. In an earlier article Edwards compared the average favorable or personal approval ratings of recent presidents and found that Reagan was among the least well-liked presidents in the past three decades.[30] Similarly, in a study of the public's attitudes toward winning presidential candidates through 1984, Martin Wattenberg found that "since the onset of academic research, no victorious presidential candidate has been more intensely disliked among his opponents, greeted with more doubts among his supporters, and hence more unpopular overall with the voters."[31]

It is plausible that there is some relationship between personal and job approval and that this relationship is reciprocal. Approval of the pres-

TABLE 1.7 Comparison of Approval of Ronald Reagan as President and as a Person (%)

Date	Job Approval	Approval as Person
1981		
July 17–20	60	78
November 13–16	49	73
1982		
February 5–8	47	70
April 30–May 3	44	69
June 11–14	45	67
1983		
August 19–22	43	67
1984		
September 21–24	57	67
1985		
November 11–18	65	81
1986		
September 3–17	63	80
December 4–5	47	75
1987		
January 16–19	48	74
April 10–13	48	75
July 10–13	49	72
1988		
December 27–29	63	79

ident's personality may buttress his job approval ratings. It seems equally likely, however, that when Reagan's job performance ratings fell, as during the recession of 1982, they had a negative influence on approval of his personality. In general, however, Americans appear to compartmentalize their attitudes toward the president. They have little difficulty separating the person from the performance.

What may be a greater influence on presidential approval and more subject to change is the way the public evaluates some of the president's job-related traits. Assessments of characteristics such as integrity, reliability, and leadership ability (as opposed to attributes such as personal warmth and charm) may change as new problems arise or as the public observes the president's performance. Certain characteristics may become more salient in response to changing conditions.

When the Iran-contra affair became news, President Reagan's decision-making style became a prominent issue, and many people evaluated the same behavior he had exhibited before—namely his focus on the "big picture" and detachment from the details of governing—in a different light. Just as the scandal was breaking in the news, a major business magazine carried a cover story emphasizing the advantages of the president's approach to running the executive branch. Such a story would not appear again. In addition, Reagan's veracity, which had not been an issue during most of his administration, became one, with a majority of Americans concluding that he had lied about his knowledge of the diversion to the contras of profits from the arms sales to Iran.[32]

Similarly, Jimmy Carter's bent for achieving command of the details of government would be criticized later as a penchant for the trivial, his deliberativeness would be condemned as indecisiveness, and his efforts to rise above politics faulted as naive. The results of two polls, taken about ten months apart, illustrate the potential for change in perceptions of a president's job-related characteristics (see table 1.8). The figures in the column on the right side of the page show that many people changed their minds about Carter's leadership abilities during a relatively short period of time.

The charm of Gerald Ford's unexceptional personal lifestyle soon gave way to the feeling that he was perhaps not up to the job of the presidency. Lyndon Johnson's political cleverness was often viewed as deceitfulness by the end of his tenure. Many presidents find behavior that was once applauded as firmness is later reproached as rigidity.

Thus, views of the president's job-related characteristics may change over time, and there is evidence that the public's evaluations of such traits influence approval of his performance in office. In earlier work Edwards found that issues of trust and evaluations of various components of lead-

TABLE 1.8 Change in Evaluation of Jimmy Carter's Job-related
Characteristics (%)

Characteristics	Agree		
	Mid-1977[a]	Mid-1978[b]	Change
Decisive, sure of himself	61	38	−23
You know where he stands on issues	42	28	−14
Has strong leadership qualities	62	36	−26
Has well-defined program for moving country ahead	43	29	−14
Uncertain, indecisive, unsure	28	55	+27
Hard to know where he stands	47	66	+19
Lacks strong leadership qualities	27	58	+31
Has no clear-cut program for moving country ahead	44	64	+20

Source: "President Carter's 'Phrase Portrait,' " *The Gallup Opinion Index* (November 1978): 9.
[a] September 30–October 3, 1977
[b] July 21–24, 1978

ership significantly influenced approval of Presidents Nixon, Ford, and
Carter.[33]

Recent research on voting behavior in presidential elections has found
that characteristics voters ascribe to candidates, such as moral character
and leadership competence, are important influences on their votes. This
finding holds for persons of all education levels.[34] Individual presidents
or candidates are easier for people to focus on than complex policy issues,
and this inclination is reinforced by the orientation of media coverage
toward the personalization of politics.[35]

Focusing on shifts in presidential approval risks missing the forest
for the trees. Predispositions such as party identification and the positivity
bias are the best predictors of the level of approval a president receives.
They provide the foundations of presidential approval and furnish it with
a basic stability. Thus the core of a chief executive's public support is the
consequence of relatively durable features of the political environment.[36]
A president's general personality characteristics seem to have little impact
on the public's evaluations, but his job-related personal characteristics play
a more important and dynamic role.

2 / CHANGES IN APPROVAL

Although some factors predispose many members of the public to approve or disapprove of the president's performance, presidential approval ratings may change while predispositions remain essentially constant. To account for such alterations in the president's standing with the public requires focusing on aspects of the environment that are more subject to change than predispositions.

The rise and fall of presidential approval has been of interest to scholars ever since the Gallup Poll and other polling organizations began making their findings public. For the past two decades scholars have sought to understand and predict changes in the president's standing in the polls and, in the process, have used a wide range of sophisticated statistical techniques. This chapter focuses on some of the principal questions involved in the investigation of the ebb and flow of presidential approval.

Variable Influences on Presidential Approval

A number of factors affect the influence that an aspect of a person's environment has on his or her evaluation of the president. For a matter to influence approval of the president significantly, it must be salient to people, they must hold the president responsible for it, and they must evaluate the president in terms of his performance regarding it. Perceptions of reality affect all these components of presidential assessment.

Salience

Understanding presidential approval requires identifying what is on the minds of Americans. If a matter is not salient to people, it is unlikely to play a role in their evaluations of the president. It cannot be assumed that all people use the same criteria in evaluating the president or that an individual always judges him by the same benchmarks. We saw in chapter

1, for example, that the salience of the president's job-related personal characteristics may vary from one period to the next.

The importance of specific issues to the public also varies over time and is closely tied to objective conditions such as unemployment, inflation, international tensions, or racial conflict. From the time the cold war developed in the late 1940s until the early 1960s, foreign affairs dominated public concern, with economic matters a strong second. Beginning in 1963, the civil rights movement ranked as the most important problem until foreign affairs, boosted by the Vietnam War, regained the top position in 1965 and stayed there in almost every most poll until 1970. For the 1970–73 period, public concern wavered; social control, foreign affairs, and the economy all shared the spotlight. From 1973 through 1983, economics was consistently the most prominent issue to Americans.[1] In 1984 foreign affairs again gained in prominence and alternated with the economy as the most important problem in the rest of Ronald Reagan's term of office.

When doing time-series analysis of the impact of an issue on presidential approval, it is important to take into consideration that the meaning attributed to a variable may change over time, although the theory underlying its use may assume that the meaning is constant. For example, although reports of the unemployment rate continue to count the percentage of the population that is unemployed, the composition of the unemployed has changed over time and the hardship caused by unemployment has been reduced. Women and youth now compose a larger percentage of the unemployed than they did in the 1950s. Since many of these people are not the primary wage earners in their families, the correspondence between hardship and unemployment is probably less now than in earlier decades. More liberal eligibility requirements for unemployment insurance and welfare programs and increased payments from these programs over time buttress the argument that unemployment has a lesser impact on people's lives today than it did in the past.

The extent to which this difference translates into a different impact on presidential approval is an open question. The point is that a change in the meaning of an issue over time may reduce the reliability of findings. Cross-sectional analysis allows one to assess the effect, if any, of an issue such as high unemployment, at different points in time to see if it has changed and if it is greater when the values of the variable are extreme.

In addition to variation over time in the prominence of issues, different issues are likely to be salient to different groups in the population at any given time. Some may be concerned about inflation, others about unemployment, and yet others about an aspect of foreign policy.[2]

Within an issue area, bad news may outweigh good in capturing the public's attention. Several scholars have found that people weigh negative information more heavily than positive; that is, it is more salient to them.[3] If the economy slumps, for example, this may be more salient to the public than if it continues to grow at a moderate rate. Thus, the president may be punished in the polls if the economy is not doing well, while he may not be rewarded for prosperity.[4] It may be that an issue only comes to the public's attention when it reaches a certain threshold—one that usually means there is a problem.[5]

The relative weight of values and issues in evaluations of the president also varies over time. Valence or style issues, such as patriotism, morality, or a strong national defense, on which there is a broad public consensus are more important than a position on a specific policy. The president's articulation of valence issues, directly and in the symbols he employs in his actions and speech, can affirm the values and beliefs that define citizens' political identities. As a result, valence issues may be powerful instruments for obtaining public support, for presidents often prefer to be judged on the basis of consensual criteria with which they can associate themselves.

There is reason to believe that valence issues augmented Ronald Reagan's standing in the polls. People liked the values he articulated more than they liked his issue stands. Americans are conservative in their basic values, such as religion and morality, pride in country, and national security, and skeptical about the government's ability to solve social and economic problems; they responded positively to the president's broad themes. As long as values and the symbols used to represent them were more salient than issues, Reagan did well in the polls. When issues were more salient, as during the recession of 1982 or in the wake of the Iran-contra scandal, he slipped.

Responsibility

Even if a matter, such as the economy, is salient to the public, it is not likely to affect people's evaluations of the president unless they hold him responsible for it.[6] Despite the prominence of the chief executive, there are several reasons why people may not hold the president responsible for all the problems they face personally or for some problems that they perceive confront the country.

Most people do not politicize their personal problems, and most of those concerned about personal economic problems do not believe the government should come to their assistance.[7] If people perceive that their economic problems are the result of their own failings or those of their immediate environment, then their personal economic circumstances should not necessarily lead to discontent with national political figures or institutions. A study asking who is "most responsible" for "economic problems" found that only 11 percent chose the president; 67 percent chose big business and big labor.[8]

Some people may feel that those who preceded the president or who share power with him are to blame for important problems. During the 1982 recession, for example, Ronald Reagan was spared the wrath of those who felt economic problems were more the fault of Carter's administration than of Reagan's, that the president had little control over the causes of inflation and unemployment, and that past presidents had been unable to control these same problems.[9] A poll taken on Election Day in 1982 found that 41 percent of the voters blamed Ronald Reagan for the recession, but 44 percent blamed the Democrats.[10]

Similarly, there is evidence that voters are sophisticated enough to recognize that current conditions do not necessarily reflect either present or future economic performance.[11] Although 36 percent termed Reagan's economic policies a failure at the midpoint of his first term and only 6 percent claimed they were a success, 49 percent felt the president's program needed more time.[12] Thus, blame is not automatic for presiding over hard times.

Perceptions of salience and responsibility may combine to influence presidential approval. A study of the 1984 presidential election found that perceived changes in personal economic circumstances affected candidate evaluations only for those who were doing worse (a small percentage) and who held government responsible.[13]

Performance

For matters that are salient to the public and for which it holds the president accountable, the quality of the president's performance becomes a factor in presidential approval. Yet there is not a consensus on the criteria by which the public evaluates presidential performance. A discussion of the most often cited issue area influencing presidential approval, the economy, will help illustrate the dimensions of the question.

The state of a nation's economy has a pervasive influence on the lives of its citizens. Their sense of self-esteem, social status, and their degree of optimism about the future are often related to the economy. So are the opportunities for their children and their life-styles.

The conventional view is that people's evaluations of the president are affected strongly by their personal economic circumstances. That is, they are more likely to approve of the president if they are prospering personally than if they feel they are not. According to Richard Neustadt, "The moving factor in [presidential] prestige is what men outside of Washington see happening to *themselves*."[14] Lyndon Johnson believed that "the family pocketbook was the root-and-branch crucial connection to all his plans and hopes for the future."[15]

Many studies have focused on the impact of economically self-interested behavior in voting for candidates for Congress or the presidency, with a wide variety of results.[16] In recent years, however, an impressive number of studies have found that personal economic circumstances are typically subordinated to other, broader considerations when people evaluate government performance or individual candidates.[17]

More specifically, some scholars have argued that citizens evaluate the president on the basis of broader views of the economy than their narrow self-interests. In other words, rather than ask what the president has done for them lately, citizens ask what the president has done for the *nation*.[18]

There are strong theoretical reasons to have confidence in such findings. On a wide range of issues, including federal tax policy, busing schoolchildren for racial integration, the Vietnam War, energy policy, national health insurance, law and order, and unemployment, scholars have found little relationship between the self-interest of respondents and their policy preferences or voting behavior.[19]

Furthermore, people differentiate their own circumstances from those of the country as a whole. For example, in a Gallup Poll taken in the fall of 1988, only 56 percent were satisfied with the way things were going in the nation, but 87 percent were satisfied with the way things were going in their personal lives.[20]

In addition, there is reason to be cautious about accepting the findings of earlier work. Most studies of presidential approval have relied on time-series analysis of aggregate data to investigate the impact of economic conditions on presidential approval.[21] In essence, scholars have compared the rise and fall in presidential approval (treated as a dependent variable) over time with the rise and fall of possible explanatory variables, such as unemployment and inflation. The implicit theory underlying such studies is that as the environment and circumstances of individuals change, their level of support for the president also changes. If unemployment and presidential approval vary together, for example, then researchers conclude that unemployment levels are part of the explanation for presidential approval.

The careful reader will note that in such analyses scholars use aggregate data (the national unemployment rate or the Consumer Price Index, for example) because they lack individual-level data. Exclusive reliance on aggregate data leaves the researcher subject to the ecological fallacy, however. Aggregate data can take a researcher only part of the way toward answering questions about how individuals react to changing circumstances or why people evaluate the president as they do, because the data do not provide information about individual behavior.[22]

Findings of covariation in such instances explain very little. Just who is responding and for what reasons? If unemployment rises nationally at the same time that presidential approval drops, what group decreases its support of the president? Those experiencing unemployment? Those worried about unemployment more generally? Or those who are not directly affected by unemployment but who feel the president is not doing enough for those who are? Or yet others?

To properly test propositions about the causes of evaluations of the president, it is necessary to obtain individual-level data and then examine them to see what (if any) circumstances or perceptions of persons are related to differences in presidential approval. Such data are not widely available, however. In general they are limited to a few polls taken in national election periods in the relatively recent past. The data in this volume help fill the gap somewhat, because researchers can specify certain groups in the population and relate their approval levels to changing circumstances. Nevertheless, the absence of individual-level data remains a constraint on explaining presidential approval.

Thus, when the public evaluates the president in terms of the economy, it is likely to look beyond narrow self-interest and personal problems. The question then is whether people rely on the overall performance of the economy as a criterion for evaluating the president's performance or whether they employ a more general notion of how he is handling economic policy. The two criteria are related, but the latter may give the president more leeway.

The public may be less harsh in its evaluations of a president who is struggling with a difficult situation, even if he is not meeting with short-term success. Franklin D. Roosevelt may have enjoyed the public's tolerance in 1933 and 1934, not only because he could not be held responsible for the Depression but also because he was seen as actively doing the best that could be done under trying circumstances.

An extensive cross-sectional analysis showed that people's perceptions of their personal finances, experiences with unemployment, the effects of inflation, business conditions, and the nation's economy did not correlate highly with presidential approval. Perceptions of presidential performance in economic policy, however, had strong relationships with more general evaluations of the president. Although it might be concluded that perceptions of the president's handling of economic policy were simply a product of more general evaluations of the president, this proved not to be true.[23]

The same principles apply to other policy areas. For example, the Vietnam War was highly salient to the American people and the president was inextricably held responsible for its conduct. Americans did not evaluate the president on the basis of their personal experiences with the war — whether they or a family member had been drafted, for example. Instead, they evaluated him on the basis of their views of his handling of the war.

Perceptions of Reality

Evaluations of the president are heavily dependent on the public's perceptions of the environment and the president's performance in handling various aspects of it. Perceptions are often distorted, however. The literature on the public's knowledge and understanding of politics and public policy is vast, and it does not paint an encouraging picture of the awareness of the typical citizen.[24]

A national poll in May 1982 found that only 27 percent of the public knew that the inflation rate had fallen. Thirty-four percent thought it had gone up, although it had in fact fallen sharply.[25] It was not until April 1983 that a majority of respondents felt inflation was less of a problem than it had been a year earlier.[26]

Another poll found that in late 1982 only 38 percent of the public was aware of the sharp drop in interest rates.[27] Even in the presidential election year of 1984, less than half the public knew of the dramatic drop in unemployment rates, and even fewer knew of the drop in the inflation rate.[28]

Similarly, economic forecasts reflect more a combination of hopes and politicized guesses about the future than they do an awareness of current economic conditions and an understanding of how the economy functions. Forecasts of the economy are not simple extrapolations based on current economic conditions and are often inaccurate.[29]

The distortion of reality due to the emphasis on negativity has already been discussed. In 1982 the public knew unemployment had risen but not that inflation had fallen.[30] This appears to be symptomatic of a more general tendency for the public to be more accurate in its recollections of unemployment than of inflation.[31]

At other times it is unclear just what "reality" is, and there may be no consensus on how well the president is doing. In a poll taken in November 1982, 39 percent of the respondents concluded that Ronald Reagan's economic policies had helped the country while another 40 percent felt they had hurt it. Forty-six percent felt Reaganomics would help the country in the future, but 45 percent believed it would hurt the nation.[32]

The role of schemas in people's thinking about politics has received substantial attention in recent years. A "schema" is an individual, informal, tacit theory of the nature of reality and the meaning of events, objects, and situations. It provides a contextual framework within which actors, groups, and events are understood. New information is interpreted in terms of prior knowledge and conceptions, the inference being that new information represents a particular instance of a more general type.

Thus, schemas are simplifying devices, reducing the cost of evaluating the president and new information about him.[33] They provide a guide to what the president should be able to do, what to expect, what information is relevant, what criteria are appropriate for judging him, and what the quality of his performance has been.

Schemas play an important role in the development of attitudes about the president, but they may oversimplify and misrepresent the world. When this potential is combined with human limitations and error plus the negativity bias and means of inconsistency reduction (including selective perception, persuasion, and projection as discussed in chapter 1), numerous limits on cognitive processing are evident. Together they represent substantial potential for misperceiving reality.

Issues and presidential actions are often accompanied by symbols that trigger associations of schemas based on prior experience.[34] These may evoke emotion and sentiment rather than simple objective appraisal of information, and in so doing they may generate an emotional response that makes the issue or event politically meaningful. As a result, such schemas may have a powerful influence on evaluations of the president.

Since the public's perceptions of issues and of the president's actions are often hazy, there is ample opportunity to influence its impressions. The White House invests considerable amounts of time and energy to influence the public's perceptions of presidential performance.[35]

There is some experimental evidence that network news helps to provide a frame of reference for some issues, and when it does, evaluations of presidents are affected. For example, if people saw poverty as a systemic outcome rather than dispositional, they were less likely to evaluate Ronald Reagan highly.[36] Another experiment found that President Carter's overall reputation and, to a lesser extent, his apparent competency, was affected by network news. The standards people used in evaluating the president— what they felt was important in his job performance—seemed to be influenced by the news they watched on television.[37]

As a result of various limitations on the accuracy of perceptions of reality, one cannot simply assume that everyone views the world through the same eyes. In addition, the aggregate social indicators that are employed in time-series analyses of presidential approval are often poor measures of the reality they purport to represent. Statistics concerning the progress of the Vietnam War, such as reports of the number of enemy soldiers killed, are notoriously suspect. Numerous articles appear in scholarly journals on the limitations of economic indicators such as the Consumer Price Index and the unemployment rate. Even to the extent that the latter is an accurate measure at any one time, the figures employed in time-series analyses may not reflect the total percentage of the population unemployed in a year. The rate may be stable while newly unemployed people replace those who found employment. Thus many more people may be unemployed in a year than the official rate indicates.[38] Rather than relying on measures that are of doubtful validity and that are not congruent with the theories ostensibly being tested, it is preferable to find out how individuals perceive their circumstances and the degree to which their circumstances have changed.

Rally Events

Sometimes public approval of the president takes sudden jumps. One popular explanation for these surges of support is that they are "rally events." John Mueller seminally defined a rally event as one that relates to international relations; directly involves the United States and particularly the president; and is specific, dramatic, and sharply focused. Such events confront the nation as a whole, are salient to the public, and gain public attention and interest.[39]

The theory behind rally events is that the public increases its support of the president in times of crisis or during major international events, at least in the short run, because he is the symbol of the country and the primary focus of attention at such times. Moreover, people will support the president because they do not fear hurting the country's chances of success by opposing him, and at such times the president has an opportunity to look masterful and evoke patriotic reactions among the people.

Conversely, there is reason to expect the "rally around the flag" effect to have limited potential. A major study of American public opinion regarding national security in 1988 found that almost half (47 percent) of the public felt that the country should *immediately* debate a president's decision to send U.S. troops to defend an invaded nation, four out of ten (42 percent) argued that people should not question the president's action, and 8 percent said it depends on the circumstances. Even with a conservative Republican, Ronald Reagan, in the White House, only a bare majority of conservatives and Republicans said they would defer to the president. Those most likely to be opinion leaders—those with postgraduate education—favored debate rather than deference by a two-to-one margin.[40]

Such views are not new. The public had more confidence in the judgment of Congress than in that of the president on the question of entry into World War II and on reorganization of the Defense Department in the 1950s (even when the president was former General of the Army Dwight Eisenhower).[41] In 1973, 80 percent of the people supported a requirement that the president obtain the approval of Congress before sending American armed forces into action outside the country.[42] With the public's support that year Congress passed the War Powers Resolution over the president's veto. The purpose of this law was to substantially limit the president's ability to continue the use of U.S. forces in hostile actions without the approval of Congress.

In 1987 only 24 percent of the public responded that they trusted President Reagan more than Congress to make the right decision on national security policy. Sixty percent had more confidence in Congress.[43] Only 34 percent of the public agreed that the president should be allowed to conduct secret operations in foreign countries without notifying Congress; 61 percent disagreed.[44] In the same year 63 percent of the public desired the president to obtain the approval of Congress to keep U.S. ships in the Persian Gulf. Only 33 percent wanted him to be able to make the decision himself.[45]

The values that predominate in the American political culture are not only less than conducive to leadership, but virtually stand as a barrier to it. According to Samuel Huntington, "the distinctive aspect of the American Creed is its antigovernment character. Opposition to power, and suspicion of government as the most dangerous embodiment of power, are the central themes of American political thought."[46] Many have commented on the importance to Americans of limited government, liberty, individualism, equality, and democracy.[47] These cultural values generate a distrust of strong leadership, authority, and the public sector in general. Americans are basically individualistic and skeptical of authority. Although some are attracted to strong leaders, they do not seem to feel a corresponding obligation to defer to their leadership. There does not seem to be a segment of the population that is deferential to the president.[48]

Thus the question of the rally phenomenon requires careful examination. To begin, there must be a means of identifying a rally. The theory underlying the rally phenomenon directs us to look for sharp increases in presidential approval. Adopting any figure as evidence of the impact of a rally event is inevitably somewhat arbitrary. When the figures for presidential approval in two polls are around the 50 percent mark, we can have 95 percent confidence that a 5 percentage point increase in approval represents some change in national approval and is not the result of sampling error (see Appendix C). It is important to note that there would have to be an increase of 10 percentage points between two polls for us to have 95 percent confidence that a change of 5 percentage points occurred.

There is a danger of overinterpreting apparent opinion change. One panel study of presidential approval found that most opinion change has a large random component.[49] An ABC News/*Washington Post* Poll taken in December 1983 asked the presidential approval question at both the beginning and the end of the poll. The authors found that 15 percent of the sample changed their evaluations of Ronald Reagan from approval to disapproval or vice versa during the course of the poll![50]

On the other hand, adopting too high a threshold for change may bias the results against finding evidence of a rally effect. Thus, a 5 percentage point increase in the national totals, the minimal threshold, will serve here as the baseline for the impact of a rally event. Readers who wish to examine the response of specific demographic groups to rally events should note that the sampling error is larger when using smaller samples.

The basic procedure is to compare changes in approval levels from the poll preceding a possible rally event to the poll following it. It is possible that the impact of a rally event will not be fully reflected in the polls, because it occurred during an interviewing period, which typically lasts from four to six days (one to two days in telephone polls). In such a case at least part of the sample would be evaluating the president without the potential influence of the rally event. In these instances, the comparison is made between the poll during which the event occurred and the next poll. Upon inspection of the data, this does not seem to pose a significant confounding factor in the analysis of response to potential rally events, but it may occasionally mask an impact.

If an event began before a poll was taken but extended through the period of the poll, the comparison is made with the previous poll. All respondents to the second poll could have been aware of the event.

Often there have been gaps in the data sets that scholars have used, gaps they either ignored or interpolated without alerting the reader. The data in this volume fill most of those gaps, but researchers should note that because of the inclusion of trial-heat questions for presidential candidates, there were no presidential approval questions asked in the periods immediately preceding elections—September and October 1956, July through October 1964, October 1968, July through October 1972, July through November 1976, and October 1980. Care should be taken not to interpret, say, the jump of 8 percentage points in Gerald Ford's approval that took place over six months in the second half of 1976 the same way a similar increase occurring between polls taken only weeks apart is interpreted.

There is no definitive list of rally events. Mueller included five categories of international events under his definition, including sudden American military intervention in another nation, major military developments in ongoing wars, major diplomatic developments, dramatic technological developments, and summit meetings between the president and the leader of the USSR.[51] Lists of potential rally events in the period 1953–88 appear in tables 2.1–2. The lists encompass a wide range of military and diplomatic activities, including all those identified by Mueller. To be fair to the rally hypothesis, the definition of rally events employed is a generous one. For example, the Hungarian uprising in 1956, the Six-Day War in the Middle East in 1967, the Soviet Union's invasion of Czechoslovakia in 1968, and the overthrow of the Marcos regime in the Philippines in 1986 did not directly involve the United States. However, there were expectations that the president would respond to them.

The tables show that most potential rally events do not produce rallies at all. Instead, the polls taken after most of them show a loss of support. Presidents average about one rally every year and a half, and most of the rallies that occur produce changes of less than 7 percentage points. In addition, several rallies have alternative explanations rooted in domestic politics and policies (these alternatives are shown in parentheses). Actually, approval is more likely to fall in spurts than to increase in response to potential rally events. On 61 occasions, 11 of them following potential rally events, approval fell by at least 5 percentage points.

Even the rallies that do occur may be short-lived.[52] For example, the famous 5 percentage point increase in approval accorded President Kennedy immediately following the invasion of Cuba at the Bay of Pigs was succeeded by a 6 percentage point decline in the next poll—despite the public's pride in the first manned U.S. space flight, which occurred before the poll. Even some rallies that sustained themselves for more than one poll had only temporary effects. Richard Nixon received a short respite from Watergate with the end of American participation in the war in Vietnam, but he soon declined in the polls. Similarly, Jimmy Carter rose substantially following the taking of American hostages in Iran in November 1979 (in fact he had two consecutive rallies as the crisis dragged on), but he fell below 40 percent approval by March 1980.

Those who have previously opposed the president rather than those in the "no opinion" category provide most of the new support for the president during a rally event,[53] and such persons turn to disapproval of the president's handling of the issue at a higher rate than other citizens.[54] Thus even when surges of support occur, the president should not expect them to be sustained. Since he is probably already receiving high support from his own partisans, those who rally to his side are likely to be In-

TABLE 2.1 Apparent Rally Effects of at Least 5 Percentage Points
between Polls

Event	Date	Increase in Approval over Previous Poll	Change in Next Poll
Eisenhower Atoms for Peace speech	1953	10	+12
Marines land in Lebanon	1958	6	− 2
Nixon visit to U.S.S.R. (Landrum-Griffin labor reform)	1959	6	− 1
Eisenhower goodwill trip	1959	10	− 9
Bay of Pigs invasion	1961	5	− 6
Cuban missile crisis	1962	13	+ 2
Marines invade Dominican Republic	1965	6	− 1
First bombing near Hanoi	1966	8	− 5
LBJ visits South Vietnam; North Korea kills 6 U.S. soldiers	1966	5	− 5
Six-Day War in Middle East	1967	7	− 4
U.S.S.R. invades Czechoslovakia (Democratic convention)	1968	7	+ 1
Pueblo crew released (three astronauts circle moon)	1968	5	a
Nixon Vietnamization speech	1969	11	− 8
U.S. pullout of Cambodia (18-year-old vote amendment)	1970	6	− 6
Vietnam ceasefire proposal	1970	7	− 1
Mining of North Vietnamese harbors; (U.S.-U.S.S.R. summit	1972	8	− 3
Vietnam peace accord (Nixon inauguration, draft ends)	1973	16	− 2
Bombing of Cambodia ends (Nixon Watergate speech)	1973	5	− 2
Mayaguez rescue	1975	11	+ 1
Panama Canal Treaties announced	1977	6	−12
American hostages taken in Iran	1979	6	+13
Marines killed in Beirut; U.S. invasion of Grenada	1983	4[b]	+ 4
TWA hijacking	1985	5	+ 2
Bombing of Libya	1986	6	− 7

[a] No further polls on Johnson.
[b] See text for explanation.

dependents or those who identify with the opposition party. The latter especially will soon be pulled by partisan ties toward opposing him.

Thus, rallies are likely to follow a pattern of impulse and decay.[55] Temporary disturbances are likely to have temporary effects on public

TABLE 2.2 Potential Rally Events for Which No Rally of 5 Percentage
Points Occurred

Event	Year	Change in Approval
Korean War truce signed	1953	+ 1
U.S.S.R. tests H-Bomb	1953	− 13
Formosan Resolution	1955	+ 3
North Korea shoots down U.S. place	1955	− 5
U.S.-U.S.S.R. summit; Open Skies proposal	1955	+ 4
Eisenhower Doctrine announced	1956	− 6
Khruschev visit to U.S.	1959	+ 1
Khruschev disrupts U.N.	1960	− 7
President's Japan trip canceled	1960	− 4
U-2 shot down; summit collapse	1960	+ 3
U-2 Pilot Gary Powers convicted	1960	− 2
U.S.S.R. shoots down U.S. plane, backs Castro	1960	− 8
Geneva summit (U.S.-U.S.S.R.)	1961	− 2
Berlin Wall erected	1961	+ 1
Reserves mobilized in Berlin crisis	1961	+ 1
Nuclear Test Ban Treaty announced	1963	+ 1
Bombing of Vietnam beings	1965	− 2
Major U.S. defense commitment in Vietnam	1965	0
Holiday truce in Vietnam	1965	− 4
LBJ confers with South Vietnamese leaders	1966	− 5
Air war in Vietnam intensifies	1966	− 8
Glassboro summit (U.S.-U.S.S.R.)	1967	− 4
Holiday truce in Vietnam	1967	+ 2
Tet begins; *Pueblo* captured	1968	− 7
Tet continues	1968	− 5
North Vietnam agrees to peace talks	1968	− 5
Bombing halt in Vietnam	1968	+ 1
Nuclear Non-Proliferation Treaty announced	1969	− 8
Invasion of Cambodia	1970	+ 2
POW rescue attempt in North Vietnam	1970	− 5
U.S.-supported invasion of Laos	1971	− 7
Publication of Pentagon Papers	1971	0
Nixon China trip	1972	+ 4
"Christmas" bombing of North Vietnam	1978	− 8
First POWs released from Vietnam	1973	− 2
U.S.-U.S.S.R. summit meeting	1973	0
Middle East war	1973	− 3
U.S. armed forces on worldwide alert	1973	0
U.S.-U.S.S.R. summit meeting	1974	− 4
Vladivostok arms limitations agreement	1974	− 6
Cambodia falls to communists	1975	− 5
Treaty limiting underground nuclear tests	1976	− 1
Camp David Accords	1975	+ 3

TABLE 2.2   (continued)

Event	Year	Change in Approval
People's Republic of China recognized	1978	− 1
Middle East Peace Treaty signed in U.S.	1979	− 2
SALT II agreement announced	1979	0
Carter criticizes Soviet troops in Cuba	1979	+ 3
U.S.S.R. invades Afghanistan; grain embargo	1979–80	+ 2
U.S. attempt to rescue hostages in Iran	1980	+ 4
Carter changes policy on flotilla from Cuba	1980	− 5
U.S. shoots down two Libyan jets	1981	+ 4
U.S. embassy in Beirut bombed	1983	+ 2
U.S.S.R. shoots down Korean airliner (KAL 007)	1983	+ 4
Reports of mining Nicaraguan harbors	1985	− 2
Achille Lauro hijacked	1985	+ 3
U.S.-U.S.S.R. summit	1985	− 2
Ferdinand Marcos flees Phillipines	1986	− 1
Iran-contra affair revealed	1986	− 16
Tower Commission report	1987	− 5
Medium Range Nuclear Arms Treaty signed	1987	0
U.S. shoots down Iranian airliner	1988	+ 3

opinion. Usually there will be nothing to sustain the impact of a rally event, and public opinion will return to a state of equilibrium. Although some researchers assume that the effects of rallies are cumulative,[56] with one rally building on another to substantially increase presidential approval, there is no evidence to support such an assumption.

It is not clear whether major milestones in the space program should be considered rally events. Because they are dramatic and have international implications, they are listed in table 2.3. Only the landing on the moon seems to have given the president's approval rating much of a boost. All but one of the remaining events were followed by lower levels of approval.

There is not much evidence here of systematic deference to the president in the broad area of national security, nor is there evidence that people reliably rally to the president's side when the United States is threatened or appears in an unfavorable light. This is nothing new. Henry Adams reported that James Madison hoped the burning of the White House by the British during the War of 1812 would evoke a strong reaction from the American public in favor of the war effort and was disappointed when no such response occurred.[57]

The impact of two classic cases of potential rally events, which occurred almost simultaneously in 1983, may have been masked by the

TABLE 2.3   Potential Rally Events in Space Exploration

Event	Year	Change in Approval
Soviet launching of Sputnik	1957	−2
First U.S. satellite	1958	−2
First U.S. manned space flight	1961	−6
First U.S. space flight to orbit earth	1962	+1
U.S. astronauts land on moon	1969	+7[a]
Space shuttle's first successful flight	1977	−1
Challenger disaster	1986	−7

[a] President Nixon lost 3 percentage points in the next poll.

dates of a poll. The first event was the bombing of the U.S. Marine barracks in Beirut on October 23, 1983, which caused the death of 241 Americans. The second was the U.S. invasion of Grenada three days later. The October 21–24 Gallup Poll recorded 49 percent approval of President Reagan, up 4 percentage points from earlier in the month, while the November poll found 53 percent approval. Thus, in a month's time the president improved 8 percentage points in the approval ratings. The CBS News/*New York Times* Poll found a similar 8 percentage point increase in the president's standing in the polls.

It is difficult to distinguish an increase in support of Reagan due to one or both of these events from the general upward trend in his support occurring at the time, and there is reason to believe that the public did not immediately rally to the president's side as a result of either of these events. The Reagan administration, which was closely attuned to public opinion, feared that it would be hurt, not helped by these events. According to White House spokesman Larry Speakes, it was only when the television cameras recorded the responses of medical students returning from Grenada that the president avoided being damaged politically:

> the medical students were grateful for the rescue . . . almost delirious with joy. When . . . the first student off the plane [from Grenada] knelt and kissed the ground and they all . . . thanked the U.S. military for rescuing them from a dangerous and chaotic situation, the public relations problem was solved.[58]

When surges in presidential approval occur, they are just as likely to happen in the absence of rally events as following them. On 23 occasions presidential approval rose by 5 percentage points or more in the absence of a rally event. The probable explanations for these increases are varied, ranging from Eisenhower's heart attack in 1955 and Johnson's withdrawal from the presidential campaign in 1968 to the assassination attempt on President Reagan.

It is difficult to identify characteristics that differentiate events that produce rallies from those that do not. Neither diplomatic activities, international agreements, the president's foreign travel, military actions, armed conflicts among other nations, successes in the space program, announcements of changes in U.S. policy, nor armed attacks on U.S. armed forces are typically followed by surges in presidential approval. This is also true for setbacks or policy failures for the United States in the international realm, which one might expect to be especially likely to produce a rally effect. Events in each of these categories are more likely to diminish than to bolster approval.

Obviously, some events are more salient to the public than others. In addition, the public responds positively to some potential rally events and negatively to others. Determining the causes of these differing responses is an important area of future research. One interesting explanation that has been advanced is that differing responses are the result of opinion leadership. The researchers argue that in potential rally situations, the public is especially dependent on information from the press and those public figures the press interviews. If the balance of elite commentary on the potential rally event is positive, then the public is more likely to rally behind the president. If it is negative, then there is less likelihood of a surge in support.[59]

Although the public may be highly dependent on a few commentators for a short period of time during an international incident, more typically there are several sources of information, not all of which support the White House. In addition, the nature of many potential rally events is such that those previously disapproving of the president will have no reason to change their evaluations. As noted earlier, the public does not display a pattern of deference to the chief executive, nor does it allow him to safely wrap himself in the flag in times of trouble.

There are several reasons in addition to the general lack of deference in American society that may depress the impact of potential rally events. Presidents who are already high in the polls, and therefore whose job performance is disapproved of by few people, have less potential for surges in support than those chief executives who are lower in the polls.

The vagaries of polling dates and history also complicate the task of evaluating the rally phenomenon. The more time that has elapsed since a rally event, the more its impact is likely to be attenuated. It is possible that short-term surges followed some events but were missed because of the timing of the following poll.

Other factors may intervene to depress the effects of a rally event. In such a case the rally would buttress the president's approval and perhaps keep it from rapidly declining but would not result in a substantial increase in approval. Long-term factors are not likely, even without a rally event, to cause public approval of the president to nosedive, and in most instances of potential rally events there is no evidence of discrete events that might counteract them.

As noted earlier, the Gallup Poll frequently did not ask the approval question during presidential election campaigns. As a result, there are often gaps for several months preceding a presidential election. In the analysis an increase of 5 percentage points over such a period was not treated as a rally, since the interval between polls was so great. There are a few possible rally events for which we have too little data to reach conclusions about their impact on presidential approval. These are listed in table 2.4.

TABLE 2.4   Possible Rally Events for Which Data Is Lacking

Event	Year
Suez crisis	1956
Uprising in Hungary	1956
Gulf of Tonkin incidents	1964
"Peace Is at Hand" speech	1972

It is possible that potential rally events that are followed by modest increases in support help build a basis for approval in the longer term. One cannot tell from the data at hand. It is possible to conclude with confidence (1) that the impact of the rally phenomenon is difficult to isolate, (2) that the preponderance of evidence indicates that it rarely appears, and (3) that the events that generate it are idiosyncratic and do not differ significantly from similar events that are not followed by surges in presidential approval.[60]

Many factors, ranging from various aspects of the economy to international conflict, are subject to change over relatively short periods of time. These elements of the public environment may explain much of the variance in levels of presidential approval over time, depending on their salience to the public, the degree to which people hold the president responsible for them, the way people evaluate the president's performance regarding them, and people's perceptions of reality. Sudden jumps in presidential approval in response to rally events are relatively rare, and it is difficult to discern patterns in the types of events that generate rallies.

3 / PRESIDENTS

This chapter presents an overview of public approval of each of the last seven presidents. The focus is on establishing the overall levels of approval of each chief executive, specifying the volatility of that approval, and identifying sources of special strength and weakness in support among particular segments of the public.

Dwight D. Eisenhower

Dwight Eisenhower served eight years in the White House in the "quiet" decade of the 1950s and enjoyed remarkably high approval ratings throughout his tenure. The former supreme allied commander never experienced a year in which he did not have on average the approval of a majority of the American public. Indeed, he only served one year as chief executive in which he obtained less than 60 percent average approval!

Eisenhower only fell below 50 percent approval twice. Once was in the recession year of 1958. The second instance occurred in July 1960 in a poll taken immediately after the Democratic National Convention. The next poll, taken only two weeks later, found 63 percent of the public approving Eisenhower's performance in office. It appears that criticism directed at the incumbent administration at the opposition party's convention depressed the president's approval for a very short period.

Eisenhower's approval levels were stable as well as high. In table 3.1 we see his average approval levels on a yearly basis. The high and low averages differed by only 7 percentage points in his first term and by 9 points in his second term. Across the entire eight years, the range was 18 percentage points. Much of this spread was due to the deviant year of 1958, in which his approval was 6 percentage points lower than in any other year.

In table 3.2 we find the high and low approval levels for each year

TABLE 3.1 Average Yearly Approval for Eisenhower (%)

Year	Approval	Disapproval	No Opinion
1953	68	15	17
1954	66	22	12
1955	71	16	13
1956	73	16	11
1957	64	22	14
1958	55	30	15
1959	64	22	14
1960	61	25	14

of Eisenhower's tenure as president. Volatility is greater here than in the yearly averages, of course, but there is still a basic stability to the figures, and, as we have seen, the low figure for 1960 is an aberration. The president consistently maintained the support of the American people for his performance in office.

The average yearly approval levels of various demographic groups are found in table 3.3. There are no significant systematic differences among the gender, age, or religious groups. On the other hand, there are notable differences among racial, regional, union, and educational groups.

Comparing the approval levels of whites and nonwhites, we find that whites gave Eisenhower on the average 11 percentage points more approval

TABLE 3.2 Yearly Extremes of Eisenhower's Approval Ratings (%)

Year	Extreme	Month	Approval
1953	High	March–April, May, August	74
	Low	November	59
1954	High	July	75
	Low	November	57
1955	High	November	78
	Low	March	66
1956	High	December	79
	Low	August	68
1957	High	January	73
	Low	October	57
1958	High	January	60
	Low	March	48
1959	High	December	77
	Low	January	57
1960	High	January	66
	Low	July	49

TABLE 3.3   Average Approval of Demographic Groups for Eisenhower (%)

	Approval							
Group	1953	1954	1955	1956	1957	1958	1959	1960
Male	68	65	71	72	63	53	63	60
Female	69	66	71	73	65	56	65	63
White	69	67	72	74	65	55	65	63
Nonwhite	54	53	63	64	56	50	55	50
East	69	65	71	77	69	59	66	64
Midwest	68	66	72	73	65	57	65	64
South	66	65	68	67	57	46	58	55
West	70	68	75	73	65	56	67	61
Protestant	69	68	72	74	68	55	65	63
Catholic	66	63	67	74	69	56	66	61
Union	62	59	70	69	62	51	59	56
Nonunion	69	69	72	74	67	58	68	63
Grade school	62	60	66	68	60	50	57	57
High school	70	67	72	74	65	55	65	63
College	75	73	79	79	69	61	71	66
Under 30	69	65	70	75	68	57	66	64
30–49	67	64	70	72	64	54	63	60
Over 50	68	69	72	73	63	55	65	62

than nonwhites (shown in table 3.4). This difference is not surprising, given that nonwhites were (and are) disproportionately Democratic. Moreover, the president's reluctance to take a firm stand on support for civil rights likely caused some reluctance on the part of minorities to approve his performance in office.

Although the East, Midwest, and West evaluated the president's job performance similarly, citizens in the South were less supportive, especially after 1955. Since this finding is largely a phenomenon of the second term, it is difficult to attribute it to the predominance of Democratic party identification in the South, which should have affected approval from the beginning. Moreover, Southerners were overwhelmingly conservative and quite accustomed to supporting Republican *presidential* candidates in the 1950s (Eisenhower won 4 of the 11 Confederate states in 1952 and 5 in 1956, including Texas and Florida in both elections). They expressed their party loyalties by supporting Democratic candidates for virtually all other offices.

It is reasonable to argue that regional differences in approval primarily reflected racial matters. The turmoil and hostility in the South engendered by the Supreme Court's *Brown* decision requiring integration of the public

TABLE 3.4   Average Presidental Approval Ratings (%)

	Approval							
	All	DDE	JFK	LBJ	RMN	GRF	JC	RR
National	55	65	71	56	48	47	47	52
Male	56	64	70[a]	57	50	46	46	57
Female	53	66	70	55	47	47	47	48
White	56	66	69	54	51	49	46	57
Nonwhite	46	55	84	75	25	29	54	22
East	55	67	75	63	46	44	46	50
Midwest	55	66	72	56	48	49	46	52
South	53	60	63	49	51	47	50	54
West	55	67	71	55	48	46	44	53
Republican	66	88	49	39	74	67	31	83
Democrat	48	49	84	69	34	36	57	30
Independent	54	67	67	49	48	48	43	54
Protestant	55	66	66	52	52	49	47	54
Catholic	56	64	84	66	45	46	48	53
Union	49	61	77	59	39	41	47	46
Nonunion	53	68	68	51	48	48	47	53
Grade school	50	60	69	56	44	38	48	39
High school	55	66	73	57	48	46	46	51
College	58	71	67	54	52	54	47	59
Under 30	56	66	77	57	46	49	51	54
30–49	55	64	73	56	48	47	46	54
Over 50	53	66	65	54	49	45	45	50

[a] The national average is 71 percent approval, but the average for both sexes is only 70 percent approval because data for each demographic group is not available for all polls.

schools and the resentment of Eisenhower's use of federal troops to implement federal court orders for the integration of Central High School in Little Rock alienated many Southerners. The president's signing of the Civil Rights Acts of 1957 and 1960 only exacerbated animosity toward the White House.

There are also some notable differences in approval between union and nonunion families and among the three educational groupings. Families with union members and people with less education were less supportive of Eisenhower than their counterparts. This is exactly what we would predict given the makeup of the Democratic coalition. Those of lower socioeconomic status were more likely not to approve of the conservative Republican president.

Despite these differences in approval levels, the overall picture of the Eisenhower years is one of public support that is both broad and deep.

Only in the South in 1958 did the president slip below 50 percent approval. Most Americans liked Ike.

John F. Kennedy

Republican Dwight Eisenhower, a conservative in domestic policy, was succeeded by Democrat John F. Kennedy, who was considerably more liberal on a wide range of domestic policy issues. Despite the change in the ideology of the president, he maintained an even higher level of public approval than his predecessor. Kennedy served in office for less than three years, of course, so we cannot know whether he would have enjoyed sustained high approval ratings throughout two terms in office. Yet during his shortened tenure he achieved the highest average approval rating of any chief executive in the post-World War II era—71 percent (shown in table 3.5).

TABLE 3.5   Average Presidential Approval for Entire Terms in Office (%)

President	Approval
Eisenhower	65
Kennedy	71
Johnson	56
Nixon	48
Ford	47
Carter	47
Reagan	52

Kennedy's *lowest* yearly average, shown in table 3.6, was a remarkably high 64 percent approval. He never fell below 56 percent approval in any individual poll, always maintaining the support of a majority of Americans. In addition the range of Kennedy's yearly approval averages over his term was only 12 percentage points.

TABLE 3.6   Average Yearly Approval for Kennedy (%)

Year	Approval	Disapproval	No Opinion
1961	76	10	14
1962	72	17	11
1963	64	24	12

Kennedy's public approval was less stable within years than across them. In table 3.7 we find that, although his public support varied very little in his first year in office, the president faced considerable instability in the public's evaluations in 1962 and 1963. Support over the second and third years of his tenure generally eroded, largely owing to loss of approval in the South associated with racial integration of educational institutions. However, this decline was interrupted by the Cuban missile crisis in October 1962, which gave him a considerable boost in the polls and also increased the volatility of his approval ratings.

TABLE 3.7   Yearly Extremes of Kennedy's Approval Ratings (%)

Year	Extreme	Month	Approval
1961	High	September, November	79
	Low	February, June	72
1962	High	January, March	79
	Low	October	61
1963	High	January	74
	Low	September	56

When we disaggregate the public into demographic groups (see table 3.8), the results are revealing. Although differences between the sexes are minimal, racial differences are significant, especially after the issue of civil rights increases in prominence in 1962 and 1963. Unlike the situation in the previous administration, however, nonwhites are more approving of the president. This undoubtedly reflects both Kennedy's commitment to civil rights and the Democratic party identification of most nonwhites.

The racial issue is also reflected in the erosion of Southern support, especially after the White House proposed a major civil rights bill in 1963. As it was under Eisenhower, the South is the major outlier among the regions, providing the president considerably lower support than the others. The East, on the other hand, accorded the New Englander somewhat greater approval than did the Midwest or the West.

Unlike the 1950s, religion was a discriminating characteristic in Kennedy's years in office. Not surprisingly for the first Catholic president, Catholics are more supportive than Protestants. It is interesting to note that Catholics approved Eisenhower's performance in office as much or more than did Protestants in the first half of 1960. But once Kennedy was nominated, once the issue of his religion came to the forefront, and once he began to attack the incumbent administration and his opponent, Vice President Nixon, Catholics accorded Eisenhower less approval than did

TABLE 3.8 Average Approval of Demographic Groups for Kennedy (%)

	Approval		
Group	1961	1962	1963
Male	77	72	62
Female	74	72	65
White	75	71	60
Nonwhite	80	85	86
East	78	76	71
Midwest	77	73	66
South	72	66	51
West	76	73	65
Protestant	72	67	58
Catholic	87	86	81
Union	83	74	70
Nonunion	75	66	57
Grade school	74	71	63
High school	78	74	66
College	73	67	59
Under 30	80	81	71
30–49	78	75	67
Over 50	71	66	57

Protestants. These differences increased to more than 10 percentage points after the election in November. Apparently Kennedy's coreligionists began rallying to his support before he even entered the White House. In addition, some of the relative lack of Protestant support for Kennedy is probably the result of the lack of support for him in the largely Protestant South and the fact that Catholics were disproportionately Democrats.

Contrary to the case of Eisenhower, education is not a particularly important predictor of presidential approval with Kennedy. Union membership remains a discriminating factor, but with a Democratic president in the White House, union members are more, rather than less, supportive. Once again, some of the difference may be attributable to the president's poor standing in the relatively nonunion South. Differences among age groups in support for the nation's youngest elected president are also evident. Younger citizens, perhaps attracted by Kennedy's vigor and youthfulness, are more supportive than are those over fifty. Part of the explanation for these differences may also be the fact that older voters were more likely to be Republican.

In sum, John F. Kennedy obtained high levels of approval from the

American public. Although the rate was lower at his death than at the beginning of his term, he never averaged less than 50 percent approval with any major socioeconomic segment of the population in any year. None of his successors would come close to matching this record.

Lyndon B. Johnson

Assuming office in the wake of President Kennedy's assassination, Lyndon Johnson began his tenure with the highest approval levels recorded during the period of our study. The shock of the national tragedy unified the nation for a time, and it rallied behind its new leader. Yet by the end of his tenure, Johnson had fallen far below the approval levels of his two predecessors.

Table 3.9 shows that the average yearly approval levels of President Johnson steadily declined throughout his tenure until they leveled off in the low 40s. By 1968 more Americans disapproved than approved of his performance in office. He had lost the approval of fully one-third of the public between 1964 and 1968. Given the turbulent times over which the president presided in the 1960s, with widespread unrest over the war in Vietnam, civil rights, and other social issues, such findings are not surprising.

TABLE 3.9 Average Yearly Approval for Johnson (%)

Year	Approval	Disapproval	No Opinion
1964	74	12	14
1965	66	21	13
1966	51	35	14
1967	44	42	14
1968	42	46	12

The figures in table 3.10 showing the variability of Johnson's support within his years in the Oval Office parallel the data in the preceding table. The president's public support was not stable, and it declined substantially and consistently. Ironically, his March 1968 decision not to seek reelection, which gave him a temporary boost in the polls, may very well have prevented Johnson's approval levels from falling noticeably lower.

The approval levels of groups within the public, shown in table 3.11, reflect patterns similar to those of Johnson's predecessor. Despite the war in Vietnam, which raised questions on the use of force in international relations about which women in later years would be especially sensitive,

TABLE 3.10   Yearly Extremes of Johnson's Approval Ratings (%)

Year	Extreme	Month	Approval
1964	High	February–March	79
	Low	December	69
1965	High	January	71
	Low	November	62
1966	High	January	61
	Low	October, December	44
1967	High	June	51
	Low	September, October	38
1968	High	April	50
	Low	August	35

TABLE 3.11   Average Approval of Demographic Groups for Johnson (%)

| Group | Approval | | | | |
	1964	1965	1966	1967	1968
Male	76	67	53	45	42
Female	74	66	50	43	42
White	74	64	48	42	41
Nonwhite	84	87	76	65	62
East	80	75	61	51	48
Midwest	77	69	50	42	41
South	69	57	44	39	36
West	72	64	49	44	44
Protestant	73	62	46	40	38
Catholic	82	77	63	55	52
Union	78	74	57	48	48
Nonunion	74	64	49	40	41
Grade school	74	66	53	43	44
High school	76	68	52	45	42
College	75	64	48	43	39
Under 30	78	70	55	44	40
30–49	76	68	53	44	42
Over 50	73	64	49	43	43

differences between the sexes in presidential approval were slight.

Race remains a good predictor of approval levels for Johnson. Not only did nonwhites provide higher levels of approval than whites, but they also were more dependable supporters. Although Johnson lost about one-third of his white support over his term, his approval among nonwhites declined by only about one-fourth. The strong legacy of President Johnson in the area of civil rights had a direct payoff in terms of political support.

It also had its costs, however. As in the case of John F. Kennedy, the conservative South, rocked by the tumult over racial integration, gave the president lower support than any other region, while the more liberal East continued to accord him the highest levels of approval. Education levels, on the other hand, exhibited only sporadic differences in approval ratings. Since the more poorly educated South provided relatively low levels of support, the figures for those with different educational backgrounds do not reflect the differences in the core national constituencies of the parties.

The Protestant Johnson continued to receive most of the advantage of his predecessor in obtaining considerably more support from Catholics than from Protestants. Labor union families were also more supportive than those without a union member. As for Kennedy, Johnson's relatively low levels of approval in the South and the traditional identification of Catholics and unions with the Democratic party largely explain these differences. Yet the gap between Catholics and Protestants, which did not occur under Eisenhower, is significant in itself.

Conversely, the disparities among age groups from which Kennedy benefited slowly faded under Johnson. As the war in Vietnam escalated, the president lost the extra increment of support he had once enjoyed from younger citizens.

President Johnson's relationship with the public was a stormy one. Although he began his tenure with an extended honeymoon, he ended it with nearly half the public disapproving of his performance in office. It was this lack of support that undermined his ability to govern and eventually drove him from office. He was not to be the last president to endure such tribulations, however.

Richard M. Nixon

If lack of public support preempted Lyndon Johnson's bid for reelection, it had even more damaging consequences for the presidency of Richard Nixon. Ultimately, low levels of approval forced Nixon's resignation and prevented him from waging an effective battle against efforts to impeach him.

Although Nixon ended his tenure lower in the polls than any president since approval ratings were initiated in the 1930s, his time in office, contrary to conventional wisdom, was not characterized by weak approval ratings. As we can see in table 3.12, the president enjoyed quite respectable average levels of approval in his first term; 50 percent was the lowest average he experienced in any year. It was not until Watergate broke as a major issue in 1973 that his public support dropped precipitously.

TABLE 3.12   Average Yearly Approval for Nixon (%)

Year	Approval	Disapproval	No Opinion
1969	61	17	22
1970	57	29	14
1971	50	37	13
1972	56	33	11
1973	42	47	11
1974	26	62	12

Table 3.13 presents the range of Nixon's approval ratings in each year of his tenure. Aside from 1973, when fallout from the Watergate scandal cost him most of his support, the figures reflect a reasonably stable base of approval; 13 percentage points is the largest difference between highest and lowest levels. In 1971 and 1972 he barely dipped below the 50 percent mark for his lowest ratings of that period. Indeed, his pre-Watergate support was substantial enough that he began his second term at a point equal to the highest level of approval he received in his entire first term (in 1969)—67 percent.

TABLE 3.13   Yearly Extremes of Nixon's Approval Ratings (%)

Year	Extreme	Month	Approval
1969	High	November	67
	Low	October	56
1970	High	January-February	64
	Low	September	51
1971	High	January	56
	Low	June	48
1972	High	May, November	62
	Low	January	49
1973	High	January	67
	Low	October, November	27
1974	High	February, May–June, June–July	28
	Low	July, August	24

The careful reader might note that Nixon's approval levels in 1971 and 1973 closely resemble those of Lyndon Johnson in his third and fifth years in office. Yet when we disaggregate the data into the various demographic groups in table 3.14, we find that the sources of his support were quite different.

TABLE 3.14   Average Approval of Demographic Groups for Nixon (%)

Group	Approval					
	1969	1970	1971	1972	1973	1974
Male	63	59	51	59	42	27
Female	60	55	49	55	41	25
White	63	60	53	60	45	28
Nonwhite	39	28	26	28	18	10
East	58	55	50	55	38	22
Midwest	62	55	49	55	42	26
South	64	60	52	60	45	30
West	60	59	48	54	42	25
Protestant	65	60	54	61	47	31
Catholic	59	54	47	55	38	20
Union	56	53	42	48	35	19
Nonunion	63	64	52	60	44	28
Grade school	54	51	45	51	38	26
High school	62	57	50	57	42	25
College	67	62	55	61	44	27
Under 30	64	56	47	52	38	22
30–49	61	58	51	56	42	25
Over 50	61	57	52	58	44	29

Differences between the sexes in support for Nixon were small, but racial differences were quite large, averaging 26 percentage points during his tenure in office. Unlike Democrats in the White House, however, Nixon's support among nonwhites was very low; it never rose above 39 percent approval. The strong partisanship of nonwhites and their perception of Nixon as not strongly committed to enforcing civil rights apparently took a toll on their support for him.

At the same time, Nixon benefited from solid approval in the South. His open appeals to social and political conservatism and his reluctance to exercise overt pressure on racial matters won him more support in the South than in any other region. Indeed, he was the first president in our study to achieve his greatest support in the South. Moreover, his absolute

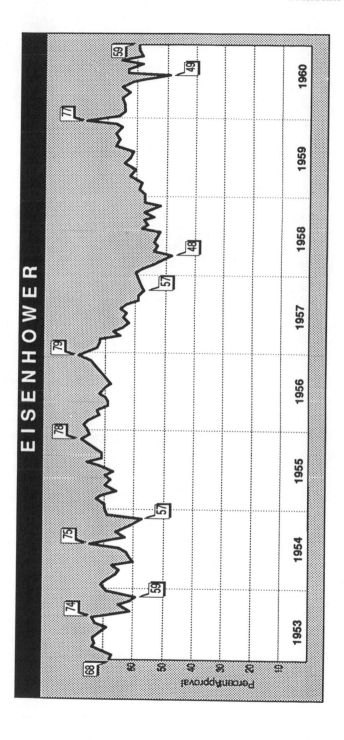

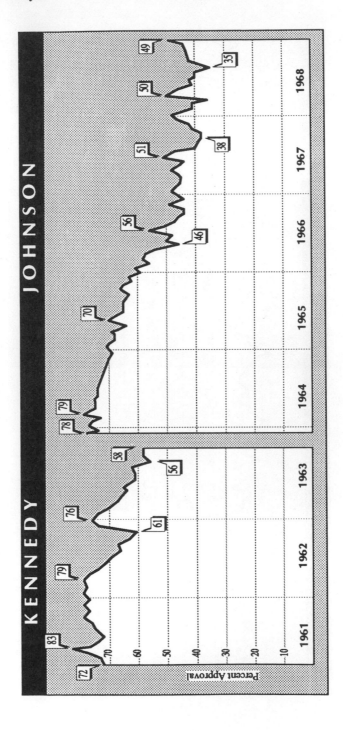

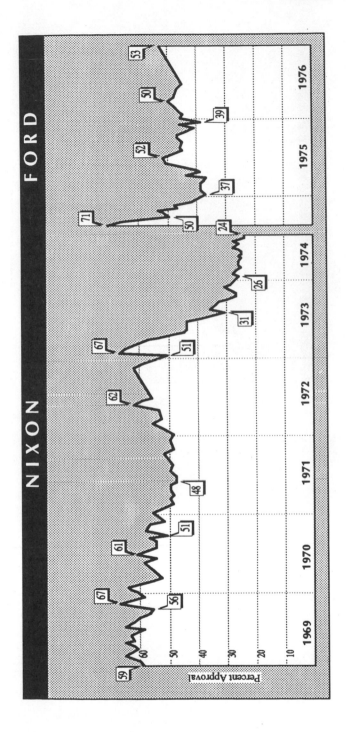

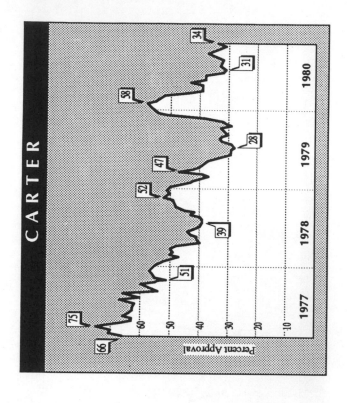

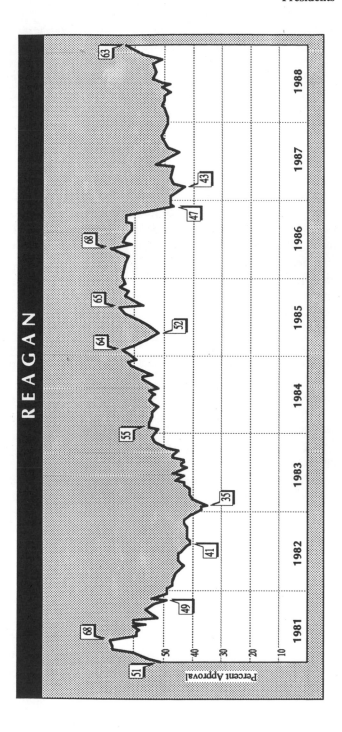

levels of approval in the South exceeded those of Southerner Lyndon Johnson in the second, third, fourth, and fifth years of their terms.

The differences among groups defined by religion, union membership, and education appear to be a reflection of the classic coalitions that compose the constituencies of the two parties. Protestants, nonunion families, and those with higher education were all more likely to be Republican and were all more likely to approve of Nixon's performance in office. The president's relatively strong support in the largely Protestant South also helped bolster the religious differences.

Age is another matter. Differences do not appear until 1971, when younger citizens became the least supportive age group. Although young people at the time were more likely to identify themselves as Democrats, the impact of partisanship was not evident in 1969 and 1970. Doubtless they became more alienated than other age groups by the continuation of the war in Vietnam and the White House's sometimes strident attacks on social liberalism.

Richard Nixon is a controversial figure in American history. Yet until the Watergate scandal broke, he experienced a significant degree of support from the public. Although there were signs of polarization in public opinion, they were fewer than we might expect from a chief executive famous for his contentious approach to politics and his hostility toward opponents.

Gerald R. Ford

Like Lyndon Johnson, Gerald Ford began his tenure with approval ratings bolstered by national unity in the wake of tragedy. The public's relief that the "long national nightmare" of Watergate was over offered the nation's first nonelected president a potentially significant advantage. Unlike Johnson's, however, Ford's honeymoon with the public was short-lived.

Ford's approval ratings were typically quite modest, as we can see in table 3.15. Only in the last few months of 1974 did he average majority approval. For 1975 and 1976 he was not supported on the average by a

TABLE 3.15 Average Yearly Approval for Ford (%)

Year	Approval	Disapproval	No Opinion
1974	54	26	20
1975	43	40	17
1976	48	39	13

majority of the public. His pardon of Richard Nixon tied him inextricably to Watergate, from which he never recovered.

The new president experienced tremendous volatility in his first two months in office. Within a few months his support fell 29 points (shown in table 3.16), mostly in response to his pardon of his predecessor. Afterwards, his approval stabilized somewhat. The next year the range of his approval was 15 percentage points, and the following year it was only 8.

TABLE 3.16   Yearly Extremes of Ford's Approval Ratings (%)

Year	Extreme	Month	Approval
1974	High	August	71
	Low	December	42
1975	High	June	52
	Low	January, March	37
1976	High	December	53
	Low	January, June	45

Differences in approval of Ford's job performance among groups in the population, shown in table 3.17, were less than those for Nixon, no doubt partially as a result of the new president's lower overall support, which reduced the potential for substantial differences. Sex, as usual, was not a discriminating characteristic, but the other variables reflected at least some differences in approval.

Whites were more approving than nonwhites, although Ford averaged slightly more support from the latter than did his predecessor, despite his lower overall approval. The gap between the two groups was smaller than under Nixon. With less racial polarization and with civil rights a less salient issue in Ford's administration, the advantage of stronger approval from the South enjoyed by Nixon evaporated. Instead, the president's native Midwest accorded him the highest support among the regions, although the differences were typically not great.

Protestants and nonunion families were a bit more supportive of Ford than Catholics and union families, but the differences were modest and in the direction we would expect on the basis of the party leanings of the groups. Similarly, and not unexpectedly for a Republican president, the more educated the group, the more likely it was to approve of Ford's handling of his job as president. Younger citizens were again somewhat more supportive of the president now that the war in Vietnam was over.

Gerald Ford assumed the presidency under unusually traumatic cir-

TABLE 3.17   Average Approval of Demographic Groups for Ford (%)

Group	Approval		
	1974	1975	1976
Male	53	42	48
Female	55	43	48
White	56	46	50
Nonwhite	38	25	31
East	51	41	43
Midwest	57	45	51
South	53	44	48
West	54	42	49
Protestant	57	45	50
Catholic	53	42	46
Union	49	38	40
Nonunion	55	45	50
Grade school	48	33	40
High school	53	42	47
College	60	51	53
Under 30	56	46	50
30–49	53	44	47
Over 50	53	40	47

cumstances and without the benefit of running on a national ticket. His pardon of Richard Nixon lost him the goodwill of a substantial segment of the American people, and he had to struggle for support throughout his term. In this environment, his average of 47 percent approval may be viewed as respectable if unimpressive.

Jimmy Carter

Jimmy Carter did not enjoy strong backing from the American people. Coming to office as an outsider who would establish a fresh relationship between the White House and the American people after the scandal of Watergate, he and his supporters had high hopes of developing a national consensus around clean, efficient government acting in the public interest. The public soon soured on Carter, however, and he became the first elected incumbent since Herbert Hoover a half century earlier to lose his bid for reelection.

It did not take long for the American public to find fault with Carter's performance in office. As we can see in table 3.18, he received approval from a majority of the people only in his first year in office. His average support for the last half of his term was less than 40 percent, and it would have been lower except for the boost he received from the Iranian hostage crisis.

TABLE 3.18   Average Yearly Approval for Carter (%)

Year	Approval	Disapproval	No Opinion
1977	62	20	18
1978	46	38	16
1979	37	49	14
1980	41	49	10

Carter's approval levels were not only unimpressive, they were also volatile, as shown in table 3.19. The range of his approval across his administration averaged 23 percentage points per year. Sixteen percentage points was the smallest difference between his highest and lowest approval levels in a given year. Thus, much of his support was ephemeral, not based on an intensely committed constituency.

TABLE 3.19   Yearly Extremes of Carter's Approval Ratings (%)

Year	Extreme	Month	Approval
1977	High	March	75
	Low	October	51
1978	High	January	55
	Low	July, August	39
1979	High	December	54
	Low	June–July	28
1980	High	January	58
	Low	June, November	31

The approval of demographic groups for the Georgian appears in table 3.20. Differences among the sexes are not significant, but racial differences remain noteworthy. Carter's advantage among nonwhites is much less than that of his Democratic predecessors, however. Over his term nonwhites averaged only 8 percentage points more approval than whites, and they gave him much lower absolute levels of support than they accorded Kennedy or Johnson. Although the president was committed to enforcing civil rights protections, his administration was not characterized by a push for new statutes. The legislation of the 1960s already provided substantial legal protection against racial discrimination. Moreover, Carter, the first modern Democratic president to have to deal with the politics of scarcity, was not in a position to propose the creation or expansion of expensive social welfare policies.

TABLE 3.20   Average Approval of Demographic Groups for Carter (%)

	Approval			
Group	1977	1978	1979	1980
Male	63	46	36	39
Female	62	45	37	42
White	62	44	36	40
Nonwhite	67	55	44	49
East	64	46	35	38
Midwest	61	44	36	41
South	64	48	41	46
West	60	43	34	36
Protestant	63	46	37	42
Catholic	66	48	37	41
Union	64	47	36	40
Nonunion	63	45	37	41
Grade school	58	50	39	45
High school	61	45	36	41
College	67	44	37	38
Under 30	68	50	40	43
30–49	63	45	36	38
Over 50	58	43	36	41

The depolarization of racial politics and Carter's Southern heritage undoubtedly helped him win his highest regional approval levels from the South. The differences among the regions were not large, however. Continuing the pattern begun in Kennedy's tenure and interrupted by the war in Vietnam, younger voters were somewhat more supportive than their seniors.

The figures for religion and union membership reveal no differences in evaluation of Carter's job performance. This is significant, because it reflects the loss of the advantages Democratic presidents had enjoyed with Catholics and union families. This pattern goes beyond presidential approval, however, and reaches to voting behavior in presidential elections as well. In addition, it is possible that Carter's conspicuous identification as a born-again Southern Baptist made some Catholics dubious about him.

The figures for education paint a clouded picture. In his first year in office the president enjoyed considerably higher approval from the most highly educated group, but after this the pattern changed to slightly more support from those with less education, as we might expect for a Democratic president. As is often the case, citizens with lower levels of education were reluctant to express an opinion about a president's performance in his first year in office. The "no opinion" response from this group averaged 24 percent in 1977, about one-fourth of those in the grade school education category.

Jimmy Carter, like his predecessor, averaged less than majority approval (47 percent) across his term in office. His Southern roots were useful in winning the presidency, but he was not able to retain the strong support of traditionally Democratic groups in the public. Limited by his own leadership style and the traditional orientations of his party, he could not redirect the Democratic coalition in an era of scarce resources. The party would not come to terms with the dominant features of the policy-making environment until the presidential election of 1984.

Ronald Reagan

Ronald Reagan's standing with the American people is legendary. In contrast to his two immediate predecessors, the public viewed him as a strong leader, and he overwhelmingly won a second term in office. This seeming love affair with the public generated commentary in the media about his ability to deflect criticism and project a favorable image. Some referred to him as the "Teflon president." As is true of much of the remembered past, however, the myth of Reagan's public support has significant fallacies. Actually, there was as much fission as fusion in his relations with the public.

President Reagan's yearly averages are shown in table 3.21. The average approval in all the polls taken in his eight years in office was 52 percent. On the whole, this is not an impressive record. As we can see in table 3.5, Reagan's approval levels fall in the middle of those of the seven presidents covered in this study and are closer to the low than the high end. Reagan did not obtain an average of even majority approval in three of the eight years. Thus, there is less than meets the eye to the myth of his strong public backing.

Reagan's support was not especially firm. In table 3.22 we can see that the ebb and flow of public approval in his two terms in office was relatively volatile. The range of his approval levels averaged 14 percentage points per year, and in 1981, 1983, and 1986 it averaged 19 to 21 percentage

TABLE 3.21   Average Yearly Approval for Reagan (%)

Year	Approval	Disapproval	No Opinion
1981	58	28	14
1982	44	46	10
1983	44	46	10
1984	55	36	9
1985	60	31	9
1986	61	29	10
1987	48	43	9
1988	52	38	10

points. There is certainly no evidence here of a Teflon-coated presidency invulnerable to the shifts in public opinion experienced by other presidents. Although Reagan did not sustain the low levels of approval experienced by Richard Nixon and Jimmy Carter, he also did not attain the heights of Eisenhower, Kennedy, or Johnson (thus the relatively low standard deviation of his approval levels, shown in table 1.3).

There are slight differences among the average approval levels for Reagan of Protestants and Catholics, those in various age groups (at least in the first term), and residents of each major region in the country (shown in table 3.23). At first glance these results may appear to support the

TABLE 3.22   Yearly Extremes of Reagan's Approval Ratings (%)

Year	Extreme	Month	Approval
1981	High	May	68
	Low	November, December	49
1982	High	January	49
	Low	July–August, August, December	41
1983	High	December	54
	Low	January	35
1984	High	November–December	62
	Low	January, May, July	52
1985	High	August, November	65
	Low	April	52
1986	High	May	68
	Low	December	47
1987	High	June	53
	Low	March	43
1988	High	December	63
	Low	May, June	48

hypothesis of a partisan realignment, with conservative Catholics, Southerners, and young voters moving into the Republican fold. Yet President Reagan's last three Republican predecessors—Eisenhower, Nixon, and Ford—also experienced reasonably uniform approval levels among these groups. Thus, the president's social conservatism, vocal anticommunism, and image as a strong leader do not seem to have altered the basic contour of approval of Republican presidents among these groups.

TABLE 3.23   Average Approval of Demographic Groups for Reagan (%)

	Approval							
Group	1981	1982	1983	1984	1985	1986	1987	1988
Male	62	48	49	59	64	65	53	57
Female	53	40	39	52	57	57	44	47
White	63	49	49	60	64	64	52	56
Nonwhite	21	14	16	20	32	35	22	26
East	55	41	40	51	58	61	46	51
Midwest	59	45	45	54	60	59	48	51
South	58	43	44	58	62	61	51	55
West	59	47	47	57	61	61	47	48
Protestant	59	46	46	58	61	62	50	53
Catholic	59	44	44	56	62	64	48	53
Union	54	36	38	48	53	55	41	44
Nonunion	59	46	45	57	61	63	48	53
Grade school	41	32	31	40	42	46	39	44
High school	58	42	42	53	58	60	46	51
College	65	52	53	62	66	67	52	54
Under 30	56	43	44	57	64	65	52	57
30–49	60	45	45	57	61	63	50	52
Over 50	56	43	43	53	56	54	43	49

Polarization is evident in the very large differences among the approval levels of groups with different levels of education, perhaps our best indicator of social class. Twenty percentage points separate the approval levels of the most and least educated groups, by far the largest gap to be found among the presidents in our study (shown in table 3.4). A smaller (7 percentage points) but nevertheless significant gap separates the support of union and nonunion households. These differences undoubtedly reflect the varying responses of different social classes to the president's policies and the predominant party identifications among the groups. The presence of such dissimilarities, but not their size, is consistent with results for previous Republican presidents. It is also significant that in Reagan's second term voters at or near retirement age accorded the president noticeably less approval than younger citizens, perhaps owing to concern about threats to social security from the president's posture of fiscal austerity toward domestic programs.

The differences between the subgroups are particularly interesting, and particularly sharp, in the categories of race and sex. The 35 percentage point difference between whites and nonwhites is unprecedented, larger than even the gaps during the Nixon administration. Because the differences between racial groups under both Eisenhower and Ford were much smaller than under Reagan, we know that extreme racial polarization is not inherent in a Republican presidency. Nevertheless, the president's openly conservative approach to civil rights and social welfare policy issues seems to have exacerbated the tendencies of racial minorities to disapprove of Republicans in the White House.

Finally, there is the "gender gap." For all other recent presidents, with the exception of a few polls under Nixon, the differences in approval levels of men and women have been negligible. For Reagan, however, there is a consistent 9 percentage point average difference, with males clearly more supportive of the president.

"Women's issues," especially the Equal Rights Amendment and abortion, do not play a major role in the gender gap; men and women have supported these policies in about equal percentages.[1] (It may be, however, that this similarity masks a more substantial impact of these issues on women's presidential approval because of their greater salience to women.)

Reactions to fundamental issues of economic and foreign policy lie at the core of the gender gap. Women consistently rated Reagan less favorably than men on his handling of both the economy and foreign policy.[2] Women are often in more vulnerable economic positions than men and thus more susceptible to economic downturns or reductions in domestic social welfare policy expenditures. In addition, in comparison with men women frequently show a greater concern for fairness, are more compassionate toward the disadvantaged, and are more concerned about international conflict.[3] Reagan's palpably hard-line conservatism may have caused the gender gap to surface for the first time during his administration.

The polarization of the public's evaluation of Ronald Reagan is especially clear in the figures for the approval of party groups. (The yearly averages are shown in table 1.2.) Ronald Reagan's average support among Republicans was 83 percent, ranging from 94 percent to 67 percent in individual polls. The figures are dramatically different for Democrats, however. Their average support was only 30 percent, with a high of 52 percent and a low of just 17 percent in individual polls. Independents, as we would expect, fall between the partisan groups with a 54 percent average.

What is most interesting about these figures is the difference between the support of the two parties. The public was polarized along party lines in Ronald Reagan's tenure more than under any president in our study. Between 1953 and 1980 the absolute difference in approval levels between Democrats and Republicans was a substantial 35 percentage points. Independents fell in between, averaging 17 percentage points difference from Democrats and 18 percentage points from Republicans. During Reagan's time in office, however, the gap between Democrats and Republicans widened to 53 percentage points. Independents, still in the middle, on the average approved the president 24 percentage points more than Democrats and 29 points less than Republicans.

This partisan gap is not the result of abnormally high levels of approval among Republicans. In fact, President Reagan had lower approval levels among Republicans than Eisenhower in either of his terms or Nixon in his first term. Only in the Watergate-marred period of 1973–76 have Republican presidents received lower average approval levels than Ronald Reagan from the Republican rank and file. The real cause of the sizable differences between the parties is the unusually low approval levels among Democrats. Even Richard Nixon averaged 42 percent approval among Democrats in his first term, and in 1973–76 Nixon and Ford averaged 30 percent approval.

Prior to Reagan, it had been Republicans rather than Democrats who tended to give presidents of the opposition party very low approval levels, especially in 1967–68 and 1978–80. Yet in these years Democrats awarded the president low approval levels as well; their average approval never reached even 60 percent for a year. Thus, members of both parties gave Johnson and Carter low support. In Reagan's case, however, clear bifurcation of evaluations reflects, but also exaggerates, the underlying partisan loyalties of the public. Partisan identification has always affected how people perceive and react to the president and the events and conditions by which they evaluate him. Under Reagan it became even more salient.

Ronald Reagan was less of a public relations phenomenon than many believe. Rather than uniting the public behind him or developing new bases of support, he increased its polarization along partisan, class, racial, and sexual lines. At the same time, he was able to maintain more support on the average than did his three immediate predecessors while leading the country in what some considered to be radical new directions in public policy. This was no small achievement.

Presidents do not appeal equally to all groups in the public. Each of the presidents in this study has experienced a different pattern of public support. There has been a considerable range in both the levels and the volatility of presidential approval (averages are shown in tables 3.24 and 3.25), and each president has had sources of special strength and weakness in support among particular segments of the public.

TABLE 3.24   High Points of Approval Ratings (%)

	Approval						
	DDE	*JFK*	*LBJ*	*RMN*	*GRF*	*JC*	*RR*
National	79	83	79	67	71	75	68
Male	79	81	80	71	70	75	74
Female	80	81	79	66	71	74	65
White	79	80	79	69	74	73	74
Nonwhite	77	95	95	49	62	85	45
East	81	83	84	66	67	73	69
Midwest	80	82	81	71	76	74	74
South	75	81	76	70	71	79	72
West	81	84	81	72	66	74	68
Republican	95	67	78	91	77	60	94
Democrat	67	92	87	56	68	84	52
Independent	82	80	76	72	70	73	75
Protestant	79	76	78	71	71	74	69
Catholic	79	91	87	70	73	78	74
Union	79	85	81	67	66	77	66
Nonunion	79	76	78	69	71	79	70
Grade school	75	80	77	66	66	69	58
High school	80	83	81	70	68	76	69
College	85	80	85	74	80	77	76
Under 30	81	88	84	70	70	77	74
30–49	78	83	81	67	69	77	72
Over 50	80	76	81	71	74	71	68

TABLE 3.25   Low Points of Approval Ratings (%)

	Approval						
	DDE	*JFK*	*LBJ*	*RMN*	*GRF*	*JC*	*RR*
National	48	56	35	24	37	28	35
Male	46	54	35	23	35	27	39
Female	50	58	34	21	38	28	32
White	49	53	32	26	40	28	39
Nonwhite	34	68	49	6	19	30	9
East	50	64	39	19	31	25	29
Midwest	51	58	31	21	36	25	35
South	36	33	30	26	36	30	35
West	49	56	33	19	33	23	35
Republican	79	30	19	48	57	12	67
Democrat	28	71	48	11	28	34	17
Independent	51	52	21	22	35	20	34
Protestant	50	51	33	28	40	29	36
Catholic	49	77	40	16	34	28	36
Union	45	69	36	16	23	24	25
Nonunion	51	57	34	25	38	29	37
Grade school	43	53	36	20	26	28	16
High school	49	58	33	22	35	26	35
College	55	49	30	22	42	22	43
Under 30	45	63	29	17	37	26	36
30–49	47	58	34	22	36	24	33
Over 50	47	51	35	25	34	26	33

PART THREE
Appendixes

APPENDIX A

The Evolution of the Gallup Poll's Presidential Approval Question

Gallup's early efforts to develop some kind of presidential "popularity" rating to reveal how Americans felt about Franklin Delano Roosevelt were confined to questions concerning whether they would vote for him again rather than whether they liked him or the job he was doing. Initially, the questions asked which candidate—Roosevelt or one of his challengers—respondents would vote for at the next presidential election or, alternatively, if they planned to vote for or against Roosevelt. Later, the question was changed to ask whether respondents would vote for or against FDR if a presidential election were held "today"—the day the poll was taken.

By August 1937, however, Gallup had abandoned the voting intention-type questions in favor of questions more akin to the current approach. At that time, Gallup started asking a sample of Americans whether they were "for or against Roosevelt today" (see table A.1).

A year later, in August 1938, Gallup first used the approve/disapprove dichotomy, asking respondents, "In general, do you approve or disapprove of President Roosevelt?" (A week later the word "today" was added to the question.)

In October 1938, the question was further modified to ask, "Do you approve or disapprove today of Roosevelt as president?"

Because of some evidence that this question measured approval or disapproval of Roosevelt personally as well as approval or disapproval of his performance in office, the question was changed three years later (May 1941) to emphasize FDR's performance. The resulting question read, "Do you approve or disapprove of the way Roosevelt is handling his job as president today?" Except for the inclusion of the word "today," which was dropped in May 1945, this is the question that Gallup has used for half a century to measure how the public rates the presidents. It has become the standard presidential approval question in the polling industry.

TABLE A.1   Evolution of the Gallup Poll's Presidential Approval Question

---

August 2, 1937
Are you for or against Roosevelt today?

August 10, 1938
In general, do you approve or disapprove of President Roosevelt?

August 16, 1938
In general, do you approve or disapprove of President Roosevelt today?

October 17, 1938
In general, do you approve or disapprove today of Roosevelt as president?

May 20, 1941
Do you approve or disapprove of the way Roosevelt is handling his job as president today?

May 29, 1945
Do you approve or disapprove of the way Truman is handling his job as president?

It should be pointed out that, in developing the presidential approval questions, Gallup regularly ran split-sample tests to determine if the cited questions as well as a number of others produced different results. Other questions tested included: "Are you for Roosevelt today?" "In general, are you satisfied today with Roosevelt as president?" "In general, do you approve of the Roosevelt administration, today?"

APPENDIX B

Questions on Demographics

Sex and Race
Check (record) whether:

White man	Nonwhite/Black/ Negro/Colored man	Hispanic man	Oriental man
White woman	Nonwhite/Black/ Negro/Colored woman	Hispanic woman	Oriental woman

Region
Questionnaire precoded by sampling point for state and region

Politics
In politics, as of today, do you consider yourself a Republican, Democrat, or Independent? [This wording was introduced July 2, 1953.]
Republican   Democrat   Independent   Other party

Religion
What is your religious preference—Protestant, Catholic, or Jewish?
Protestant   Catholic   Jewish   Other   None

Labor Union
Are you (or is your husband/wife) a member of a labor union?
    Yes, I am.
    Yes, both are.
    Yes, he/she is.
    No.

Education
What is the last grade or class you completed in school?
    None, or grades 1–4
    Grades 5, 6, 7
    Grade 8
    High school incomplete, grades 9–11

High school graduate, grade 12
Technical, trade or business
College, university, incomplete
College, university graduate

Age
And what is your age? _____

APPENDIX C
Sampling, Weighting, and Sampling Tolerances

Personal Interview Sample

Sample Design

The sampling procedure used for the personal interview surveys in this study provides for interviewing in over three hundred sampling locations and was designed to produce an approximation of the adult civilian population living in the United States, except those persons in institutions such as prisons or hospitals. Persons in the eighteen- to twenty-year-old group were first included in the sample in June 1971 when the Twenty-sixth Amendment to the Constitution, according this group the right to vote, was ratified.

The design of the sample is that of a replicated, probability sample, down to the block level in the case of urban areas and to segments of townships in the case of rural areas.

The current sample design includes stratification by these seven size-of-community strata, using 1980 census data: (a) incorporated cities of population 1,000,000 and over; (b) incorporated cities of population 250,000 to 999,999; (c) incorporated cities of population 50,000 to 249,999; (d) urbanized cities not included in (a)-(c); (e) cities over 2,500 population outside of urbanized areas; (f) towns and villages with less than 2,500 population; and (g) rural places not included within town boundaries. Each of these strata are further stratified into four geographical regions: East, Midwest, South, and West. Within each city size-regional stratum, the population is arrayed in geographic order and zoned into sampling units of equal size. Pairs of localities are selected in each zone, with probability of selection and each locality proportional to its population size in the most recent census, producing two replicated sample of localities.

Within each selected subdivision for which block statistics are available, a sample of blocks or block clusters is drawn with probability of selection proportional to the number of dwelling units. In all other subdivisions or areas, blocks or segments are drawn at random or with equal probability.

In each cluster of blocks and each segment so selected, a randomly selected starting point is designated on the interviewer's map of the area. Starting at this point, interviewers are required to follow a given direction in the selection of households until their assignment is complete.

Interviewing is conducted at times when adults in general are most likely to be at home, which means on weekends, or if on weekdays, after 4:00 P.M. Allowance for persons not at home is made by a "times at home" weighting procedure, which is a standard method for reducing the sample bias that would otherwise result from underrepresentation in the sample of persons who are difficult to find at home.[1]

Weighting Procedures

The procedures for weighting the survey data collected are designed to reinforce the projectability of the data, the more basic foundation for which is supplied by area probability sampling procedures. More specifically, by assigning an individual weight to each respondent in the survey based on his or her particular combination of demographic characteristics (and hence assigning a weight to his or her answers in any tabulation of the survey data), the Gallup Organization guards against a variety of possible errors, both random and systematic, that might otherwise impair the generalizability of survey results.

The weighting of this personal data is a three-step procedure. The first step is to compute a "times-at-home" weight for each respondent that is based on the estimated probability that the respondent would be found at home at the time when the interview was completed. This weighting is designed to correct bias that might result from underrepresentation of respondents who are relatively unlikely to be found at home during normal interviewing hours.

The second weighting step uses a demographically based sample balancing (iterative marginal fitting) program. By using a statistical algorithm (suggested by demographic statistician W. E. Deming in his book *Statistical Adjustment of Data* [New York: Wiley, 1943]), the overall (marginal) distributions of several variables may be adjusted by assigning weights to individual respondents in order to bring all the distributions into alignment with population parameters, or "true distributions," of these variables. The Gallup Organization uses the most recent national data available from the Bureau of the Census for sex, race, region, age, and education.

The weights output by this program for individual respondents have two limitations. The program only fits marginal distributions to census parameters (e.g., it requires the proportion of women in the weighted sample to correspond to the Census Bureau's best estimate of the proportion of women in the adult population and does the same for four categories of education, but it does not take into account the nature of the relationship between sex and education). Moreover, it sets no limitations on the permissible size of the final weights. This latter aspect is important because it seems unreasonable to assign any particular interview very much more weight than any other interview. Both of these limitations are addressed in the third stage of weighting.

The third and final weighting step is again demographically based, but it is a ratio estimation procedure that takes both marginal distributions and interrelationships among demographic variables into account. For this purpose a full weighting matrix of region by sex by age by education is derived from Current Population Survey information. This procedure incorporates the times-at-home weight and the weight derived from the sample balancing procedure as input (or beginning) values. Finally, it allows the specification of a range of weights that may not be exceeded. The weights assigned to an individual respondent upon the completion of weighting are usually restricted to range between 1.0 and 4.0.

Note on "Times at Home"

In these surveys interviewers made one attempt to contact a qualified respondent. Given this level of effort to reach a respondent at home, persons infrequently at home tend to be underrepresented. Since they are less often at home, there is less chance of catching them at home. Similarly, persons usually at home tend to be overrepresented because the chances of finding them at home when the call is made are very good.

To correct for the differential probability of inclusion in the sample of respondents frequently at home versus those infrequently at home, a weighting is used. This respondent-specific weight is a function of the estimated probability of each respondent's being at home at the time the interview was actually conducted. Specifically, the weight is the reciprocal of the probability of being at home; the "at-homeness" probability is estimated by asking each respondent whether he or she was home at the time of day of the interview on other days when interviewing might have occurred.

For example, if a respondent was interviewed on a Saturday afternoon, and indicated in response to specific questions that he or she was at home on the three other occasions asked about, that respondent is assigned an estimated "at-homeness" probability of 1.0 (i.e., at home four out of four possible times, at home on this Saturday and three previous Saturdays asked about, or 4/4 = 1.0). The reciprocal of 1.0 is 1.0, so the times-at-home weight for this respondent would be 1.0.

Consider a second case in which a respondent interviewed at a given time reported being at home at that same time on only one of three other dates. This respondent would be assigned an estimated "at-homeness" probability of 0.5; that is, he or she was at home on two of four possible times (for the interview and on one other date). The reciprocal of 0.5 is 2.0, which is the times-at-home weight assigned to this respondent.

In a similar manner, one could compute probabilities of "at-homeness" and use the reciprocals as times-at-home weights for respondents at home on one of four dates (P = 0.25, wt. = 0.4) and respondents at home on three of four dates (P = 0.75, wt. = 1.33).

Using this method, respondents rarely at home are given larger weights, and the representation of rarely at home respondents in the weighted sample is increased.

It is important to keep in mind that this times-at-home weight is not used by itself. Other weighting factors are combined with the times-at-home weight to produce a final weight for each respondent.

Telephone Sample

Sample Design

The Gallup Organization's standard national telephone samples are unclustered, random-digit-dial (RDD) samples, based on a proportionate stratified sampling design.

The random digit aspect of the sample is used to avoid "listing" bias. According to the most recent estimates from the Bureau of the Census, there are 90.8 million households in the United States, and just over 92 percent of them contain one or more telephones. Telephone directories only list about 71 percent of such "telephone households," and numerous studies have shown that households with unlisted telephone numbers are different in several important ways from listed households. Moreover, nearly 15 percent of listed telephone numbers are "discontinued" owing to household mobility and directory publishing lag, and it is reasonable to assume that a roughly equal number of working residential numbers are too new to be found in published directories.

In order to avoid these various sources of bias, a random-digit procedure designed to provide representation of both listed and unlisted (including not-yet-listed) numbers is used. The design of the sample ensures this representation by random generation of the last two digits of telephone numbers selected on the basis of their area code, telephone exchange (the first three digits of a seven-digit telephone number), and bank number (the fourth and fifth digits).

The selection procedure produces a sample that is superior to random selection from a frame of listed telephone households, and the superiority is greater to the degree that the assignment of telephone numbers to households is made independently of their publication status in the directory. That is, if unlisted numbers tend to be found in the same telephone banks as listed numbers and if, in general, banks containing relatively few listed numbers also contain relatively few unlisted numbers, then the sample that results from the procedure described below will represent unlisted telephone households as fully as it represents listed households. Random number selection within banks ensures that all numbers within a particular bank (whether listed or unlisted) have the same likelihood of inclusion in the sample, and that the sample so generated will represent listed and unlisted telephone households in the appropriate proportions.

A data base of listed telephone numbers for the continental United States is geographically stratified, and a sample of listed "seed" numbers is drawn so that states, counties, and telephone exchanges are represented in their appropriate proportions. That is, the number of telephone numbers randomly sampled from within a given exchange is proportional to that exchange's share of listed telephone households in the set of exchanges from which the sample is drawn.

Only working banks of numbers are used for the selection of seed numbers. A working bank is defined as 100 numerally sequential telephone numbers containing three or more residential telephone listings. By eliminating nonworking banks of numbers from the sample, the likelihood that any sampled telephone number will be associated with a residence increases from only 20 percent (where all banks of numbers are sampled) to between 60 and 70 percent. The sample of telephone numbers produced by this method is thus designed to provide an unbiased random sampling of telephone households in the continental United States.

Within each contacted household, an interview is sought with the youngest man eighteen years old or older who is at home. If no man is at home, an interview is sought with the oldest woman eighteen or older who is at home. The time of day and the day of the week for callbacks is varied so as to maximize the chances of finding a respondent at home.

All interviews are conducted on weekends or weekday evenings so that potential respondents who work full-time can be contacted. Overall quotas are set for males and females in order to ensure that the gender distribution approximates census bureau estimates.

Weighting Procedures

The final sample is weighted so that the region by age by sex by education distribution and the region by sex by race distribution of the sample matches current estimates derived from the U.S. Census Bureau's Current Population Survey for the adult population living in telephone households in the continental United States.

Sampling Tolerances

In interpreting survey results, it should be borne in mind that all sample surveys are subject to sampling error—that is, the extent to which the results may differ from what would be obtained if the whole population surveyed had been interviewed. The size of such sampling errors depends largely on the number of interviews.

The following tables may be used in estimating the sampling error of any percentage in this study. The computed allowances have taken into account the effect of the sample design upon sampling error. They may be interpreted as indicating the range (plus or minus the figure shown) within which the results of repeated samplings in the same time period could be expected to vary, 95 percent of the time, assuming the same sampling procedure, the same interviewers, and the same questionnaire.

Table C.1 shows how much allowance should be made for the sampling error of a percentage for a personal interview sample. The table can be used in the following manner: Let us say a reported percentage is 33 for a group that includes 1,000 respondents. First we go to the row headed "percentages near 30" and go across to the column headed "1,000." The number at this point is 4, which means that the 33 percent obtained in the sample is subject to a sampling error of plus or minus 4 points. Another way of saying it is that very probably (95 chances out of 100) the average of repeated samplings would be somewhere between 29 and 37, with the most likely figure the 33 obtained.

In comparing survey results in two samples, such as, for example, men and women, the question arises as to how large must a difference between them be before one can be reasonably sure that it reflects a real difference. In the following tables the number of points that must be allowed for in such comparisons is indicated. The top half of table C.2 is for percentages near 20 or 80, the bottom half for percentages near 50. For

TABLE C.1   Personal Interview Sample: Allowance for Sampling Error
of a Percentage

	Size of Sample (Percentage points—at 95 in 100 confidence level[a])							
	1,500	1,000	750	600	500	400	300	200
Percentages near 10	2	2	3	3	3	4	4	5
Percentages near 20	3	3	4	4	5	5	6	7
Percentages near 30	3	4	4	5	5	6	7	8
Percentages near 40	3	4	5	5	6	6	7	9
Percentages near 50	3	4	5	5	6	6	7	9
Percentages near 60	3	4	5	5	6	6	7	9
Percentages near 70	3	4	4	5	5	6	7	8
Percentages near 80	3	3	4	4	5	5	6	7
Percentages near 90	2	2	3	3	3	4	4	5

[a]The chances are 95 in 100 that the sampling error is not larger than the figures shown.

percentages in between, the error to be allowed for is between those shown in the two tables.

Here is an example of how the tables would be used: Let us say that 50 percent of men respond a certain way and 40 percent of women respond that way also, for a difference of 10 percentage points between them. Can we say with any assurance that the 10-point difference reflects a real difference between men and women on the question? The sample contains approximately 600 men and 600 women.

Since the percentages are near 50, we consult table C.2, and since the two samples are about 600 persons each, we look for the number in the column headed "600" that is also the row designated "600." We find the number 7 here. This means that the allowance for error should be 7 points, and that in concluding that the percentage among men is somewhere between 3 and 17 points higher than the percentage among women we should be wrong only about 5 percent of the time. In other words, we can conclude with considerable confidence that a difference exists in the direction observed and that it amounts to at least 3 percentage points.

If, in another case, men's responses amount to 22 percent, say, and women's 24 percent, we consult table C.2 because these percentages are near 20. We look in the column headed "600" that is also in the row headed "600" and see that the number is 6. Obviously, then, the 2-point difference is inconclusive.

Tables C.3 and C.4 provide the same information for a telephone interview sample.

TABLE C.2 Personal Interview Sample: Allowance for Sampling Error of the Difference

Sample Size	Percentages near 20 or near 80 (Percentage points—at 95 in 100 confidence level[a])							
	1,500	1,000	750	600	500	400	300	200
1,500	4							
1,000	4	5						
750	5	5	5					
600	5	5	6	6				
500	5	6	6	6	6			
400	6	6	6	7	7	7		
300	6	7	7	7	7	8	8	
200	8	8	8	8	9	9	9	10

	Percentages near 50 (Percentage points—at 95 in 100 confidence level[a])							
1,500	5							
1,000	5	6						
750	6	6	7					
600	6	7	7	7				
500	7	7	7	8	8			
400	7	8	8	8	9	9		
300	8	8	9	9	9	10	10	
200	10	10	10	10	11	11	12	13

[a]The chances are 95 in 100 that the sampling error is not larger than the figures shown.

TABLE C.3   Telephone Interview Sample: Allowance for Sampling Error of a Percentage

	Size of Sample				
	(Percentage points—at 95 in 100 confidence level[a])				
	1,000	*500*	*400*	*300*	*200*
Percentages near 10	2	3	3	4	5
Percentages near 20	3	4	4	5	6
Percentages near 30	3	4	5	6	7
Percentages near 40	3	5	5	6	7
Percentages near 50	3	5	5	6	8
Percentages near 60	3	5	5	6	7
Percentages near 70	3	4	5	6	7
Percentages near 80	3	4	4	5	6
Percentages near 90	2	3	3	4	5

[a]The chances are 95 in 100 that the sampling error is not larger than the figures shown.

TABLE C.4   Telephone Interview Sample: Allowance for Sampling Error of the Difference

	Percentages near 20 or near 80				
	(Percentage points—at 95 in 100 confidence level[a])				
Sample Size	*1,000*	*500*	*400*	*300*	*200*
1,000	4				
500	5	5			
400	5	6	6		
300	6	6	7	7	
200	7	7	7	8	9

	Percentages near 50				
	(Percentage points—at 95 in 100 confidence level[a])				
1,000	5				
500	6	7			
400	6	7	8		
300	7	8	8	9	
200	8	9	9	10	11

[a]The chances are 95 in 100 that the sampling error is not larger than the figures shown.

APPENDIX D
Sample Compositions

Note: The numbers provided in these tables are for statistical testing purposes and represent approximations of the unweighted distributions of interviews for surveys conducted in the years indicated. The actual numbers, of course, vary from survey to survey. The exact unweighted distributions vary from survey to survey and can be obtained from the Roper Center in Storrs, Connecticut.

TABLE D.1 Sample Compositions (Unweighted) for 1500 Interview Surveys

	1953	1954	1955	1956	1957	1958	1959	1960	1961	1962	1963	1964
National	1500	1500	1500	1500	1500	1500	1500	1500	1500	1500	1500	1500
Male	750	750	750	750	750	750	750	750	750	750	750	750
Female	750	750	750	750	750	750	750	750	750	750	750	750
White	1350	1350	1350	1350	1350	1350	1350	1350	1350	1350	1350	1350
Nonwhite	150	150	150	150	150	150	150	150	150	150	150	150
East	450	450	450	450	440	440	440	440	440	430	430	430
Midwest	450	450	450	450	460	460	460	460	460	440	440	440
South	380	380	380	380	380	380	380	380	380	400	400	400
West	220	220	220	220	220	220	220	220	220	230	230	230
Republican	460	500	450	450	440	440	440	440	400	400	400	370
Democrat	670	680	680	680	680	680	680	690	700	700	740	770
Independent	330	290	320	320	320	320	320	330	330	330	330	320
Protestant	1040	1040	1040	1040	1040	1040	1040	1040	1040	1030	1030	1030
Catholic	340	340	340	340	350	350	350	350	350	360	360	360
Union	400	400	400	400	380	380	380	380	380	370	370	370
Nonunion	1100	1100	1100	1100	1120	1120	1120	1120	1120	1130	1130	1130
Grade School	460	460	460	460	450	450	450	450	450	390	390	390
High School	760	760	760	760	750	750	750	750	750	780	780	780
College	250	270	270	270	270	270	270	270	270	320	320	320
Under 30	290	290	290	290	240	240	240	240	240	270	270	270
30-49	690	690	690	690	670	670	670	670	670	630	630	630
Over 50	500	500	500	500	570	570	570	570	570	590	590	590

TABLE D.1 (continued)   Sample Compositions (Unweighted) for 1500 Interview Surveys

	1965	1966	1967	1968	1969	1970	1971	1972	1973	1974	1975	1976
National	1500	1500	1500	1500	1500	1500	1500	1500	1500	1500	1500	1500
Male	750	750	750	750	750	750	750	750	750	750	750	750
Female	750	750	750	750	750	750	750	750	750	750	750	750
White	1350	1350	1350	1330	1330	1330	1330	1330	1330	1330	1330	1330
Nonwhite	150	150	150	170	170	170	170	170	170	170	170	170
East	430	430	430	430	430	430	430	410	410	410	410	410
Midwest	440	440	440	440	440	440	440	420	420	420	420	420
South	400	400	400	400	400	400	400	420	420	420	420	420
West	230	230	230	230	230	230	230	250	250	250	250	250
Republican	400	400	400	400	400	400	400	410	340	340	320	330
Democrat	690	690	690	680	630	630	630	630	640	640	660	690
Independent	330	330	330	390	430	430	430	430	480	480	480	440
Protestant	1030	1030	980	980	980	980	980	900	900	900	900	900
Catholic	360	360	390	390	390	390	390	420	420	420	420	420
Union	370	370	370	370	370	370	370	340	340	340	340	340
Nonunion	1130	1130	1130	1130	1130	1130	1130	1160	1160	1160	1160	1160
Grade School	390	390	340	340	340	340	340	290	290	290	290	290
High School	780	780	770	770	770	770	770	770	770	770	770	770
College	320	320	350	350	350	350	350	400	400	400	420	420
Under 30	270	270	290	290	290	290	290	410	410	410	410	410
30-49	630	630	600	600	600	600	600	500	500	500	500	500
Over 50	590	590	600	600	600	600	600	560	560	560	560	560

TABLE D.1 (continued)   Sample Compositions (Unweighted) for 1500 Interview Surveys

	1977	1978	1979	1980	1981	1982	1983	1984	1985	1986	1987
National	1500	1500	1500	1500	1500	1500	1500	1500	1500	1500	1500
Male	750	750	750	750	750	750	750	750	750	750	750
Female	750	750	750	750	750	750	750	750	750	750	750
White	1330	1320	1320	1320	1320	1320	1310	1310	1310	1310	1310
Nonwhite	170	180	180	180	180	180	190	190	190	190	190
East	410	410	410	410	410	410	410	370	370	370	370
Midwest	420	420	420	420	420	420	420	400	400	400	400
South	420	420	420	420	420	420	420	430	430	430	430
West	250	250	250	250	250	250	250	300	300	300	300
Republican	330	340	320	350	440	380	360	450	490	470	440
Democrat	670	670	660	680	620	660	650	590	550	570	600
Independent	480	480	480	430	440	420	450	420	420	420	420
Protestant	900	900	900	900	900	880	880	880	880	880	880
Catholic	420	420	420	420	420	420	420	420	420	420	420
Union	340	340	340	340	340	300	300	300	300	300	300
Nonunion	1160	1160	1160	1160	1160	1200	1200	1200	1200	1200	1200
Grade School	220	220	220	190	190	150	150	150	150	120	120
High School	800	800	800	800	800	800	700	700	670	670	670
College	420	450	450	500	500	500	640	640	670	700	700
Under 30	430	430	430	430	430	370	370	300	300	300	300
30-49	500	500	500	500	500	520	520	570	570	570	570
Over 50	540	540	540	540	540	600	600	620	620	620	620

Table D.2   Sample Compositions (Unweighted) for 1000

Interview Surveys

	1984	1985	1986	1987	1988
National	1000	1000	1000	1000	1000
Male	500	500	500	500	500
Female	500	500	500	500	500
White	870	870	870	870	870
Nonwhite	130	130	130	130	130
East	240	240	240	240	240
Midwest	270	270	270	270	270
South	290	290	290	290	290
West	200	200	200	200	200
Republican	260	330	310	290	290
Democrat	390	370	380	400	400
Independent	280	280	280	280	280
Protestant	590	590	590	590	590
Catholic	280	280	280	280	280
Union	200	200	200	200	200
Nonunion	800	800	800	800	800
Grade School	100	100	80	80	80
High School	470	450	450	450	450
College	420	440	460	460	460
Under 30	200	200	200	200	200
30-49	380	380	380	380	380
Over 50	410	410	410	410	410

NOTES

INTRODUCTION

1. See, for example, George C. Edwards III, *At the Margins: Presidential Leadership of Congress* (New Haven: Yale University Press, 1989), chap. 6; Charles W. Ostrom, Jr., and Dennis M. Simon, "Promise and Performance: A Dynamic Model of Presidential Popularity," *American Political Science Review* 79 (June 1985): 349; Douglas Rivers and Nancy L. Rose, "Passing the President's Program: Public Opinion and Presidential Influence in Congress," *American Journal of Political Science* 29 (May 1985): 183–96; David W. Rohde and Dennis M. Simon, "Presidential Vetoes and Congressional Response: A Study of Institutional Conflict," *American Journal of Political Science* 29 (August 1985), 397–427; George C. Edwards III, *Presidential Influence in Congress* (San Francisco: W. H. Freeman, 1980), chap. 4.

1. PREDISPOSITIONS

1. The figures in table 1.1 are from the National Election Studies (NES) rather than the Gallup Poll because the NES question asks with which party a respondent "usually" identifies. The results are less volatile than responses to the Gallup question, which asks with which party a person identifies "today."

2. See, for example, Sidney Kraus and Dennis Davis, *The Effects of Mass Communication on Political Behavior* (University Park: Pennsylvania State University Press, 1976); Leon Festinger, *A Theory of Cognitive Dissonance* (Evanston, Ill.: Row, Peterson, 1957); Jack W. Brehm and Arthur C. Cohen, *Explorations in Cognitive Dissonance* (New York: Wiley, 1962); John S. Steinbruner, *The Cybernetic Theory of Decision* (Princeton: Princeton University Press, 1974), chap. 4.

3. The seminal work on perceptual screening is Bernard R. Berelson, Paul F. Lazerfeld, and William N. McPhee, *Voting: A Study of Opinion Formation in a Presidential Campaign* (Chicago: University of Chicago Press, 1954). See also Benjamin I. Page, *Choices and Echoes in Presidential Elections: Rational Man and Electoral Democracy* (Chicago: University of Chicago Press, 1978), 184–86.

4. Alan I. Abramowitz, "The Impact of a Presidential Debate on Voter Rationality," *American Journal of Political Science* 22 (August 1978): 680–90; Robert S. Erikson, Norman R. Luttberg, and Kent Tedin, *American Public Opinion*, 3rd ed. (New York: Macmillan, 1988), 260–62.

5. See, for example, Charles W. Ostrom, Jr., and Dennis M. Simon, "The President's Public," *American Journal of Political Science* 32 (November 1988): 1096–1119. See also Angus Campbell et al., *The American Voter* (New York: Wiley, 1964), chap. 5; and Roberta S. Sigel, "Effect of Partisanship on the Perception of Political Candidates," *Public Opinion Quarterly* 28 (Fall 1964): 483–96 for a discussion of the impact of party identification on candidate evaluation.

6. See Morris P. Fiorina, *Retrospective Voting in American National Elections* (New Haven: Yale University Press, 1981) for a discussion of party identification being at least partly a result of retrospective evaluations of party performance.

7. Philip E. Converse and George Dupeux, "De Gaulle and Eisenhower: The Public Image of the Victorious General," in *Elections and the Political Order*, Angus Campbell et al. (New York: Wiley, 1966), 324–25.

8. The averages that appear in many of the summary tables that follow may be influenced by the number of polls taken during a given period. For example, if there were more polls taken during a portion of the year when the president was high in the polls than when he was low, his average for the year might be inflated. In practice, however, distortion usually does not occur or is very minor.

9. In this calculation we control for the party of the president to remove the distortions caused by the large shifts in approval that occur when the party of the president changes.

10. Martin P. Wattenberg, *The Decline of American Political Parties, 1952–1984* (Cambridge: Harvard University Press, 1986) found parties less salient. On the other hand, Stephen C. Craig, "The Decline of Partisanship in the United States: A Reexamination of the Neutrality Hypothesis," *Political Behavior* 7, no. 1 (1985): 57–78; John E. Stanga and James F. Sheffield, "The Myth of Zero Partisanship: Attitudes toward American Political Parties, 1964–84," *American Journal of Political Science* 31 (November 1987): 829–55; and Raymond E. Wolfinger, "Dealignment, Realignment, and Mandates in the 1984 Election," in *The American Election of 1984*, ed. Austin Ranney (Durham, N.C.: Duke University Press, 1985), 77–296, have found a limited long-term decline in partisanship.

11. Bruce E. Keith et al., "The Partisan Affinities of Independent 'Leaners,' " *British Journal of Political Science* 16 (April 1986): 155–85.

12. See, for example, Wattenberg, *The Decline of American Political Parties*, 23–24.

13. See Mark Peffley, Stanley Feldman, and Lee Sigelman, "Economic Conditions and Party Competence: Processes of Belief and Revision," *Journal of Politics* 49 (February 1987): 100–21 for evidence that prior beliefs and partisanship minimize the effects of new information on views of party competence in handling the economy.

14. Research has not focused directly on this question, but there is some support for the argument that party identification is at least partially a response to evaluations of public policy. See, for example, Fiorina, *Retrospective Voting in American National Elections*; Benjamin I. Page and Calvin C. Jones, "Reciprocal Effects of Policy Preferences, Party Loyalty, and the Vote," *American Political Science Review* 73 (December 1980): 1071–89; Gregory B. Markus, "Political Attitudes during an Election Year: A Report on the 1980 NES Panel," *American Political Science Review* 76 (September 1982): 538–60; Charles H. Franklin and John E. Jackson, "The Dynamics of Party Identification," *American Political Science Review* 77 (December 1983): 957–73.

15. For an overview of positivity, see David O. Sears, "Political Socialization," in *Micropolitical Theory*, vol. 2 of *Handbook of Political Science*, ed. Fred I. Greenstein and Nelson Polsby (Reading, Mass.: Addison-Wesley, 1975), 177; David O. Sears, "Political Behavior," in *Applied Social Psychology*, vol. 5 of *Handbook of Social Psychology*, 2nd

ed., ed. Gardner Lindzey and Elliot Aronson (Reading, Mass.: Addison-Wesley, 1968), 424–31; David O. Sears and Richard E. Whitney, "Political Persuasion" in *Handbook of Communication*, ed. Ithiel de Sola Pool, Wilber Schramm, et al. (Chicago: Rand McNally, 1976), 271–76 and sources cited therein.

16. Positivity bias does not seem to be an artifact of the survey instrument employed, however. See Richard R. Lau, David O. Sears, and Richard Centers, "The 'Positivity Bias' in Evaluations of Public Figures: Evidence against Instrument Artifacts," *Public Opinion Quarterly* 43 (Fall 1979), 347–58.

17. Martin P. Wattenberg, "The Reagan Polarization and the Continual Downward Slide in Presidential Candidate Popularity," *American Politics Quarterly* 14 (July 1986), 219–45.

18. I. H. Paul, "Impressions of Personality: Authoritarianism and the fait accompli Effect," *Journal of Abnormal and Social Psychology* 53 (November 1956): 338–44; George Stricker, "The Operation of Cognitive Dissonance in Pre- and Postelection Attitudes," *Journal of Social Psychology* 63 (June 1964): 111–19; Bertram H. Raven and Philip S. Gallo, "The Effects of Nominating Conventions, Elections, and Reference Group Identification upon the Perception of Political Figures," *Human Relations* 18 (August 1965): 217–29; Lynn R. Anderson and Alan R. Bass, "Some Effects of Victory or Defeat upon Perception of Political Candidates," *Journal of Social Psychology* 73 (October 1967): 227–40; Larry R. Bass and Ian B. Thomas, "The Impact of the Election and the Inauguration on Identification with the President," *Presidential Studies Quarterly* 10 (Fall 1980): 544–49. For exceptions to these findings, see Dan Nimmo and Robert L. Savage, *Candidates and Their Images: Concepts, Methods, and Findings* (Pacific Palisades, Calif.: Goodyear, 1976), 168–81, including their summary of a paper by Allan J. Cigler and Russell Getter, "After the Election: Individual Responses to a Collective Decision" (paper presented at the annual meeting of the Southwestern Political Science Association, Dallas, March 1974).

19. Sears and Whitney, "Political Persuasion," 275.

20. For this argument in the seminal study of presidential approval, see John E. Mueller, *War, Presidents, and Public Opinion* (New York: Wiley, 1970), 205–6.

21. "Remarks of the President at a Meeting with Non-Washington Editors and Broadcasters," Office of the White House Press Secretary (September 21, 1979), 11–12.

22. News release, CBS News/*New York Times Poll*, Pt. 1 (January 18, 1982), table 34.

23. "Institutions: Confidence Even in Difficult Times," *Public Opinion* (June–July 1981): 33.

24. Wattenberg, "The Reagan Polarization Phenomenon."

25. Richard E. Neustadt, *Presidential Power: The Politics of Leadership from FDR to Carter* (New York: Wiley, 1980), 70.

26. *Gallup Opinion Index* (November 1978): 8–9.

27. Interview with Richard Wirthlin, Princeton, New Jersey, April 4, 1987.

28. William C. Adams, "Recent Fables about Ronald Reagan," *Public Opinion* (October/November 1984): 7–8; Austin Ranney, "Reagan's First Term," in *The American Elections of 1984*, ed. Austin Ranney (Washington, D.C.: American Enterprise Institute, 1985), 33–34. See also Barry Sussman, "Reagan's Policies Are the Key—Not His Personality," *Washington Post Weekly Edition* (February 13, 1984): 37.

29. Everett Carll Ladd, "Is Election '84 Really a Class Struggle?" *Public Opinion* (April/May 1984): 42–43.

30. George C. Edwards III, "Comparing Chief Executives," *Public Opinion* (June/July 1985): 51. There were no data on Richard Nixon during the Watergate period.

31. Martin P. Wattenberg, "The Reagan Polarization Phenomenon."

32. For example, see "Reagan and the Contras," CBS News/*New York Times* Poll news release (August 25, 1987), table 8.

33. George C. Edwards III, *The Public Presidency* (New York: St. Martin's Press, 1983), 239, 243.

34. George E. Marcus, "The Structure of Emotional Response: 1984 Presidential Candidates," *American Political Science Review* 82 (September 1988): 737–62; Arthur H. Miller, Martin P. Wattenberg, and Oksana Malanchuk, "Schematic Assessments of Presidential Candidates," *American Political Science Review* 80 (June 1986): 521–40; David P. Glass, "Evaluating Presidential Candidates: Who Focuses on Their Personal Attributes?" *Public Opinion Quarterly* 49 (Winter 1985): 517–34.

35. For a review of the literature on this issue, see Edwards, *The Public Presidency*, chap. 4.

36. On how first impressions color later evaluations of the president, see Jon Hurwitz, Mark Peffley, and Paul Raymond, "Presidential Support during the Iran-Contra Affair," *American Politics Quarterly* 17 (October 1989): 359–85.

2. CHANGES IN APPROVAL

1. Tom W. Smith, "America's Most Important Problems, pt. I: National and International," *Public Opinion Quarterly* 49 (Summer 1985): 264–74.

2. Charles W. O. ~rom, Jr., and Dennis M. Simon, "The President's Public," *American Journal of Political Science* 32 (November 1988): 1096–1119.

3. David J. Lanoue, *From Camelot to the Teflon President* (New York: Greenwood Press, 1988); Howard S. Bloom and H. Douglas Price, "Voter Response to Short-Run Economic Conditions: The Asymmetric Effect of Prosperity and Recession," *American Political Science Review* 69 (December 1975): 1240–54; Samuel Kernell, "Presidential Popularity and Negative Voting: An Alternative Explanation of the Midterm Congressional Decline of the President's Party," *American Political Science Review* 71 (March 1977): 44–66; Richard R. Lau, "Two Explanations for Negativity Effects in Political Behavior," *American Journal of Political Science* 29 (February 1985): 119–38. But see Morris P. Fiorina and Kenneth A. Shepsle, "Is Negative Voting an Artifact"? *American Journal of Political Science* 33 (May 1989): 423–39.

4. David J. Lanou, *From Camelot to the Teflon President*; George C. Edwards III, "Comparing Chief Executives," *Public Opinion* (June/July 1985): 54. But see Michael S. Lewis-Beck, *Economics and Elections* (Ann Arbor: University of Michigan Press, 1988).

5. Ostrom and Simon, "The President's Public."

6. See for example, Jon Hurwitz and Mark Peffley, "The Means and Ends of Foreign Policy as Determinants of Presidential Support," *American Journal of Political Science* 31 (May 1987): 236–58.

7. Richard A. Brody and Paul Sniderman, "From Life Space to Polling Place," *British Journal of Political Science* 7 (July 1977): 337–60; Paul Sniderman and Richard A. Brody, "Coping: The Ethic of Self-Reliance," *American Journal of Political Science* 21 (August 1977): 501–22. See also Stanley Feldman, "Economic Self-Interest and Political Behavior," *American Journal of Political Science* 26 (August 1982): 449–52; Kay L. Scholzman and Sidney Verba, *Injury to Insult: Unemployment, Class, and Political Response* (Cambridge: Harvard University Press, 1979).

8. K. Jill Kiecolt, "Group Consciousness and the Attribution of Blame for National Economic Problems," *American Politics Quarterly* 15 (April 1987): 203–22.

9. Mark Peffley and John T. Williams, "Attributing Presidential Responsibility for National Economic Problems," *American Politics Quarterly* 13 (October 1985): 393–426.

10. NBC News/Associated Press Poll discussed in William Schneider, "Reaganomics Was on the Voters' Minds, but Their Verdict Was Far from Clear," *National Journal* (November 6, 1982): 1892–93. Also see John R. Petrocik and Frederick T. Steeper, "The Midterm Referendum: The Importance of Attributions of Responsibility," *Political Behavior* 8, no. 3 (1986): 206–29.

11. William R. Keech and Henry W. Chappell, "A New View of Political Accountability for Economic Performance," *American Political Science Review* 79 (March 1985): 10–27.

12. NBC News/Associated Press Poll discussed in Schneider, "Reaganomics Was on the Voters' Minds." Also see Petrocik and Steeper, "The Midterm Referendum."

13. Alan I. Abramowitz, David J. Lanoue, and Subha Ramesh, "Economic Conditions, Causal Attributions, and Political Evaluations in the 1984 Presidential Election," *Journal of Politics* 50 (November 1988): 848–65.

14. Richard E. Neustadt, *Presidential Power: The Politics of Leadership from FDR to Carter* (New York: Wiley, 1980), 73.

15. Jack Valenti, *A Very Human President* (New York: Norton, 1975), 151.

16. For a guide to the early literature on this question, see George C. Edwards III, *The Public Presidency* (New York: St. Martin's Press, 1983), 263–64, n. 35.

17. Lee Sigelman and Yung-mei Tsai, "Personal Finances and Voting Behavior: A Reanalysis," *American Politics Quarterly* 9 (October 1981): 371–400; Pamela Johnston Conover, Stanley Feldman, and Kathleen Knight, "Judging Inflation and Unemployment: The Origins of Retrospective Evaluations," *Journal of Politics* 48 (August 1986): 565–88; Pamela Johnston Conover, "The Impact of Group Economic Interests on Political Evaluations," *American Politics Quarterly* 13 (April 1985): 139–66; Stanley Feldman, "Economic Self-Interest and the Vote: Evidence and Meaning," *Political Behavior* 6, no. 3, (1984): 229–52; M. Stephen Weatherford, "Evaluating Economic Policy: A Contextual Model of the Opinion Formation Process," *Journal of Politics* 45 (November 1983): 866–88; D. Roderick Kiewiet, *Macroeconomics and Micropolitics: The Electoral Effects of Economic Issues* (Berkeley, Calif.: University of California Press, 1983); William Schneider, "Opinion Outlook: A National Referendum on Reaganomics?" *National Journal* (October 9, 1982): 1732; M. Stephen Weatherford, "Economic Voting and the 'Symbolic Politics' Argument: A Reinterpretation and Synthesis," *American Political Science Review* 77 (March 1983): 158–74; Jeffrey W. Wides, "Perceived Economic Competency and the Ford/Carter Election," *Public Opinion Quarterly* 43 (Winter 1979): 535–43; Gregory B. Markus, "The Impact of Personal and National Economic Conditions on the Presidential Vote: A Pooled Cross-Sectional Analysis," *American Journal of Political Science* 32 (February 1988): 137–54; John R. Owens, "Economic Influences on Elections to the U.S. Congress," *Legislative Studies Quarterly* 9 (February 1984): 123–50; Lewis-Beck, *Economics and Elections*; Donald R. Kinder, Gordon S. Adams, and Paul W. Gronke, "Economics and Politics in the 1984 American Presidential Election," *American Journal of Political Science* 33 (May 1989): 491–515; Donald R. Kinder and Walter R. Mebane, Jr., "Politics and Economics in Everyday Life," in *The Political Process and Economic Change*, ed. Kristen Monroe (New York: Agathon, 1983), 141–80.

18. See, for example, Donald R. Kinder, "Presidents, Prosperity, and Public Opinion," *Public Opinion Quarterly* 45 (Spring 1981): 1–21; Richard Lau and David O. Sears, "Cognitive Links Between Economic Grievances and Political Responses," *Political Behavior* 3, no. 4 (1981): 279–302.

19. See for example, Michael R. Hawthorne and John E. Jackson, "The Individual Political Economy of Federal Tax Policy," *American Political Science Review* 81 (September 1987): 757–74; David O. Sears et al., "Self-Interest vs. Symbolic Politics in Policy Attitudes

and Presidential Voting," *American Political Science Review* 74 (September 1980): 670–84; David O. Sears, Carl P. Hensler, and Leslie K. Speer, "Whites' Opposition to 'Busing': Self-Interest or Symbolic Politics?" *American Political Science Review* 73 (June 1979): 369–84; David O. Sears et al., "Political System Support and Public Response to the Energy Crisis," *American Journal of Political Science* 22 (February 1978): 56–82; Douglas S. Gatlin, Michael Giles, and Everett F. Cataldo, "Policy Support within a Target Group: The Case of School Desegregation," *American Political Science Review* 72 (September 1978): 985–95; Richard R. Lau, Thad A. Brown, and David O. Sears, "Self-Interest and Civilians' Attitudes toward the War in Vietnam," *Public Opinion Quarterly* 42 (Winter 1978): 464–83; John B. McConahay, "Self-Interest versus Racial Attitudes as Correlates of Anti-Busing Attitudes in Louisville: Is It the Buses or the Blacks?" *Journal of Politics* 44 (August 1982): 692–720; Donald R. Kinder and D. Roderick Kiewiet, "Economic Discontent and Political Behavior: The Role of Personal Grievances and Collective Economic Judgments in Congressional Voting," *American Journal of Political Science* 23 (August 1979): 495–527; Kinder and Mebane, "Politics and Economics in Everyday Life" and sources cited therein.

20. *Gallup Report* (January 1989): 5–8.

21. See, for example, John E. Mueller, *War, Presidents, and Public Opinion* (New York: Wiley, 1970), chaps. 9–10; Samuel Kernell, "Explaining Presidential Popularity," *American Political Science Review* 72 (June 1978): 506–22; Kristen R. Monroe, *Presidential Popularity and the Economy* (New York: Praeger, 1984); Douglas A. Hibbs, Jr., "The Dynamics of Political Support for American Presidents among Occupational and Partisan Groups," *American Journal of Political Science* 26 (May 1982): pp. 312–32; Charles W. Ostrom, Jr., and Dennis M. Simon, "Promise and Performance: A Dynamic Model of Presidential Popularity," *American Political Science Review* 79 (June 1985): 334–58 and sources cited therein.

22. But see Gerald H. Kramer, "The Ecological Fallacy Revisited: Aggregate- versus Individual-Level Findings on Economics and Elections and Sociotropic Voting," *American Political Science Review* 77 (March 1983): 92–111.

23. Edwards, *The Public Presidency*, 226–53. See also Edwards, "Comparing Chief Executives," 54.

24. See, for example, Edwards, *The Public Presidency*, chap. 1.

25. News release, CBS News/*New York Times* Poll (May 27, 1982): 3.

26. ABC News/*Washington Post* Poll, cited in "Knowing the Cost of Almost Everything," *National Journal* (May 5, 1984): 894.

27. News release, CBS News/*New York Times* Poll (October 30, 1982), tables 28a and 29a.

28. Michael J. Robinson and Maura Clancey, "Teflon Politics," *Public Opinion* (April/May 1984): 16.

29. Pamela Johnston Conover, Stanley Feldman, and Kathleen Knight, "The Personal and Political Underpinnings of Economic Forecasts," *American Journal of Political Science* 31 (August 1987): 559–83.

30. News release, CBS News/*New York Times* Poll (October 30, 1982), tables 28a and 30.

31. Conover, Feldman, and Knight, "Judging Inflation and Unemployment."

32. NBC News/Associated Press Poll discussed in Schneider, "Reaganomics Was on the Voters' Minds."

33. Bruce Buchanan, *The Citizen's Presidency* (Washington, D.C.: Congressional Quarterly Press, 1987): 48–52; Donald R. Kinder and Susan T. Fiske, "Presidents in the Public Mind," in *Political Psychology*, ed. Margaret G. Hermann, (San Francisco: Jossey-Bass, 1986), 193–218.

34. Hurwitz and Peffley, "The Means and Ends of Foreign Policy as Determinants of Presidential Support."

35. See, for example, Edwards, *The Public Presidency*, chaps. 3, 4; Samuel Kernell, *Going Public* (Washington, D.C.: Congressional Quarterly Press, 1986); and Michael Baruch Grossman and Martha Joynt Kumar, *Portraying the President* (Baltimore: Johns Hopkins University Press, 1981).

36. Shanto Iyengar, "Television News and Citizens' Explanations of National Affairs," *American Political Science Review* 81 (September 1987): 815–31.

37. Shanto Iyengar, Mark D. Peters, and Donald R. Kinder, "Experimental Demonstrations of the 'Not-So-Minimal' Consequences of Television News Programs," *American Political Science Review* 76 (December 1982): 848–58.

38. See, for example, United States Department of Labor *News* (July 20, 1982): 1–2.

39. Mueller included the inaugural period of a president's term, which we dealt with earlier, as a rally event. *War, Presidents, and Public Opinion*, 208–13.

40. Market Opinion Research, *Americans Talk Security,* no. 12 (January 1989): 31–32, 106.

41. Hazel Erskine, "The Polls: Presidential Power," *Public Opinion Quarterly* 37 (Fall 1973): 499–500.

42. George H. Gallup, *The Gallup Poll: Public Opinion 1972–1977,* vol. I (Wilmington, Del.: Scholarly Resources, 1978), 210–11.

43. News release, CBS News/*New York Times* Poll (July 9, 1987), table 4.

44. News release, CBS News/*New York Times* Poll (July 17, 1987), table 11.

45. News release, CBS News/*New York Times* Poll (September 23, 1987), table 14.

46. Samuel P. Huntington, *American Politics: The Promise of Disharmony* (Cambridge, Mass.: Belknap, 1981), 33.

47. See Huntington, *American Politics*; Bert A. Rockman, *The Leadership Question* (New York: Praeger, 1984); Daniel Boorstin, *The Americans*, 3 vols. (New York: Random House, 1958, 1965, 1973); Louis Hartz, *The Liberal Tradition in America* (New York: Harcourt, Brace and World, 1955); Richard Hofstadter, *The American Political Tradition and the Men Who Made It* (New York: Vintage, 1957).

48. Jon Hurwitz, "Presidential Leadership and Public Followership," in *Manipulating Public Opinion*, ed. Michael Margolis and Gary A. Mauser (Pacific Grove, Calif.: Brooks/Cole, 1989), 222–49.

49. Kent Tedin and Richard Murray, "Predicting the Stability of Presidential Support: A Panel Analysis" (paper presented at the Annual Meeting of the American Political Science Association, August 1983, Chicago).

50. Barry Sussman, "Why Both Parties Are Courting 50 Million Opinion-Switchers," *Washington Post National Weekly Edition"* (January 16, 1984): 37. Questionnaire bias may also have produced changes in responses.

51. Mueller, *War, Presidents, and Public Opinion*, 210–11.

52. See also Michael B. MacKuen, "Political Drama, Economic Conditions, and the Dynamics of Presidential Popularity," *American Journal of Political Science* 27 (May 1983): 165–92.

53. See also John Wanat, "The Dynamics of Presidential Popularity Shifts: Estimating the Degree of Opinion Shift from Aggregate Data," *American Politics Quarterly* 10 (April 1982): 181–96; Mueller, *War, Presidents, and Public Opinion*, 250.

54. Lee Sigelman and Pamela Johnston Conover, "The Dynamics of Presidential Support during International Conflict Situations: The Iranian Hostage Crisis," *Political Behavior* 3, no. 4 (1981): 303–18.

55. On this concept in another setting, see Edward G. Carmines and James A. Stimson, *Issue Evolution: Race and the Transformation of American Politics* (Princeton: Princeton University Press, 1989), 139–41.

56. See for example, Theodore J. Lowi, "An Aligning Election, A Presidential Plebiscite," in *The Elections of 1984*, ed. Michael Nelson (Washington, D.C.: Congressional Quarterly Press, 1985), 284–85.

57. Henry Adams, *History of the United States of America During the Administration of James Madison* (New York: Library of America, 1986), 1069.

58. Larry Speakes, *Speaking Out: The Reagan Presidency from Inside the White House* (New York: Scribner's, 1988), 159.

59. Richard A. Brody and Catherine R. Shapiro, "Policy Failure and Public Support: Reykjavik, Iran, and Public Assessments of President Reagan" (paper presented at the Annual Meeting of the American Political Science Association, Chicago, September 1987); Richard A. Brody, "A Reconsideration of the Rally Phenomenon in Public Opinion" (paper presented at the Annual Meeting of the American Political Science Association, Washington, D.C., August 1986).

60. For other findings on the lack of impact of rally events, see R. Darcy and Sarah Slavin Schramm, "Comment on Kernell," *American Political Science Review* 73 (June 1979): 544–45.

3. PRESIDENTS

1. Robert Y. Shapiro and Harpreet Mahajan, "Gender Differences in Policy Preferences: A Summary of Trends from the 1960s to the 1980s," *Public Opinion Quarterly* 50 (Spring 1986): 42–61; Martin Gilens, "Gender and Support for Reagan: A Comprehensive Model of Presidential Approval," *American Journal of Political Science* 32 (February 1988): 19–49.

2. See, for example, Barry Sussman, "Most Explanations of the Gender Gap Don't Hold Up," *The Washington Post National Weekly Edition* (February 20, 1984): 36.

3. Pamela Johnston Conover, "Feminists and the Gender Gap," *Journal of Politics* 50 (November 1988): 985–1010; Gilens, "Gender and Support for Reagan."

APPENDIX C. SAMPLING, WEIGHTING, AND SAMPLING TOLERANCES

1. See Alfred Politz and William Simmons, "An Attempt to Get the 'Not at Homes' into the Sample without Callbacks," *Journal of the American Statistical Association* 44 (March 1949): 9–31; "Note on 'An Attempt to Get the "Not at Homes" into the Sample without Callbacks,' " *Journal of the American Statistical Association* 45 (March 1950): 136–37.

INDEX